Just and Lasting Change

JUST AND LASTING CHANGE

When Communities Own Their Futures

DANIEL TAYLOR-IDE

AND CARL E. TAYLOR

With the Assistance of
Mabelle and Raj Arole, Abhay and Rani Bang,
Zeng DongLu, Ann Hawthorne, Patricia Paredes,
Robert Parker, Jac Smit, Betsy Taylor,
Henry Taylor, and Miriam Were

The Johns Hopkins University Press
Baltimore and London

In Association with
Future Generations

The Johns Hopkins University Press
2715 North Charles Street
Baltimore, Maryland 21218-4363
www.press.jhu.edu

Library of Congress Cataloging-in-Publication Data
Taylor-Ide, Daniel.
Just and lasting change : when communities own their futures /
Daniel C. Taylor-Ide and Carl E. Taylor.
p.   cm.
Includes bibliographical references and index.
ISBN 0-8018-6825-4 (pbk. : alk. paper)
1. Community health services. 2. Community development.
3. Environmental health. 4. Rural health. I. Taylor, Carl E. II. Title.
RA427 .T39 2002
362.1′2—dc21   2001001755

A catalog record for this book is available from the British Library.

To Mary
who taught us to accent the positive

Sustainable human development is development that not only
generates economic growth but distributes its benefits equitably; that regenerates the environment rather than destroying
it; that empowers people rather than marginalizing them. It
gives priority to the poor, enlarging their choices and opportunities, and provides for their participation in decisions affecting
them. It is development that is pro-poor, pro-nature, pro-jobs,
pro-democracy, pro-women, and pro-children.

JAMES GUSTAV SPETH
former Administrator,
United Nations Development Program

CONTENTS

FOREWORD

The SEED-SCALE concepts presented in this book were first published in
Community-Based Sustainable Human Development (New York: UNICEF,
1995). Jim Grant wrote the foreword to that monograph—the last words he
wrote before his death. In memory of Jim (and his father, John, whose seminal work is mentioned in chapter 7), we reprint a portion of Jim's essay.

As the World Bank's *World Development Report* for 1993 stated, there has
been more improvement in child survival in the past fifty years than in all
previous human history. A major part of that improvement has resulted from
the specific interventions promoted by what UNICEF has referred to as the
Child Survival Revolution. . . .

A major concern is sustainability of these achievements. . . . Mobilization
should start with national leaders, but its sustainability depends on continuing community participation. Demand for services must be stimulated and
maintained at the community level. Science-based interventions should be
simplified so as to be applied in the home either by family members or by
easy access to peripheral health workers. The most important responsibility
of health and other services is to promote the capacity of families and communities to solve their own problems with self-reliance.

Area-based programs have tended to be successful in local areas, but there
have been problems of their not readily "going to scale." There are, however,
examples of successful extension. . . . Drs. Daniel Taylor-Ide and Carl Taylor
have made a worthy effort in drawing important lessons from such examples,
and they have proposed a set of measures that could guide future efforts. . . .
Their process places special emphasis on: equity, a long-standing UNICEF
goal of reaching the unreached; adaptation and innovation under diverse

local conditions; and capacity building through collaboration between communities, government officials, and experts.

I want to thank Drs. Daniel Taylor-Ide and Carl Taylor for the important ideas that they have synthesized here in concise and practical ways.

JAMES P. GRANT
Executive Director, UNICEF, 1980–1995

Just and Lasting Change

Prologue

In 1914 Drs. Beth and John Taylor came to the foothills of the Himalaya as district medical missionaries. In doing so they began a family tradition of observing and participating in the processes of community change. Nearly sixty years later John described those first efforts to help: "We traveled by oxcart out into the jungles, setting up our large three-room tent, staff tents, cook tent, and medicine tent, making camp for a week or ten days at a time . . . mornings were taken up dispensing medicines. The village folks came early, bringing their sick. We set up a folding table, often under the shade of a mango tree; medicines stacked on top of the table and in boxes underneath. Beth took one side of the table and treated the women as they lined up, and I treated the men on the other side."[1]

John knew firsthand the challenges of the hard life the villagers led; he had broken Kansas sod with a plow and later wild broncos to pay his way through medical school. Before and during her medical education, Beth had taught women dressmaking through a church group. India was lonely then; a letter sent home to the United States during the summer might get an answer before Christmas. Beth and John dispensed pills and poultices during the day; in the evenings they presented magic-lantern shows teaching new health habits, new agricultural methods, and the values embodied in the life of Christ. In their view, a better life had both spiritual and physical aspects.

As they traveled each year among the villages, first by oxcart and then by Model T, they started involving children in their work. A friend who had come for some months to their tented camps described one scene: "a teenage girl came in one morning, a girl with a tumor over her eyebrow the size of a hickory nut. The patient squatted on the ground in front of the doctor who was seated on a camp stool. Dr. John removed the tumor with a local anesthetic; the girl gave no fuss or screaming. Dr. Beth assisted, and Carl, age 13, held the basin."[2]

It was an age when only quite simple things were available to make life safer and easier: medicines, soap, new kinds of vegetables, netting to keep away mosquitoes, curved iron blades on ox-drawn plows. But for most people in India a century ago, even these innovations cost too much. So as Beth and John dispensed care from their folding camp table, they taught: "Wash out a wound with soap," "Eat more vegetables and drink milk to feed the baby inside you," "You can't skip to the head of the line because you're of higher caste; wait in your place." They taught people a few at a time. Today, for a fifth of the world's people the same simple tools remain too expensive.

In these same years Mahatma Gandhi was mobilizing Indians by the millions. His inspirational example brought simple improvements to traditional livelihoods; he showed people how to stand up, organize, and create a better life; he taught them that achieving change is rooted in self-reliance and self-improvement. Their acquaintance with Gandhi challenged Beth and John, like many others, to expand both their thinking and their actions.

Each of Beth and John's children recast the family mission in a different way. Carl graduated from Harvard Medical School and after World War II went to India with wife Mary and infant son Daniel to work in a mission hospital. In those days institutions were seen as the foundation for reaching out to communities; creating and strengthening institutions was viewed as a parallel path to Gandhi's strategy for mobilizing people.

But the birth of a new India was a violent one. With independence in 1947 the land was partitioned into Muslim Pakistan and Hindu-dominated India. As almost twenty million people struggled to flee to communities of their coreligionists, blood flowed as old schisms surfaced. Beth and John joined with their sons and several friends to create a relief group. In one report in August 1947 Carl wrote: "The most common and worst killing was when gangs . . . stopped refugee trains loaded with 5,000 or more people . . . the slaughter was mostly with hand weapons: swords, spears, and pole axes. Our team [picked] up survivors . . . and we would operate for several days on emergency cases . . . What was it that caused normally civilized men to . . . kill children whose parents believed in another religion?" One of the most painful moments in the relief operations came "when I held in my arms the body of a beautiful three-year-old Sikh girl. Across her head I counted six deep sword cuts into the brain. What powerful psychological force would drive a man to rage so strong that he couldn't stop hacking even when the little baby was clearly dead?"[3]

The relief efforts during the partition riots focused on addressing individual needs, but the riots themselves pointed to the need for solutions to systemic problems. Carl left direct medical care and went back to Harvard for a doctorate in public health. In 1952 he returned to India with Mary and their children, Daniel, Betsy, and Henry. Working at the Ludhiana Christian Medical College in the Punjab and using Mary's expertise as an educator, they developed practical methods to teach medical providers how to understand community needs and move the definition of health beyond clinical care. Other medical schools in India adopted this model, developing teaching health centers in community settings. Carl, Mary, and others established a research center in Narangwal (Chapter 10) to learn the health needs of whole communities. Who didn't come to hospitals, and why? What did people do instead?

At Narangwal the children became involved in the work. When data from questionnaires showed that mortality was much higher for girls than for boys, eight-year-old Betsy suggested, "Maybe the girl children are dying because I notice that they eat after the boys and get what's left over." Each child's interests took a different direction. Henry's fascination with small mammals expanded into an interest in the health of whole communities. Betsy focused always on problems of inequity among cultures. Teenage Dan'l started searching for the Yeti.

In 1961 the family returned to America, where Carl launched the Department of International Health at Johns Hopkins. Dinnertime conversations continued to tie together lessons from daily work. Mary, in her faculty position at Towson State College, had begun setting up programs to train the most disadvantaged how to read. One such program was at the Maryland Training School for Boys, and at the table one evening, she told us about three children who had been brought into the state home that day—ages eight, ten, and eleven. They had stolen a car in Maryland and were headed to Florida but got picked up by the police in Georgia.

Henry was eleven, himself, and quite impressed. "How could kids get away with that?" he asked.

"Stealing was the easy part," Mary explained. "They took a car that had the keys hanging in the ignition. To drive, the littlest sat on the floor and pushed the pedals when those up above told him. The biggest turned the wheel, assisted by the third who handled the levers and knobs."

But Henry had practical concerns. "How did they pull into gas stations and get tanked up? It takes many tankfuls to get from Maryland to Georgia."

"When the kids were booked at the prison today," said Mary, "they bragged, 'We almost made it! We'd get gas in tins, saying our dad was down the road and had run out. But in Georgia, we really did run out, and the police caught us.'"

Thirteen-year-old Betsy was thrilled with the story. "If those children could figure out how to drive a car, Mom, you can teach them to read!"

"Betsy, how about *you* teaching them to read? Could you get some of your friends from school to work with them?" Mary's programs to teach reading—and her willingness to enlist her own kids in her work—helped teach us how to use volunteers to solve societal needs. With appropriate training, community members could be as effective as professionals.

In 1969 Dan'l finished graduate training and joined the worldwide campaign to lower population growth. He was stationed in Nepal by the U.S. Agency for International Development in a project shaped not by local realities but by outside political priorities. The U.S. Congress, concerned that population growth was undermining international economic potential and Earth's natural resources, offered hundreds of millions of dollars' worth of condoms, pills, and vasectomies to other governments to solve the problem. In 1972 Dan'l realized that although the problem was real, the solution did not seem appropriate; the massively financed program had no solid population-based research to show this approach would work. For Dan'l there were also ethical questions about using money to buy poor people's cooperation in what someone else had decided was good for them. How did this approach differ from that of prescriptive missionaries?

Dan'l left the top-down approach to try the bottom-up one. With wife Jennifer he moved to West Virginia, an isolated and beautiful part of America, and joined others in starting an action learning center, the Woodlands Mountain Institute. Over twenty years the institute undertook experiments in hands-on education: courses to strengthen family relationships, courses for children using the outdoors as the classroom, programs to foster responsibility in youngsters in trouble with the law, and training teachers in experiential education. All these efforts improved our understanding about how to teach when the real world is the classroom.

Meanwhile Carl's students were launching projects and partnerships in communities around the world. Several of the successes (Jamkhed, Gadchiroli, and Kakamega) are discussed in this book. The failures taught us that an outsider's good intentions are generally a bad starting point and that community successes tend to evaporate once governments or donors assume control.

Carl applied these lessons when in 1978 he coauthored the background documents for the World Conference on Primary Health Care in Alma Ata, Soviet Kazakhstan. In the documents he focused on "three pillars of primary health care": infrastructure for peripheral health services, community participation, and intersectoral cooperation. Sadly, within six years international donors abandoned the three-pillar strategy, redirecting funds into programs that promised quicker solutions for more narrowly targeted problems. During this period we were traveling extensively, observing the negative impact at the community level.

Noting that dedicated leaders had played essential roles in the successes at Jamkhed, Gadchiroli, Kakamega, and many other places, and that for more than two centuries the people of West Virginia had been unable to rise out of poverty, poor education, and ill health despite the state's enormous wealth in timber, coal, natural gas, and industrial development, in 1983 Jennifer and Dan'l launched a program to develop a statewide cadre of leaders. Every year a hundred eleventh graders chosen by the West Virginia Scholars Academy for their initiative or academic or technical promise worked one on one with more than five thousand high school students to increase college attendance among the state's youngsters. In 1983 West Virginia ranked forty-ninth in the nation in percentage of college attendance; in 1986 it moved to forty-eighth, and in 1990 it rose to forty-sixth. But the program was wholly outside-funded, and a change in the donor's leadership eliminated that outside support. A program that was trying to build leadership itself crumbled for lack of leadership.

In 1984, after twenty-three years of teaching and fieldwork in sixty-two countries, Carl became professor emeritus at Johns Hopkins and was invited to lead a new UNICEF program in China. Seeing this as a unique opportunity to integrate top-down and bottom-up approaches on a national scale, he helped launch China's Model Counties Project (Chapter 18).

In 1983, after twenty-five years of searching, Dan'l discovered the scientific reality behind the ancient legend of the Yeti. While he and brother-in-law Nick were climbing in a high remote valley east of Everest, Nick spotted fresh tracks belonging to a big animal, maybe five feet tall. The Abominable Snowman proved to be a bear, an adaptation by the Asiatic black bear, one that lived primarily in trees and had primatelike paws to hold on, leaving humanlike footprints when it traveled through deep, wet snow. To Dan'l, who had grown up in the Himalaya and watched human populations double and animal populations tumble, it was clear that the future for this bear was bleak. Dan'l teamed with the Nepalese and Chinese governments to establish national parks on the slopes of Mount Everest. The intent was to help people live better lives and simultaneously protect the environment and ultimately the bear. Over time the Makalu-Barun National Park in Nepal and the Qomolangma National Nature Preserve in China evolved comprehensive solutions that integrated development with conservation (Chapter 16).

As we work on understanding the process of intentional community—and in some cases regional—change, the transgenerational dialogue continues. A fourth generation—Jesse Oak, Christopher, Tara, Ruth, Luke, Caleb, and Anna—has grown up walking Himalayan trails with us, critiquing our approach. Whether or how they will take up the quest remains uncertain, but their participation has greatly informed the discussions in this book. In 1999 Luke ran along the trails of Nepal with his butterfly net, comparing butterfly counts with what his grandfather had found fifty years before. On this same survey expedition, Ruth interviewed women about their nutrition needs, and Caleb kept notes on the games children were playing. Jesse Oak had just finished work with local hunters ferreting out mysteries in their jungle in the northeast corner of India. His article in the September 2000 issue of *National Geographic* describes a phase in his engagement with this quest:

We're an unusual group: two wildlife officers of the state of Arunachal Pradesh, both Apatani born and raised in the jungle; the "boys"—six young Apatani hunters; and me, a 17-year-old American raised on

Himalayan expeditions. We're camped at 7,800 feet on a plateau in the heart of some of the wildest jungle and cloud forest left on Earth. Thick bamboo carpets the valley floor. At night, birds—the mountain scops owl and the large hawk cuckoo—call in the trees above, while somewhere below, unseen and unheard, a hunting cat stalks its prey.

We've come . . . to encourage local people in Arunachal Pradesh and across the border in Tibet to improve health care and education in their communities and to manage their forests, wildlife, and other resources in a sustainable manner.

Nani Sha and I are also engaged in a personal quest: to capture on film the elusive *Neofelis nebulosa,* the clouded leopard. This magnificent cat takes its name from the cloud forest it inhabits and the hazy markings that allow it to blend with the shifting shadows of the jungle canopy. My family's connections to these Himalayan jungles go back to my great-grandfather John Taylor Sr. and his wife, Elizabeth, in 1914 . . .[4]

Introduction

Today 6 billion neighbors share our planet. Some live in hugely wealthy, fast-moving societies, but 1.3 billion of us scratch out a living on a dollar a day in circumstances that do not improve.[1] Our diversity is so great that most descriptions of our commonalities seem either farfetched or trite. Options are expanding so rapidly that it seems impossible to coordinate the choices. But for the 1.3 billion there are very few choices.

It is possible to reduce the gap between rich and poor. The megaforces of globalization can be directed. Damage to the environment can be dramatically reduced. Community-based solutions are the way to attain these goals—and achieving them can be rapid and cost-efficient. Positive examples of communities taking control of their futures are found in every country, every economic situation, and every ethnic group. Today most people live longer and in more material comfort than their grandparents did. Most children grow up with fewer physical and mental disabilities. Most older people enjoy unprecedented care and security. Expanding telecommunications are creating a "one world" perspective and causing many people to believe that their futures will consistently improve.

But at the same time environmental limits threaten to cap progress. Our lives are increasingly subject to the caprices of corporations and to other large forces controlled by determinants so distant that they feel as arbitrary as the weather. Millions of people migrate daily, moving across the landscape like rising and falling tides, seeking opportunity amid a sea of global change that preferentially rewards the affluent. Although opportunities have increased for three-quarters of us, genetic and geographic factors discriminate even among this privileged group, keeping the pace of improvement uneven. With mounting social and economic inequities, civil strife grows. Against this vision of promise, we equally often daily face greed, ego, cruelty, racism, and shortsightedness.

Seeing the enormity of the challenge, some among us wring our hands and lament that there is just too much to do. But by twos, tens, and thousands, as communities and as nations, others among us are acting. As we learn together, beginnings grow into larger solutions. Progress often starts small and seems unsophisticated, but year by year in these communities more and more people are seeing opportunities and taking a hand in shaping how they live. Thus while some aspects of planetary change spin toward uncertainty, some communities are pulling ahead—just as certain communities have always pulled ahead in the past.

This book identifies a pattern in our collective history that shows how we can reduce the gaps between those who have, those who want to have, and those who have given up. It describes how the process can not only continue but expand rapidly, going to quite significant scale. The process is complex, and the strategies are still evolving; the paradigm outlined in the following pages will no doubt be more usable and more efficient a few years hence. But already we have a clear enough understanding of how each of us can act.

Action must be sensitive simultaneously to the environments, cultures, and economies in which people live. Success must build in radiating self-assembly, with each iterative effort going beyond those tried earlier. This is an organic process, much like the growth of an animal population, with family units reproducing in increasing numbers of places. Each unit grows in accord with the circumstances prevailing in its own specific place.

The most vital management feature of this process is that those in authority must relinquish control, gently and more quickly than they may think comfortable—just as a parent must learn to trust increasing capability in a child as he or she grows up. Learning is a process of making mistakes and then building from them, not of starting all over from the same place. It is hard for leaders and experts to let go as fast as communities gain capacity to act on their own. But when the right organic process is found, change can radiate rapidly across a region, and it does this best when outsiders restrict their roles to enabling that change instead of prescribing how it must occur.

The following chapters distill this process into a sequence that almost any community or cluster of communities can replicate. We call it SEED-SCALE

(Self-Evaluation for Effective Decisionmaking and Systems for Communities to Adapt Learning and Expand). SEED-SCALE synthesizes many schools of thought regarding development and conservation as well as many participatory methods. It appears to transcend cultures and economies even as it relies on, and enhances, communities.

The lives we lead as people do not follow a single theme or even a systematic structure. Our lives are fluid, folding back, starting and being cut off, reforming. It would be false to suggest that building a better future can be as organized a process as, say, building a factory. In writing this book we struggled to capture this complex and manifold recursiveness. We therefore present our perspectives on this recursive process before summarizing the themes. These themes resurface throughout a series of case studies. The final chapters set forth the SEED-SCALE process in the form of handbooks.

SEED-SCALE is a form of action that individuals can launch in their communities, and it is a process that governments can enable on a regional or national scale. SEED generates the local database; it can be viewed as creating community-specific DNA, the guiding codes that tell social units how they can evolve according to their comparative advantages. SCALE defines the growth process, how a variety of features nurture the self-assembly of communities. Although the terminology is quite new, the case studies demonstrate that the process has been used for generations. Field trials around the world confirm that the process is effective under very different political and economic systems.

We first outlined the SEED-SCALE process in two monographs prepared for the 1995 United Nations World Summit for Social Development.[2] A great many helpful responses came in from around the world as people tested the ideas against their experiences. In our own continuing field-based research we initiated projects in several countries as prospective case studies to test the approach. The Narangwal, China Model Counties, Tibet, and CLAS cases in this book are some of these field trials. Other case studies in Parts II, III, and IV confirm that the process works. Continuing feedback and adjustments will undoubtedly make the process still more useful. This volume makes available what is known so far, so that others can also test its utility.

Over the six years of writing this book we shared drafts with colleagues. Those leading field projects wanted more operational details, which we provide in the handbooks in Part V. Academic colleagues wanted more data and more elaboration of the methods used in the case studies. Activist colleagues, such as Halfdan Mahler, the inspirational former director general of the World Health Organization, said, "Get this book out to launch more field trials worldwide and to inform the paradigm." Colleagues who wanted to start projects (from administrators of donor agencies to graduate students) sometimes dismissed the successes of Chapters 7–19, suggesting that the achievements were the results of special situations, or that they depended on charismatic leaders, or that most circumstances were too constraining to permit implementation of this type of approach. We acknowledge that distinctive features did contribute to many of the case studies. But as the approach evolves, it grows increasingly usable.

The urgency to act, however, is also increasing. People in communities around the world want a reliable, replicable process with which to respond to the outside forces that push them around. As the privileged gain more advantage, the poor are becoming more disadvantaged. Planetary processes are teetering on the brink of irreversible imbalance. Civil stability is unraveling. Change looms as a threat rather than a promise. While a great deal has been accomplished with the resources and models that exist today, they are not enough to promote a just and sustainable future for all people, including that poorest 1.3 billion, and for generations of people not yet born. A new paradigm is needed by which change can be reshaped in positive ways.

The choice ultimately is whether we are ready to take collective, intentional action to deal with both the challenge and the positive potential. The approach described in this book is a synthesis of lessons from world experience, thinking and observations from four generations of our family's work, and large field trials over the last three decades where we tested and refined the method. It is a process based on partnership, objective data, and systematic work plans. Its consequences are designed to extend to everyone.

The familiar slogan "Think globally, act locally" endures because it is a hopeful, directed statement. It assumes that we can shape today's fast-moving and complex forces to build a meaningful future for ourselves and for the generations that will follow us. The words define the scope of the problem, but they do not offer a clear-cut solution. In today's world, as we seesaw between promise and pessimism, this book advances a practical path for locally based action at whatever scale communities are capable of aggregating. If we disregard the imperative for locally based action, we face a future of exploitation. If we disregard the imperative for thinking globally, we also face a future of exploitation. But if we heed and act upon both, we can assure ourselves and our neighbors a better future.

As we begin this book, it is important to clarify a concept: the dimensionality of development. Change is commonly viewed in one dimension, but in reality there are at least three dimensions: bottom-up actions by people, top-down policies from government, and outside-in contribution of ideas and skills. These categories delineate the space within which communities operate—much the way latitude, longitude, and altitude define geographical space, or the x, y, and z dimensions define mathematical space. A similar nomenclature is needed for development. How do communities work with government, experts, and donors?

Our search of developmental literature did not uncover existing multidimensional vocabulary. So we created a terminology. SCALE One defines the axis of change at the community level. SCALE Squared outlines the axis that brings in knowledge and skills. SCALE Cubed is the enabling environment of policies and financing. Each of these three dimensions describes *where* actions are occurring. Who is doing the acting may vary—for example, community-based actions are not limited to actions by the community, nor is bringing in knowledge and skills a function solely of experts.

These multiple perspectives may be confusing at first, because our thinking on community change has typically occurred linearly, focusing on one aspect, not three. And, because we have thought linearly, we often came forward with simplistic solutions. It is going to be hard to appreciate the merit of another's position. Each partner's perspective was typically the axis along which he or she stood: top-down if official or international bureaucrat; outside-in if donor, academic, or international expert; bottom-up if community member or progressive outsider. But now, with a vocabulary that is based on interconnections, discussions and decisions can show each partner his or her role in relation to those of the other partners.

Just as the world is not flat, social change is not one-dimensional. When our perspective considered the planet flat, the world was Europe, Asia, and

Africa—lands now known as the Old World. But when our quest crossed the horizon in 1492, we learned that the world was a sphere. What had been West became the way East. Flat became round, and the same place could be gained by going in opposite directions. Viewing the world as a sphere changed our understanding of it. In more ways than the physical finding of the Americas, a New World was discovered. The modern age began when we learned that the earth was round.

Winds and currents of new understanding about societal change are coming today from distant corners of the Earth; we need appropriate ways to describe and deal with these. SEED-SCALE is one technique. It is specifically designed to help each community find itself within the complexity of options—then help the community move step by step along a curve of change that it desires and can implement. To find the starting point, we use the process of SEED. To describe each role, we use SCALE One, Squared, and Cubed. To find the actions to make the next year's move, we offer the seven annual steps.

PART I

The Claim

A Just and Lasting Future Is Achievable

CHAPTER 1

Getting Started

Positive Change Is Possible

On December 17, 1903, Wilbur and Orville Wright launched a "crate of sticks, linen, and wire" into the air from an obscure American beach. On that day men broke free from Earth's gravitational grip, but for five years the public scarcely noticed that people could fly. Then in 1908 Wilbur took to the sky over Paris in two successive flights. Crowds poured out of the city to see a human being riding in an "air ship."

Within a year Louis Bleriot flew across the English Channel. A year later, Alberto Santos-Dumont had an airplane for sale for pleasure flying. By 1913, the end of the first decade of aviation, metal was replacing sticks and linen, Igor Sikorsky was operating a huge four-engine craft in Russia, and more than forty thousand people had taken to the air in at least thirty-nine countries. The year 1919 saw the first flight across the Atlantic and another from England to Australia. By the 1920s ordinary people were going for joyrides in airplanes. Flying was affordable: pay a dollar to see the roof of your house. Twenty-five years after the Paris demonstration, commercial airplanes were carrying passengers, by the 1950s jets were circling the globe, and in 1969 a few people even went to the moon.

The surge in air travel did not start with the first flight. It started in 1908 with the first flight that people actually *saw.* The flight in 1903 was a technical breakthrough, but the revolution that continues to transform our lives began with ordinary people understanding that flight was possible. Similarly, the key to building better lives is not technical breakthroughs but changing behavior at the community level. This is a book about how to change the way we behave. Three principles are key to planned, intentional community change, but all three center on the same objective: changing people's behavior in ways that fit local circumstances. Such transformation requires confidence that new ways are possible, and that confidence both stems from and contributes to building capacity in communities. Playing an essential role in these processes are the formation and maintenance of a genuine three-way partnership among people in the community, experts from outside, and government officials.

Earlier efforts to define the dynamics of social change often failed because they focused on only one kind of leadership. Most professionally led approaches stressed top-down, prescriptive systems, seeking to direct people rather than helping them discover how to direct themselves. Another group of approaches failed because they stressed empowering people without taking into account the larger, more complex systems that are required for people to learn how to take advantage of opportunities.

Effective change grows from the community level, but bottom-up growth does not happen on its own. Grass provides an analogy. To grow from the roots, grass needs top-down nourishment from sun and rain (government help) and outside-in nourishment from fertilizer and micronutrients (expert help). Likewise, the SEED-SCALE approach builds from what should be self-evident: on their own, communities are unlikely to make significant change. If simple grassroots change were possible, then more and more communities, recognizing their self-interest, would have achieved it long ago. Mobilizing community growth is a complex process, requiring a three-way partnership of top-down support from government, outside-in innovation from experts, and bottom-up hard work from local people.

But even a three-way partnership faces huge challenges. Change at the local level is subject to two increasingly powerful global factors: international trade controlled by and for corporations, and accelerating change in the world's climate. These two megaforces introduce more and more complexity into launching community-based change. Adding to the difficulty is the increasing stress on our human social systems in the forms of fear, intracommunity violence, and disruption of family and community stability.[1]

The lengthening reach of the global corporate enterprise, particularly through expansion in trade, outpaces every other factor that can be quantified. International trade grew from $31 billion in 1950 to $3.6 trillion four decades later (in 1990 U.S. dollars)—a more than elevenfold increase—while world output grew only fivefold, from $3.8 trillion to $28.9 trillion.[2] The trend is not only not slowing; it is moving beyond the abilities of even the strongest governments to regulate it. This growth is supported by mega-agencies (the World Trade Organization, the World Bank, the International Monetary Fund, and the like) that introduce their own versions of supportive frameworks and restructure supposedly sovereign governments so that trade grows further and faster. Some of this global trade benefits communities, and some damages them. The beneficial aspects of international trade need to be preserved but in many cases refocused.

The only meaningful counterbalance to corporate globalization is communities. The momentum of globalized trade cannot be stopped, but it can be redirected. Communities are small enough to be able to understand their own self-interest, yet large enough to be able to access resources and generate efficiencies of scale. When communities are weak, they are inevitably exploited. To take advantage of corporate growth and not be its victims, communities around the world must rapidly increase their strength and ability to organize.

Even more undermining to society is environmental degradation. In its 1995 report to the United Nations, the International Panel on Climate Change acknowledged that human activity is changing the Earth's climate, and evidence has continued to mount ever since. Rising world temperature has now been associated with rising sea levels. Weather patterns are shifting along with air and ocean currents. Rising world temperature makes our habitat less healthy; a warmer climate extends the range of tropical diseases such as malaria even as globalization extends the potential range of epidemics of the heretofore localized Ebola and West Nile viruses. Lifestyle, international economics, and world politics may have to find new balances. To respond to these challenges, we need more-effective strategies. The most practical and accessible way to shape a collective response is to grow appropriate solutions at the community level that take into account the large and complex forces impinging on them.[3]

Community, as we use the term, is any group that has something in common and the potential for acting together. Usually communities consist of people who live in a geographic region and interact as a cohesive social unit.

But there are other communities—unions, religious groups, ethnic alliances, and the like—that can also collectively organize to change. Most people are members of multiple communities. A defining characteristic is that a community functions best if it is small enough that people know one another, or about one another, and can organize for joint action.

Community action need not be limited to a small scale. It is possible to build systematically from one or several specific community-based projects and, using these as learning centers, to "scale up" to a whole region or nation. Such expansion occurs best when a larger framework reinforces community-level action throughout the process. As community activity grows in scope and strength, solutions can self-assemble across a region. SEED-SCALE is our name for the way to manage this process so that it is effective, rapid, and efficient. In contrast to approaches that prescribe one universal solution for all—religious dogmas, Marxism, politicians seeking office, even advertisements from the global consumer society—SEED-SCALE helps people find solutions that are appropriate to their own place and time. Over time these community-specific solutions can build into an aggregate force strong enough to resist and redirect the large forces now threatening societies and environments worldwide. The process grows through the annual iteration of seven steps.

Annual Action to Get Localized Solutions

There are now visible (and visitable) successes, in villages, cities, and jungles, on which to model future efforts. In all these examples of successful change, activities seem to cluster into annual cycles much like agricultural or academic years, with each cycle creating a staging point for the next. To establish such a cycle we advocate that each year a series of seven simple steps be repeated. If even one step is made so complicated that it cannot be accomplished in a given year, the other steps will not follow. Each year each community *must* run the whole cycle of steps. We cannot overstate the centrality of this point. A farmer who spends all his time plowing will never get to planting . . . let alone the harvest. A perfectionist student who takes too much time to complete individual assignments will not successfully finish the school year. The annual seven steps (under three group headings) are:

Building Capacity

1. Create or recreate a coordinating committee and use it to mobilize the community and engage with outside agencies. An individual attempting to lead community action tends to get caught between competing factions or demands. A coordinating committee brings groups together and distributes responsibilities among those who will act.

2. Identify past successes. What a community has done successfully is the most likely base for future success. On its own a community may not see what really are its successes and strengths. Experts can help identify these and can help redirect action so as to build potential.

3. Study successes and visit other communities. Find options that have worked for other people and adapt these to each local situation. Send people for these visits who will actually do the work (not just the powerful) so that the backbone of the community gets practical training.

Choosing a Vision: SEED (Self-Evaluation for Effective Decisionmaking)

4. Evaluate the situation objectively (self-evaluation). Create a community-specific database instead of working only from people's opinions. Gather information on problems and resources, and identify those in the community with specific skills or potential and the ability to forge agreement.

5. Discuss sources of problems, explore possible solutions, and decide which problems are most urgent (effective decisionmaking). Once people in the community have agreed on the priorities, they can draw up a work plan that assigns jobs and functions to all.

Taking Action

6. Involve as many people in the community as possible. Start projects that will be popular because they respond to felt needs. Aggregate activities so that momentum converges and builds.

7. Monitor momentum and identify gaps in action to make midcourse corrections in how work is actually performed. Then reallocate functions. It is less important to get action right at the beginning than to try options, adapt them, and keep improving.

This ongoing process of our collective change requires working together. We opened this chapter with a sketch of the expansion of the technology of flight. But improving our lives and redefining our future does not depend fundamentally on technical solutions, money, new infrastructure, or even management. Those are merely components of the process. Reshaping our future is about changing how we live, and to highlight the point that we are sentient creatures, capable of responding to circumstance and turning it to adaptive advantage. From time to time in this book we present biological parallels rather than the static engineering or commercial metaphors commonly used by development experts. In this instance, birds offer nature's lessons about how to fly. How does nature move a whole flock of birds?

Consider the goose. The striking V formation of a flock in flight reveals a number of natural lessons about how to move collectively. A flock can travel up to a thousand miles without resting, whereas a single bird cannot go much more than half that distance. The discipline of their flying V allows geese to utilize lift coming off the tips of one another's wings, so the flock gets a 60 percent greater flying range than if each bird flew alone. Because the leader tires without benefit from the lift of others' wings, the leadership role rotates: the lead bird drops behind to ride in the draft, and others move forward. When a goose moves out of formation, the increased drag on its wings reminds it to fall into position to gain the collective lift. In a common endeavor encouragement helps, so as geese fly together, they honk, offering support and identifying their position to those who share their effort. Should a bird become sick, wounded, or exhausted, when it descends from the flock a couple of other geese drop out to protect it. They remain together until they are able to fly as a threesome or join another passing flock.

The parallels to ourselves are obvious. One worth emphasizing here is the importance of the whole-flock perspective. Nature supports a dominant, alpha leadership position only when organizational needs are short-term, as in the cases of protection against direct threats to life and of carnivores' pursuit of food. When the task is to move long distances, the organizational needs are different; no individual can assume sole leadership without weakening the group, so nature summons collective action. The organizational principle of development is partnership—cooperation among individuals and groups to get lift, rotate leadership, honk encouragement, and shelter the weak even if it means temporarily abandoning flight.

Several years ago we worked with the White Mountain Apache tribe in the American Southwest, helping them to adapt these concepts. Before their contact with Europeans the Apache hunted, gathered, and farmed according to their own set of values. The new American nation confined them to a smaller area and imposed upon them a radically different set of values and lifestyle. In discussions with the Apache about how to put together a vision that drew its guidance from Apache culture, we asked them: "How would you describe a just and sustainable future?" They answered: "Our whole community walking forward together." The Apache statement, like the long-distance flight of the geese, acknowledges the central importance of collective interdependence during a great journey.

A whole community walking together along the path of change has no losers—except those who choose not to participate. Each new step forward is a step into unknown territory, where the options are uncertain and the hazards unknown. A person walking alone into such territory can easily lose the way or simply stand still, afraid to go forward. But if we walk together and walk sensitively, we will feel when we've stepped off the path—like geese that feel the increased drag. No detailed road map exists to show each community the precise way to go, but a process does exist that tells how to find the next step, the one that is right for each community. Walking the path together, we build the potential for generations to come, just as earlier generations built the present we enjoy today.

Four Examples of Development with Worldwide Impact

Four examples of intentional action in the past show how societywide change can take off. None is perfect; each has done less than it could or should have to reduce inequities between rich and poor, each has had unintended negative consequences, and none offers a guarantee of continued benefits for future generations. But they do show that intentional action can launch large-scale change.

Development Expansion in the United States

From the 1860s to the 1960s the United States evolved an enabling context for communities that allowed the entire nation to progress from a land of soil-scratching farmers where diarrhea was the number-one killer, illiteracy was more common than literacy, and the primary business medium was barter, to the most developed nation on Earth, with predominance in trade, education, military power, and the popular media. Other parts of the world in the mid-nineteenth century also had skilled people, open land, innovation, abundant natural resources, and intensive external investment. Why did this particular former colony move so dramatically to preeminence? The actions of two presidents in particular made major contributions to this outcome.

In the 1850s the United States was far from being a world power in any sphere. One indicator of its low status was that the British government paid a higher hardship allowance to its diplomats posted in mud- and malaria-ridden Washington, D.C., than to its diplomats in Calcutta. But in 1861 a cluster of enabling acts was launched, creating reinforcing feedback loops that strengthened community capacity. The Industrial Revolution was under way in many countries, along with exploitation of natural resources and the availability of low-cost labor from large-scale migration. In the United States, however, government joined with business and experts to create an environment that nurtured large-scale mobilization, educated people by the hundreds of thousands, and supported experimentation.[4] As a result this society overtook England, France, and China, which in differing ways were developmentally ahead at the time, and outpaced Canada, Brazil, Russia, Japan, and Australia, which were also launching intentional development action and had great potential for building their economies. In the United States compulsory, publicly financed education accelerated and built up a skill base. Roads, canals, and railroads created transportation linkages throughout the nation. Poor people were able to acquire land and initiate large agricultural expansion. Policies enabled individual initiative to grow into community initiative, especially by fostering entrepreneurship. A critical mass of individual changes coalesced to promote societal change.[5]

Abraham Lincoln played a crucial role in launching this enabling context.[6] While the Civil War and the issue of slavery consumed most of Lincoln's attention—and has certainly consumed most of history's—under his administration the U.S. government redirected the way it supported the American people. Many of the changes were justified under the political cover of the national crisis as officials established sweeping new frameworks for action. The Civil War did more than fire up America's industrial engine, transforming its manufacturing capacity; equally important, Lincoln used the war to fire up America's societal engine.

Lincoln understood the importance of the flow of information. During his administration he spent more time in the telegraph office across the street from the White House than in any other single place outside the White House. Often he made the trip three times each day, crossing the lawn with a gray plaid woolen shawl wrapped around his shoulders and settling his lanky frame into a chair to read the stack of waiting messages. It was while sitting in that telegraph office, waiting for other messages, that Lincoln drafted the Emancipation Proclamation.[7] Recognizing the role information could play in people's lives, Lincoln embraced the new information technology. When he entered office, the Pony Express was considered an innovation. But the Pony Express, though imbued with romance, benefited only a few and did not change the flow of information. Lincoln pressed to expand communication services to the public. In 1861, only months into his administration, the first transcontinental telegraph line was completed, supplanting the Pony Express. In the same year Lincoln pressed through passage of the Pacific Railroad Act and actively supported construction of a transatlantic telegraph cable. But the change that made the biggest difference in people's lives was the inauguration of swift and reliable postal service, with three classes of mail, the introduction of postcards, and free home delivery in cities. Delivery became faster as employees sorted mail in special postal cars on trains, picked up postal sacks from hooks, and threw them out as trains sped through stations.

Lincoln also launched important educational initiatives. In 1862 the Land Grant Colleges Act opened opportunities for higher education to people at all economic levels in every state, whether they came from farms or from industrial manufacturing centers. In this era, advanced learning was a privilege of the wealthy; two more generations would pass before most European countries made low-cost higher education available.

Lincoln's administration restructured the movement and management of money, and in doing so made it better serve common people. Three initiatives stand out: a national banking system, a standard currency (the "greenback"), and the postal money order. While the national banking system and standard currency helped keep Lincoln's government solvent as war debts mounted, the money order helped ordinary people directly. In an era when most communities did not have a bank, post offices were authorized to issue money orders, supporting the safe transfer of small sums. Money orders gave commoners a secure currency that allowed them to act economically in another community. This move especially helped rural people at a time when barter was still common.

Lincoln's administration initiated a number of financial-security policies, including several that supported the growth of corporations (as opposed to family businesses) by shielding individual shareholders from direct legal liability. These measures opened up more diverse investment, commercial risk-taking, and experimentation; but as additional measures over the next several decades shielded corporations more and more, what had started out as a benefit to development became an increasingly intractable problem, contributing to greater inequities in America.[8]

As a result of his farm upbringing, Lincoln understood the support farmers needed, and he acted quickly with several agricultural initiatives. In March 1862 his administration created the Department of Agriculture, and passage of the Homestead Act in May 1862 gave farmers free land. Lincoln's administration also supported The Grange, a nongovernmental organization that gave expert help to farmers at the community level.

Finally, Lincoln risked the nation itself to press for equity through the abolition of slavery. His initiatives strengthened the country not by direct government action, but by using government to create an enabling context that supported community action.

Another major figure in promoting an enabling framework for equity was Theodore Roosevelt, who pursued parallel priorities of Progressive era populism and environmental action.[9] In his effort to control the monopolies that had become rogue economic forces, he created the Bureau of Corporations to gather data on the monopolies and with that information broke up more than forty, including John D. Rockefeller's Standard Oil. In 1905 with the Hepburn Act he weakened the influence of the railroads by regulating fares.

To counterbalance business interests' direct access to the White House, Roosevelt reached out to the growing communities of workers, including unions, and intervened in several standoffs, the most important being the one involving the United Mine Workers. His administration also investigated the conditions of factory workers and began testing consumer products. With passage of the Meat Inspection Act, he created the Food and Drug Administration in 1906.

Roosevelt made environmental action a priority for national government. His administration started the National Forest Service, protecting 150 million acres of watersheds. Through the Interior Department he created five national parks, eighteen national monuments, and fifty-one federal bird reservations. Many of Roosevelt's measures, such as the Reclamation Act of 1902, integrated people with land protection. Environmental concerns recur throughout his speeches, even those not directly seeking environmental action, showing concern for watersheds, sensitivity to ecosystem dynamics, and his early awareness of the importance of people within those systems.

Roosevelt focused not only on issues of populist equity but also on the budding forces of globalization. His active promotion of the Panama Canal is well known; less remembered today are his key roles in keeping Germany out of Venezuela in 1902, his mediation in the Russo-Japanese War in 1904–5, and his peacemaking in the Moroccan crisis of 1906. This global activism did not go unnoticed; Teddy Roosevelt was the first American to win the Nobel Peace Prize.

Both Lincoln and Roosevelt had their tawdry sides (Lincoln's "darky" jokes and his plans to export blacks back to Africa are examples, as are Roosevelt's elitism and his fondness for killing rare animals); but these leaders promoted positive change as part of larger partnerships; remarkable people in their administrations helped launch their more visionary programs. Both presidents saw government as a means of enabling ordinary people. Neither tried to tell communities what their solutions should be; rather, they worked to create an environment in which communities could evolve their own solutions.

In the 1960s this unique century of development came to an end. National enabling frameworks began to erode as narrow interests gained special access to officials and large groups were more and more excluded. National policy began to focus on regulation and accountability instead of incentives and empowerment. The effect was to reinforce behaviors of confrontation rather than collaboration. Even so, this sketch shows vividly the processes involved in taking development to national scale through creation of a web of community-enabling policies.

The Green Revolution

Over the last four decades of the twentieth century, a series of scientific contributions known collectively as the Green Revolution increased world food supply so dramatically that famines, which had been a growing worldwide threat in the 1940s and 1950s, virtually disappeared. Today, although hunger persists worldwide, and although food distribution remains inequitable, there is greater food security in all countries despite the fact that twice as many people must be fed.[10] Major negative effects also accompanied this revolution: commercialization of food security, consolidation of agriculture into the hands of wealthy farmers, huge ecological pressure on soil and water supplies, and loss of genetic diversity. But the Green Revolution was one of the first planned development initiatives to succeed on a global scale; it more than doubled world food production, largely by adapting its farming breakthroughs to local conditions.

The Green Revolution expanded in three phases. First, scientists in many parts of the world developed packages of technical interventions for each of the major cereal grains. Next researchers at agricultural centers adapted the packages to regional environments, cultures, and economies, monitoring nitrogen and other nutrients to create the most-productive fertilizers, promoted irrigation to accelerate growth and extend growing seasons, selectively breeding high-yield seeds, and advocating the use of powered machinery. In the second phase, demonstration farms in each subregion further modified the packages of innovations and encouraged farmers to visit to see the results. Third, governments opened new land, created new financial mechanisms, improved food storage, built factories to make the machinery, and supported more-efficient food distribution. Throughout this process, farmers received incentives from international donors and wide-ranging subsidies from national governments to adopt and continue to implement the packages of interventions.

The Child Survival Revolution

During the second half of the twentieth century the Child Survival Revolution reduced child mortality worldwide more than in all previous human history. Research centers in the developing world (discussed further in Chapters 6 and 10) achieved simplified technical breakthroughs that enabled parents to diagnose and treat the leading causes of child death and communities to develop and expand potable water supplies, public health education, family planning, immunization, breast-feeding, and infant and child nutrition. Most important, however, was not the medical or scientific intervention, but the widespread education of girls. Collectively the changes filled gaps in existing health services, and their simplicity promoted rapid change in behaviors in homes and communities; millions of lives were saved as a result.[11] One of the most beneficial and important consequences was the realization that the most important health workers in the world are not physicians or surgeons but mothers.

As in the case of the Green Revolution, negative consequences attended the Child Survival Revolution. The strong push to deliver specific services and meet targets created unsustainable vertical programs that fractured the primary-health-care systems of many poor countries. Massive financial contributions from international donors helped countries to achieve their goals but also made them dependent on outside funding. Even so, the speed and effectiveness with which the movement went to scale make it a useful example of social mobilization and behavior change.

The Transportation Revolution

Over the past four decades the transportation revolution has expanded bus and airline travel in all countries of the world with steady gains in cost-effectiveness; every year, long-distance travel becomes more reliable, less expensive, and available to greater numbers of people. In turn this revolution has leveraged change in other sectors, increasing economic activity, access to information, and communication among communities. It has also contributed to air pollution, warming of the atmosphere, high accident rates, and depletion of nonrenewable resources.

The catalyst in the transportation revolution has been a partnership between government and business: governments created enabling policies and financial frameworks, and businesses implemented the services. Today an array of small and large companies responds to local needs, continually gathering data on their customers' destinations, finances, and scheduling preferences to make services more effective.

Who Needs to Develop?

Most people today feel that their margin for failure is thin and that they are generally better off being cautious. They change only if change comes with low risk or potentially high returns. Comprehensive community change feels too ambitious, and wealthy communities are likely to be even less willing than poor ones to take risks.

Yet a new framework of development is as much needed among wealthy communities as among poor ones, for they face the same perils. For rich and poor alike, the expansion of trade, changes in the Earth's environment, and the unraveling of social systems make the future uncertain. Even wealthy societies are increasingly unable to care for their growing numbers of poor, alienated youth, forgotten elderly, marginalized mothers, hostile homeless, and exploited minorities. In many ways, the rich have more to lose, and the need for a fundamental change in values and behavior is even more urgent. It seems that even those with great wealth have not arrived but, like the poor, are still "developing."

To achieve a more just and lasting future we must continually update our definition of development. We can advance more confidently and effectively into that unknown territory by drawing lessons from past successes—and from past failures—and by tailoring solutions for each community to its specific hopes, capabilities, and resources. The approach we describe in the following chapters streamlines the earlier and slower processes that brought the benefits we enjoy today and offers a way to build continuing progress for all.

CHAPTER 2

Synopsis of SEED-SCALE

SEED (Self-Evaluation for Effective Decisionmaking) + SCALE (System for Communities to Adapt Learning and Expand) = SEED-SCALE

The conversations that ultimately grew into this book began in the Punjab of northern India during the 1950s. Then this father-and-son team would drive each week through high *sarkanda* grass that extended as far as our eyes could see. We were headed to isolated villages to run medical clinics. The father drove the jeep, and the ten-year-old son rode proudly by his side. A generation earlier, the father had been the son, two hundred miles to the east, in the foothills of the Himalaya, riding in an oxcart beside his medical missionary parents, bouncing over rutted jungle tracks as that generation also headed out to run clinics.

Each year during our drives we became more aware that the animals were getting fewer; human progress was causing the *sarkanda* to disappear. During the day we worked in a village clinic where the father, Carl, would see the patients, many of whom had waited hours for care. Thump, thump, ahhhh, where does it hurt? After the diagnosis the patients walked to the table where sat the young Danny. He read the father's gnarly handwriting, counted the right number of pills from the right bottle, folded these inside a paper, and the patients returned to their fields scattered among the high grasses.

After the last patient we shut the door and turned to our search for food. With evening casting a red glow over the grass, we drove out along the Sutlej River. The land near the river was laced with waterways, nearly dried up for months each year except during the monsoon; in the mud were waterholes where wild boar, blue antelope, foxes, and occasional leopards came. We scanned especially for black buck, which sometimes ran in herds of hundreds through the high grass. They, and the blue antelope or wild boar, were meat to share with our neighbors who could not afford chickens or goats from the bazaars.

Today the black buck is an endangered animal, and the savannas we once drove through are now endless wheat fields. Like the United States, whose prairies and herds of bison have long since disappeared, India has sacrificed its natural environment to the goal of self-sufficiency in food production. India's population, like America's, has grown enormously, and so have the expectations of its people. Following different paths of development, both nations have sacrificed ecology for economy. Both India and the United States have achieved their development goals; life in both countries is better today for most people than it was in the 1950s. But in the drive to development they have lost precious environmental capacity, and their peoples have benefited unequally. Across generations we have asked ourselves and many others: how could we make development more just and sustainable?

Today our family's transgenerational quest to improve the lives of people in greatest need has extended to a fourth tier, the children of that ten-year-old son. But we know that we are tiny figures in a vast cavalcade extending back in time to the dawn of our species. The particular challenge may once have been how to make a fire and keep warm, but although the technical challenges are now hugely different, the process remains the same: we kindle one flickering success into more and larger fires that can warm more people. We can do this only by working in partnership, gathering data about our circumstances and then distributing the workload.

A manageable number of people with common interests and the potential for action—we call them a community—achieve one success, and they adapt some ideas, work together, and achieve another. Just and lasting change in a community builds from cumulative successes. Development grows out of hope. The process of community development parallels the process of successful parenting: a child must believe in his or her capacity and build on strengths. Communities that are skeptical about their potential may endure, accommodate, or pretend, but they will not develop. Privileged starting points and resources do not matter nearly as much as positive conviction about the future. A vision that is shared in the community, a conviction that the common future will be better, is the foundation for development.

Once such hope is mobilized, the challenge is to find concrete ways to build community capacity. To achieve successes, communities must form partnerships with outsiders, officials and experts. But infusions of outside resources (such as money, training, and technology) do not guarantee a better life. Resources from outside can create jobs, improve health indicators, send children to school, and construct roads, but they don't necessarily mobilize community energy. In fact they often drain away self-reliance and make a community dependent.

We advocate flexible growth following patterns defined by the lifestyle of communities and their families. Development changes relations in a community. As priorities change in response to chronic everyday problems, and as goals are tailored and retailored every year to the community's specific economic need, culture, and ecology, multiple activities generate new relationships, firing up community energy. When participants see that joint activities are solving their needs, they adapt solutions to fill their own local niches, and the energy replicates and spreads.

Community energy can be neither bought nor coerced. It is internal. Outsiders and outside resources are crucial to it, but their role is to stimulate commitment and practical alternatives, not to do the actual work. Technology, training, incentives, and regulations expand possibilities; good sales pitches stimulate curiosity. And when successes appear, other communities can learn from them and achieve their own. For this outward radiation to proceed, government must create an enabling environment, experts must assist with ongoing technical breakthroughs and education—and both government and experts must relinquish control as capacity grows among multiple communities. Guidance nurtures hope by adapting, using, and sharing benefits.

Three Basic Principles for Community Action

Principle One: Three-Way Partnerships

Community energy seldom mobilizes by itself. Communities need help from officials, who can adjust policies and regulations, facilitate cooperation among factions, and channel essential resources. Communities also need help from experts, who can build capacity and skills by training, introduce new ideas and techniques, and help monitor change, ideally bringing multiple perspectives—academic, business, and nongovernmental—to the process.[1] Progress comes from collaborative bottom-up (community), top-down (officials), and outside-in (experts) activity, with no one sector deciding that it alone is "in charge."

Relationships among the partners must change throughout the process. At the start, entrepreneurial leadership is important both in the community and among officials. In the middle stages experts can lead training, monitoring, and experimentation, helping communities make midcourse corrections. Later, systems are needed to help communities share their vision and capacity, and officials and experts must relinquish more and more control to support the growth of community self-reliance.

The principle of the three-way partnership denies the central importance of a charismatic leader with a vision and the capacity to mobilize and organize people behind it. Charismatic leaders are hard to find, and even harder to replace. Charismatic leaders often start out on track but stray as others stop checking their missteps; after this they become arrogant. In the very complex situations of community development, a single leader does not bring together enough diversity of perspectives. The three-way partnership avoids these pitfalls. It can use a charismatic leader if one is present, but it must be vigilant lest this one individual take control. There are exceptions to this rule: in emergencies, construction and engineering projects, professional accreditation, and other focused development work, a single leader is the preferred, and more efficient, solution.

Principle Two: Action Based on Locally Specific Data

Action must be grounded in objective local data. Lacking such data, participants will base decisions on transitory shifts in opinion influenced by who talks most convincingly or is most powerful at the moment. Decisions not grounded in local data often are isolated from the people; they are made by officials who tend to be out of touch and out of date, and the experts' thick reports are usually based on earlier studies done elsewhere and on deductions from theory. Focusing on local data, community members, with guidance from officials and experts, can blend practical local realities with the best of worldwide understanding.

The advantages of working from truly local data become self-evident as soon as a community effort is launched. Expecting local people to have the time, resources, and expertise required for gathering modern, scientific data is wildly unrealistic and impractical in most circumstances. But when all three partners share in the effort, they combine their separate skills: the experts design an easy-to-do process, the officials create an enabling context, and the local people do the fieldwork. Collective data-gathering fosters wider acceptance of the findings and creates a coalition for later action. When the whole community invests time in both collecting and interpreting the data, scientific data no longer belong to experts but are owned by everybody. Having objective facts allows comparisons between the past and present and also between communities. Parallel data-gathering from multiple sources allows people to synthesize science with indigenous wisdom.[2]

Some methods for obtaining locally specific and community-gathered data are already well established, such as Rapid Assessment Procedures (RAPs), Participatory Rural Appraisals (PRAs), and Planning, Learning, and Action (PLA). Our comprehensive data-gathering method, called SEED (Self-Evaluation for Effective Decisionmaking) and presented in Chapter 21, combines earlier methods of participatory data-gathering with expert-led, science-based data collection and analysis.

Principle Three: Changes in Community Behavior

People can come together in partnerships and can agree on objective data, but to achieve lasting results they must also change their behavior. Most members of the community can start simply by gaining new skills. Those in positions of power—community leaders, officials, or experts—have to learn to share power. This means giving up exclusive control, shifting to guidance that empowers rather than fostering dependency. This shift is difficult, but when officials and experts demonstrate humility community enthusiasm becomes contagious. This feedback loop sets new expectations and standards for everyone. As one change supports another, social pressure builds, and those who do not cooperate may be bypassed or overrun by the momentum.

Calling for genuine behavior change may seem about as practical as proposing a religious awakening. Behaviors are embedded in community norms. Established traditions do not shift easily. But behaviors do change when, one by one, individuals and families see that a particular change is in their self-interest. Ideas offering obvious benefit become entry points for blending traditional interpretations with modern scientific findings. The process may then spread quickly as a mass movement, but more often it permeates gradually, evolving societal change.

A particularly striking recent mass behavior change is the worldwide shift in family-planning practice. During the early 1960s changing sexual behavior seemed to be among the tougher challenges of civil society, since it is genetically grounded, supported by religious dogma, and protected by strict norms of privacy. But during the last forty years we have seen a worldwide change as more and more people realized that smaller families do better economically and that slower-growing communities can achieve higher quality in their services and their lives.

The Three Dimensions of SCALE

As it expands through a cluster of communities (or even through a region or nation), development unfolds along multiple dimensions. We have clustered the development process into three dimensions:

- SCALE One selects, learns from, and promotes successful community projects (Successful Change As Learning Experiences).
- SCALE Squared transforms demonstration projects into learning centers for others (Self-help Centers for Action Learning and Experimentation).
- SCALE Cubed promotes systematic extension throughout regions and societies (Systems for Collaboration, Adaptive Learning, and Extension).

When it is used to apply to all three dimensions, the SCALE acronym stands for System for Communities to Adapt Learning and Expand. This multilevel acronym, which probably appears both overly ornate and reductionist to English-speakers in the developed world, provides a useful standard formula when the process is taught at the field level in other languages.

Sometimes SCALE One comes first, especially when the change is spontaneous. One or more communities see potential and make changes that then spread to other neighborhoods. At other times SCALE Squared begins the process, particularly when experts start demonstrations at centers for training and promoting extension. More commonly now, SCALE Cubed starts the sequence, with government creating an enabling environment and putting in place key demonstrations; then innovation takes off in multiple places, to be refined through adaptation and training.

SCALE One finds or, if necessary, creates examples and conviction in communities that lead to a growing sense of empowerment. Some communities are already innovators: even in very traditional areas, certain groups are always trying new things. Even in unstable slums that have high violence, there may be an innovative edge. Successes can be found anywhere. A nongovernmental organization may have spent one or more decades developing a community-based project. A group of entrepreneurial businessmen may have conditioned a community to take risks. Their successful project may be a health clinic, a conservation effort, a jobs program, or a road. The activity matters far less than how the choices were made and the work done. What is crucial is to find an activity that empowers momentum for change, with one success adding to another. When people become aware that they can benefit from change, their self-concept, capacity, and conviction grow.

For change that does not seem to be merely the result of good luck, communities need examples and training. These are formalized in a SCALE Squared center, a particular place that other communities can go to. Or a cluster of communities with the potential to change can become a SCALE Squared center. At these centers, however they might be defined, people need to be able to see changes that they can use. The SCALE Squared dimension has two important parallel functions. One is to offer demonstrations of action learning and experimentation. The other is to promote cooperation among communities in a region, moving them beyond concern about their own development to sharing and supporting change in others.

In the action learning and experimentation role, the SCALE Squared center welcomes people from other communities to see how they can help themselves. These visitors are encouraged to ask questions and to take part in workshops or formal training as they come to believe that change is possible for people like themselves. In addition, they can try out ways to improve their circumstances, to make them fit local needs, tinkering with them and adjusting components to fit their resources.

The SCALE Cubed dimension involves expanding development to all communities in a region. Experience shows that communities left to their own resources do not consistently extend their experience to others. For example, from the 1930s to the 1950s the Rockefeller Foundation established model primary-health centers in many countries. Benefits were evident in most local situations, but they did not go to scale. Full regional expansion occurred (for example, in Sri Lanka and India's Kerala) only when systems promoted training and governments devised enabling policies.

The SCALE Cubed dimension is built on three systems that are essential to the creation of this enabling environment. These systems use external stimuli such as professional role reallocation, training, policy change, and financial incentives. They focus on new values, local as well as global influences, comprehensive rather than narrow programs, sustainability instead of immediate gain, and a concern for all rather than just the advancement of leaders and the elite. When all systems are in place, development can grow exponentially.

System for sustainable collaboration. Several structures and activities are needed to promote collaboration among communities, officials, and experts. To assemble site-specific processes of development in each community a larger environment needs to be in place to encourage local groups to create their own appropriate solutions. They need a supporting framework to help them with:

Changing policies, regulations, administrative infrastructure, financing, and information systems. In addition, ownership, transport, marketing, and communications may need adjustment.

"Seed grants" to leverage community financing and mobilize internal resources.

Communication among communities to share what others are doing in promoting innovations from SCALE Squared centers, and objective critiques by other communities.

Opportunities to attend special regional events such as fairs, competitions, concerts, workshops, and festivals to create a sense of being part of a larger, expanding movement.

System for adaptive learning. Each year needs to add another step of growth, and for that cumulative evolution communities require a system for learning about themselves. Traditionally this was a hit-or-miss process for communities; they might grab a good initiative one time but not be so lucky the next. Visits and workshops at the SCALE Squared center to learn new ideas and skills are part of scaling up. But new ideas and skills will not automatically fit every community. Communities need support from the centers in adapting and testing new ideas.

SEED provides a regular database that efficiently supports self-reliant innovation. SEED has two components: self-evaluation, or objective data-gathering, in which communities assess their changing circumstances and set priorities; and effective decisionmaking, in which communities, experts, and sometimes also officials join in analyzing the causes of local problems, choose their priorities, then analyze the functions to be performed and assign roles to distribute shared responsibility and accountability fairly.

System for extension. A central authority cannot orchestrate the details of community-based development over a large region. Government bureaucracies and their highly paid professionals have typically shown arrogant incompetence when they sought to remote-control the extension of development. Since every community is different, local solutions must be different, and as change becomes more complex, external control, formerly concentrated in the hands of a few people, must be relinquished or shared. A few activities—such as quality control and promoting equity—must always be retained as top-down functions. However, since this essential outside role also tends to create dependency rather than building self-reliance, its controlling function needs to be reduced (but never totally relinquished) as communities grow steadily more confident and capable. To develop, communities need a nurturing, enabling environment. Since they cannot make all the adjustments on their own, structural changes at the government level can support such extension, building a system for collaboration that helps communities, officials, and experts work in partnership.

Three basic changes must take place. First, policies must be changed, and with them laws, regulatory bodies, and administrative infrastructure. These policies affect trade, transport, marketing assistance, information access, many types of training, and ownership of common resources such as land or water. Second, financing mechanisms must be changed. Ordinarily lending and saving mechanisms tend to favor the financiers rather than the recipients. Yet the welfare of a society depends on financial institutions' making equity in development a continuing priority. Societies advance as a whole when they bring along their most disadvantaged segment; otherwise advancement remains fragmented. When this longer-term and wider vision is continually expanded and restructured, the financial institutions will prosper because the overall community health is improving. Third, the administrative framework must be changed so as to encourage support for extension from existing service personnel in health, agriculture, education, public affairs, and other sectors. These agencies generally focus only on solutions to problems in their area of responsibility and often complain that intersectoral cooperation is difficult. In SCALE Cubed they can learn to collaborate in helping individuals and communities learn the most appropriate answers to their practical questions. Retraining of development professionals is usually essential to reorient them to new roles.

The three dimensions require different leadership skills among the three partners. SCALE One requires initiative and capacity to incubate change, to see opportunities even in bleak circumstances, and to act with imagination. Entrepreneurs do well here. SCALE Squared involves more deliberate research and development, with practical educational skills and experimental creativity. Hands-on academic types are needed here. Larger implementation and the generation of new systems in SCALE Cubed require managers and politicians who do not try to direct the jobs themselves but who facilitate collaboration among others. Good bureaucrats are a treasure here. People may succeed in one dimension but fail in others unless they change their attitudes and skills. In each dimension there are roles for everyone—but the role of each partner changes.

Six Criteria for Testing Action

Six criteria help participants in community efforts to monitor whether particular changes and events are positive or will create later problems. These tests are not as firmly established as the three principles described above. Communities need to tailor their own definitions and uses of these criteria to the local situation. For example, equity will be measured differently in the United States from in the Czech Republic, China, or Tchad. Imposing outside definitions will cause resentment and impede cooperation.

1. *Collaboration.* A community develops efficiently when people as a group agree on the direction they want to go. When people's vision is grounded in an understanding of what is realistic for them, they develop a general sense of cooperation that spreads internally through the community. As we use the term, *collaboration* within the community differs from partnership, which relates to cooperative action among the three larger partners of community, officials, and experts. Collaboration comes from agreement within the community to pull together, not from oratory or injunctions. It builds on pragmatism, which counteracts unrealistic visions nourished by sales pitches, bank-loan officers, and personal aspirations. Collaboration creates a mutual support structure that encourages behavior change. The indicators of how widely a vision is shared include who shows up at community meetings, who does the talking, who decides, who volunteers for what kinds of work, who seeks credit, and how benefits are distributed.[3]

2. *Equity.* Too often groups that can afford to take risks seize emerging advantages, and the less educated, the poor, and the ethnic and religious minorities fall behind. When socialist alternatives were more widely promoted, there was greater acceptance of the need for equity. Equity is a justifiable goal for more than moral reasons. An

organism cannot be healthy when certain organs are diseased, and a community cannot be healthy when groups within it are disenfranchised. But community-based equity will not evolve on its own, because in most societies local patterns of discrimination are deeply entrenched. Controls are needed to ensure that, with a rising tide, those who have bigger boats do not swamp those whose boats are smaller and have leaks. Only outside pressure for equity from a government-led enabling environment will convince local elites that their own future will improve when everyone benefits.[4]

3. *Sustainability.* Testing for environmental, economic, and cultural sustainability helps decisionmakers recognize when development is producing short-term gains but not lasting benefits. Is development exhausting water, forest, and energy resources or increasing air, soil, and water pollution? Are debts being incurred that cannot be repaid? Most important, sustainability must retain a human face: is change undermining the transmission of cultural values to the next generation?[5]

Development will always bring multiple trade-offs: resources will be consumed, economic costs will mount, and cultures will be forced to adapt. Moving to something new will always involve the loss of something old. Technology, training, and invention will constantly seek to make development more efficient, but they never can make it totally efficient. So each community as it approaches new opportunities must ask: Are the gains worth the costs? Sometimes communities may conclude that they do not want a particular development, that the changes are not progress according to their vision of the future.

4. *Interdependence not dependency.* The antithesis of development is dependency. Action for just and lasting development enhances interdependence within and among communities and reduces vulnerability to the victimization that so often accompanies dependency. Interdependent development does not advocate that communities try to stand on their own but that they create links that foster great, cumulative strength.

A more just and lasting future cannot be bought. Donors, seeking faster results, may offer to pay the costs of some service. Government officials seeking votes may promise to provide popular services. New outside assistance may at first appear to improve conditions, but capacity within the community fades when people cling to unrealistic expectations of help from outside. Donors who thought they were promoting development find that instead they have instigated dependency. Outside resources are certainly needed, but they should be accepted only if they do not shift control outside the community.

5. *Holistic action.* Many development efforts have tended to look at people as patients, students, bus riders, consumers, or statistics, but this is not how people see themselves. People are whole beings, individuals with unique needs. Breaking development into sectoral programs such as health, education, and transport does not address the larger reality of multifaceted well-being. By contrast, an orientation that addresses combinations of needs promotes synergistic interactions and quantum shifts, especially when a particular behavior change solves more than one problem. Action in one area stimulates progress in other areas; together they strengthen the fabric of community and family life and foster a rising tide.

6. *Iterative action.* Successful development matures through sequential learning and through continual adjustments in complex relations. An idea is attempted; on the next try, implementation gets a little better; in a third trial, the outcomes are even more useful. Iterative action is quite different from simply repeating a job endlessly the same way a machine would. In development, tasks and practices need to be adjusted with each trial. As in operations research, iteration is situation- and time-specific. If out of a dozen variables a few are not functioning, the whole system may be in jeopardy. By using methods such as annual SEED surveys it is possible to identify loose ends and determine which to tie down and which to trim.

In many places, an all-or-none law operates; here, iteration helps communities to find a balance. A community may be making money and expanding services, but if it is not attending to key changes or excluded groups, it may not be enjoying real development. Iterative action identifies problems and monitors the effects of change in an ecological way, sensitive to links among elements in the system. Development comes alive when partnerships, data, and changed behavior fit together; and as precision builds with each iteration, pieces fall into place.

The Cumulative Cycle of Crafting the Future

People in communities naturally think not in terms of work plans, but in terms of annual cycles such as an agricultural, fiscal, or academic year. The development year can be conceived of in a similar way, with seasons of building capacity, choosing direction, and taking action. This seasonal approach expands on UNICEF's experience in its world nutrition program, which was the "Triple A" process of assessment, analysis, and action to break program activities into a repeating sequence to keep action informed by both local reality and mounting experience.

Building Capacity

A time should be set each year, perhaps coinciding with the beginning of the school year, for the community systematically to expand the vision and skills of its people. Three people nurturing activities are helpful:

- Promote evolving leadership. Development leadership is likely to be more effective if it is not limited to a single person. Communities are strengthened when they feel that they are reaching commonality. A local coordinating committee is helpful in building partnerships, encouraging planning on the basis of local data, getting the cooperation of longstanding and recent factions, and fostering changed behaviors. An initial committee of volunteers is reconstituted in phases as people rotate off and others fill their places.
- Determine what has already worked. Plans for the future will seem more achievable if they grow out of past successes. Action that

draws on experience—and avoids abruptly swinging to new tasks requiring unfamiliar skills—helps to build both coalitions and practical efforts.

- Encourage as many people as possible to visit other projects and talk with people like themselves who are making changes. When people see a fishpond and learn what is involved in building and maintaining it, they are more likely to try the fishpond option and to experiment with other options.

Choosing a Direction

Each community must decide how much of its future development it will allow to be shaped by outside forces and how much responsibility it is willing and able to assume in finding the direction the community prefers. Every year the community grows stronger if it reviews its needs and direction (self-evaluation), identifies sources of problems, and produces a functional analysis that assigns jobs to everyone (effective decisionmaking). Self-evaluation involves conducting an annual assessment of all households and environmental conditions, using key indicators to make increasingly complex assessments over time. Such assessments are best done by a partnership of women, students, men's user groups, and experts from a SCALE Squared center. Effective decisionmaking involves analyzing the data to determine the causes of problems and to create a practical annual work plan. A functional analysis involving all partners balances needs and the use of time, finances, government services, and natural resources to determine the tasks people will perform in the coming year. Outsiders work with the local coordinating committee to manage the process in locally appropriate ways.

Taking Action

Although work continues throughout the year, certain periods bring greater bursts of effort. But communitywide change depends mostly on volunteer action; hiring others is seldom affordable. The real-world activities of getting the job done and monitoring the impact on the identified priorities must be scheduled flexibly to allow people with many other real-life commitments to do them.

Once people have agreed on a doable priority, follow-up with action should get under way while interest is high. Benefits must usually demonstrate at least some quick results. Those who are taking the risk to pioneer new methods need support and appropriate recognition from the coordinating committee. Failures will be frequent. A failure in such situations is an opportunity for learning. Getting the action right the first time is not as important as getting the action going, discovering any flaws, and then keeping action going while the reasons for failure are worked through. Accepting mistakes is part of learning and fosters creativity.

As communities move forward, they must also constantly look sideways and backward to monitor results and to deal with inevitable speculation and rumors about the success of the effort. This 360-degree perspective will guide adjustments in program goals, finances, training, regulations, surveillance for equity, and sustainability. All the activities are recursive—moving forward, stepping back, looking around in a process that grows with parallel action and building from repeated cycles. Management improves with each annual evaluation and finer tuning.

The key is to keep action moving forward and, once success starts to build, to keep action under the control of the local coordinating committee. Patience will always be needed to keep time-driven outsiders (who are reporting to yet other outsiders with other priorities) from taking over. Discipline will be required to keep their offers of assistance from throwing the local partnership out of balance. Ultimately it is the real success at the local level that best serves the interests of outsiders as well as the people who must live with the results.

CHAPTER 3

Making a Large and Lasting Impact

From October through December 1949, Carl E. Taylor was a member of the first scientific expedition to enter western Nepal, and as a member of that expedition he conducted that nation's first health survey. On October 28, 1999, fifty years after Carl's first visit, his grandson, Luke Taylor-Ide, aged twelve, a member of the fourth tier of this transgenerational discussion, ran down the same trail, sweeping the air with his butterfly net. Swoosh. And with a flick of his net, the thirteenth butterfly species of that day was caught.

Three generations of our family were walking that day through the spine of the Himalaya, on our way from the plains of India to the high Tibetan plateau. We were spending a month surveying the same villages covered by the 1949 expedition, to determine the patterns that had unfolded in Nepal's development. In 1949 Nepal had been closed to all but a very few outsiders; but by now large changes had reached even this remote part of the Earth. In 1999, 67,000 tourists would walk the trail that had opened in 1949, and some of the Nepalis from the villages were now so wealthy that they could go to Bangkok and Hong Kong for their medical treatments.

Fifty years earlier Carl had also swung a butterfly net over lantana bushes at this spot beside the Kali Gandaki River, catching butterflies as he walked from one village to the next conducting his health assessments. Butterflies are sensitive to habitat and can be used as indicator species of ecological niches. Carl had named this particular spot "butterfly paradise," having found more species here than anywhere else in his journey. Fifty years later, as Luke chased down the trail repeating his survey, this particular site was still fluttering thick with many species.

Why, after half a century, when Nepal had experienced so many changes, were butterflies still so thick in this spot? The answer came from Bob Fleming

Jr., the ecologist son of the leader of the 1949 expedition, who was along on this fifty-year follow-up trek. The butterflies were here because of the lantana, a shrub that had come in after a landslide swept the hillside above into the Kali Gandaki River. Lantana, though, is a plant from Mexico. Unknown years before the first people from the New World had walked up this trail, this flowering shrub from Mexico had arrived and firmly established itself on this slope. People had made their greatest impact on the environment not in the past fifty years, when we had thought Nepal was first opening, but during the hundred years before that. A century earlier the slopes had been cleared of their trees and carved out to create thousands of terraces on the hillsides. This beginning of environmental change coincided with the beginning of Nepal's population growth rather than with the country's opening to development.

Moreover, the through-passage of 67,000 tourists a year and the demands for firewood by the hundreds of new lodges and restaurants had not destroyed the forests here. The loss of trees and biological species was greater in the area lower down in the valley, where few foreign tourists came. But it was not tourism that had fostered environmental preservation. A partnership among communities, experts, and government had catalyzed the large-scale mobilization needed to restore the environment as well as to use tourism to make local money. The partnership was led by a national nongovernmental agency that in 1985 had organized communities in the region to create the Annapurna Conservation Area Project. A host of projects were under way, and each year they were becoming more effective. Whereas environmental conditions were worsening lower in the valley, where there was no organized response, at higher elevations, where the environment was more delicate and the potential for destructive impact was greater, environmental conditions were improving.

This partnership allowed locally owned tourist lodges to spring up in response to foreign tourism, and in turn the number of tourists rose each year as they discovered there was local capacity to accommodate them. Forested areas were expanding in this high-altitude, environmentally sensitive region. Large golden mountain goats, *thar,* which had been absent in 1949, were now returning to the Himalayan crags. Leopards also now passed through villages at night. Like the Qomolangma (Mount Everest) National Nature Preserve in

Tibet (see Chapter 18), the Annapurna Conservation Area Project had engaged local people in protecting the land.

The contribution of the Annapurna Conservation Area Project was significant, but its role in development remained a catalytic one, augmented by government, donor, and private initiatives. Now people were wearing machine-made clothing, their feet were protected by shoes, their skin was washed, and their homes had glass windows and in many cases electricity and running water too. School buildings stood in every town. Most homes had gardens containing at least half a dozen vegetables not present in 1949. Even communities that were not part of the formal conservation program were trying to protect their trees and shrub-covered slopes.

Outwardly, it appeared that widespread change was occurring. There was a strong collective effort under way to create a better future, but the people lacked a systematic supporting framework. A look at the data showed that fifty years of changes had benefited approximately 80 percent of Nepal's population. For four-fifths of the people, those who had started out with a small parcel of land, a core business, a modicum of education, or the ability to leave their village as a soldier or porter for a job that paid wages, the arrival of modern technologies had opened new opportunities and provided a tide on which to rise. But our data also showed that progress had left the poorest 20 percent behind. Health clinics and schools required fees that these people lacked. Without land beside the trails walked by the tourists, it was impossible to open even a tiny tea stall. There was still demand for porters to carry loads, but Nepal's population had tripled in these fifty years, so by 1999 there was a long line of eager applicants even for these jobs. Getting a place at the front of that line commonly required a bribe to the porter broker, and porters who showed up wearing rags at the bus stop where tourists got off found themselves passed over for porters wearing cast-off mountaineering clothing and speaking a few words of English. When the processes of change are left to the tug and pull of a marketplace that favors those with some, even small, initial advantage, socioeconomic change does not benefit the absolute poor.

In 1949 a more level economic playing field had existed. The commodity of exchange had been barter: a farmer could trade produce for a poorer person's labor. In a barter economy almost every person had something to trade. But by 1999 the marketplace required money; it wasn't possible to stand in a rice shop and offer a chicken in trade, or to take one's child to school (or get on a bus, or pay for a phone call) and propose paying for the service by carrying loads. The marketplace of 1999 made it impossible for those without money, in at least small amounts, to reap the benefits of development. In Nepal, while opportunities for most people are increasing, so are the societal burdens of those being left behind.

All of Nepalese society suffers as a result. Change that leaves the poorest 20 percent behind creates lopsided, fragmented communities. As disparities grow between haves and have-nots, progress remains only partial. Modern changes have not yet penetrated to the level where change is most needed. Nepal remains one of the most stunningly beautiful places in the world, with some of the most charming people. But each year a crisis moves closer. Nepal does not need more development assistance; it has had a disproportionate share. The solution lies in a systematic, community-based process that creates locally appropriate solutions.

Nepal's experience is not unique. The pattern worldwide is the same: the rich are getting richer, the poor are being left behind, and the environment is coping remarkably well under severe stress but posing a potential peril to all. The security of all people is in jeopardy. Fear grows along with awareness of our practical and moral obligations to the desperately poor. No longer is any one part of the world isolated from another. Planetary systems are far more tightly interlinked than fifty years ago, and the human imprint on the Earth is far heavier. With our growing awareness of the wholeness of the world and our impact on it, the need for action becomes ever more urgent.

The last half-century has witnessed an explosion of projects seeking to advance human well-being and protect an increasingly endangered environment. These projects have tried many ways of extending services. Each project points to its successes, and its advocates try to convince others to replicate their methodologies. Amid the successes, however, are a profusion of failures, and one reason for those failures is that many projects used the wrong extension approach for the objectives they intended.

One of the most baffling challenges for development planners has been how to support a success that was occurring in one community so as to go to scale with that innovation across a region. At least four distinct scaling-up philosophies are operating today in programs worldwide.[1] Most have been oriented to outside control; a few reflect the enabling approach that this book advocates. Each has gone partially to scale in certain applications. The SEED-SCALE approach may not be appropriate for all large-scale development programs. The choice of how these four approaches will be used in a particular scaling-up effort depends on how much community-based action will be needed for each specific set of problems, and these differ under various cultural and ecological conditions and in the timing of the opportunity.

The Blueprint Approach

The most common method used in mass development programs is a "blueprint" approach. To scale up to large societal needs, a "fix" is fashioned, then a plan is drawn up for replicating that fix. The process tends to mimic top-down social engineering. The centrally planned economies of the former Soviet bloc attempted this approach. The Peace Corps used it to distribute superchickens in thousands of villages in developing countries. International development banks use this approach to promote rapid extension of micro-credit for women. Conservationists have standardized what a nature preserve should be, and these blueprints are then adapted to be "locally appropriate" around the world.

Blueprints have become both more sophisticated and more locally sensitive, with provisions for environmental impact assessments, participatory planning, total quality management, and various other "humanizing" approaches. But the process remains expert driven. Experts look at local needs, refer to successes in other places, develop a design adjusted to local circumstances, and prescribe a package of interventions to be administered through hierarchies of government or nongovernmental agencies. The solution comes down from the top or in from the outside, and communities can comment on how (but not what) the implementation will be. The style feels right for those doing it, since it continues to apply formal techniques of government oversight, industrial production, and business management. It is often associated with the term *professional approach*.

The approach is most useful when tasks are mechanical, straightforward, and do not require site-specific modification, when the solution does not need to be shaped by the wisdom of the people's voice. Infrastructure construction projects are likely candidates (building a network of schools, bridges, telephone systems, or water-supply projects). Blueprints are often effective early in development activities when communities have low technical skills and when the technical voids are much apparent.

But although experts may speak the local dialect and drink tea at the right times, the blueprint approach remains an outside solution. It is hard to create a blueprint so humanly prescient as to be effective in changing people's behaviors. Therefore, often these blueprints build in incentives or disincentives. People will, of course, do as they're told if adequately scared, paid, or coerced. But when greed or fear is the primary motivation, people are still working for an external reason. Behavior change must occur for internal reasons, when people are convinced of the merits of changing to improve their own circumstances; and long-term development projects succeed best when they achieve behavior change.

Externally based designers seldom have adequate local information or enough knowledge about factors outside their fields of expertise to make the site-specific adaptations needed. At best, community opinions are superficially incorporated in the blueprint; they are seldom the source of inspiration. Blueprints may seem to work over the short term, but at the end of the funding cycle, when the incentives and disincentives are being withdrawn, the intended beneficiaries do not permanently adopt the new behaviors needed to sustain progress.

The Explosion Approach

The explosion approach has been effective in addressing large-scale, temporary, specific needs, such as repairing roads and telecommunications after a flood, immunizations in response to epidemics or global eradication efforts, or food in time of famine. Government leaders like to visit disaster sites in helicopters and show solidarity. Donors get gratification and credit if they produce quick and obvious benefits. Such interventions fit nicely within the short cycles of funding preferred by government or donor agencies, and they provide measurable indicators of success. Assistance can be provided swiftly, and after a heroic rescue the givers can move on. This approach avoids the pitfalls of dependency.

The explosion approach is good at solving a massive one-time problem. It is not good at changing societal or natural systems that may be contributing to the problems. In Chapter 6 we describe how crises (which often require an explosion approach) can open up opportunities for longer-term change (which usually requires one of the two approaches that follow).

The speed and efficiency of the explosion approach often tempt people to adopt it for complex situations for which it is not appropriate. For example, on the basis of success in protecting soldiers from malaria after World War II, a worldwide program was launched to eradicate malaria by spraying endemic areas with DDT. Deaths from malaria dropped to tantalizingly low levels—but mosquitoes developed genetic resistance to DDT and the window of opportunity while mosquitoes were susceptible closed and halted the final eradication. A more thorough biological approach was needed.

On the other hand, a piggybacking of the explosion approach on earlier blueprint approaches had spectacular success in the worldwide campaign to eradicate smallpox. Instead of simply sending out teams to inoculate everyone with smallpox vaccine, the World Health Organization and government agencies first achieved major reductions in smallpox by using local primary-health services to achieve wide vaccination coverage. Then systematic surveillance in every country found the embedded, localized outbreaks. In the second phase, action focused on the identified problem areas, using the explosion model to eliminate the virus in military-style campaigns.

Those considering an explosion approach should first address issues such as whether the returns really justify the costs of setting aside all other action, and what happens after the campaign target is met to maintain the benefits achieved. For example, an immunization campaign that commandeers all personnel and transport to get vaccinations to the countryside usually takes people away from routine services providing basic care. Depending on how it is done, such a massive redeployment can strengthen or weaken the primary-health-care system. The first level of immunizations will have been delivered, but with a weakened primary-health-care system continuing immunizations will be difficult, and in the meantime other health needs have not been met.

The explosion approach is often effective in introducing a service, but sustaining the benefits requires integrating the new activity into and strengthening routine services. Those planning the integration must also recognize the potential difficulties of phasing specially funded, often technologically so-phisticated interventions into services where technical skills and resources are modest, and are supported with even more modest local funding. If external support cannot move to internal self-support, after the explosion makes its impact the problem is likely to come back, as in the case of malaria.

The Additive Approach

Proponents of bottom-up development typically use an additive approach. In its pure form this focuses on adapting programs to local conditions, with local people using local resources to address local problems. Projects that take the additive approach have popular appeal because the people associated with them usually have a passionate fervor that stimulates high-quality work.

The term *additive* refers to the manner of replication as projects get added one by one. Ten years or more are commonly invested in developing an activity in a cluster of villages. Development grows neighborhood by neighborhood (unlike the blueprint and explosion approaches, which grow much faster). Replication is slow and follows an arithmetic progression. As areas are added, projects are eventually joined together. As local leaders mature, as people transform local materials by using modern technology, as local values are respected and perhaps featured, such projects often assume showcase status.

Worldwide the additive approach has been undeniably effective. It is much favored by nongovernmental organizations and religious mission groups. These agencies make a commitment to one site, learn local conditions, train people, adapt interventions, and develop site-specific funding. Usually there is much attention to building capacity and a concentration on grassroots mobilization, but in many such projects the organization holds on to the leadership role, turning control over to local people somewhat reluctantly.

Although such projects work beautifully in one site, they inevitably face long-term challenges precisely because they have been so carefully and personally nurtured. Those in charge of such projects must ask: What happens when the outside support phases out? Can the project sustain itself using local resources? How will the project shift leadership to local control? How can the community pay key people who were funded from the outside and have grown accustomed to outsider salaries? Externally the sponsoring agency also faces fundamental questions: Did the initial success come just from local leadership, from special resources, or from some other feature? Does the donor have enough money to pay for new staff and seed capital to start new projects? Does the donor have the patience to work yet another time through the slow, early stages?

Organizations using the additive approach often claim that they are creating demonstrations and that someone else (or the government) should solve the larger problems. They usually want to be pioneers and prefer to be independent, but they seldom devote time and energy to fitting their work with the work of others. They usually seek a virgin area so they can show more dramatically that their methods or models work. Most large agencies, whose mandate is not to pioneer but to make a difference for many people, believe that the additive approach is just too slow.

If the objective is to conduct research or to prove a philosophical point, then the additive approach makes sense. In a similar way it makes sense if the area of interest is only a few communities, some place where the outside group wants to focus for some reason, such as building community support for a nature conservation program. But if the objective is to scale up and build interactive momentum, this is not the way.

The Conundrum of Control

Each of the three approaches described so far shows that, left on their own, communities are unlikely to initiate change unless they happen to have an enlightened, motivated leader, perhaps someone who has gone away, received training or a new vision, and then returned with enhanced credibility and authority. In the case study of Curitiba in Chapter 11, a visionary mayor played such a crucial role. More commonly it is outsiders (either experts, officials, or a donor) who come in and start the transformation process. They recommend a design, usually sweetening their proposal with incentives, or they motivate the community by describing dangers the people had not known about. But although outsiders often build solid working relationships through community participation, they stay in control, and their projects generally fail to build community capacity and ownership. When outsiders introduce and run a project, the great danger is that they will build dependency, not community commitment.

Because the blueprint, explosion, and additive approaches are either very top-down or are launched by outsiders, they all face the challenge of eventually relinquishing control. These projects may change and expand, but they will build community capacity only if the outside partners give up control. The concept is easy to grasp, but actual transfer is difficult. With time and preparation, communities can take the initiative from a founding agency and deliberately shift the locus of control as more and more local people are trained. As in raising a child, however, control must usually be abandoned faster than the "parent" partner is ready to accept the need.

Another approach is possible: to share ownership of control from the beginning. In such a model, control shifts flexibly, and ownership remains dynamic. Ideally this is what occurs in the biological approach described below and used by SEED-SCALE. Repeating the seven steps each year provides a regular, incremental way to adjust and reallocate responsibilities.

The Biological Approach

The biological approach explores and experiments in one population unit to find a mix of actions suited to local circumstances and then provides an enabling environment for rapid growth and extension. Consider the parallel to nature: a new species evolves slowly within an ecological niche where evolution is optimal; after making additional evolutionary adjustments, that species replicates quickly throughout the niche. The biological approach combines the advantages of the additive approach—beginning slowly and adapting to the local situation—with the potential of the other two models for rapid expansion. Three characteristics define the biological approach: the potential for exponential expansion, healthy and integrated relationships, and tensegrity.

Exponential Growth

A unique feature of replication by complex beings is that growth happens through the simultaneous expansion of multiple subsystems throughout the body, not in one unit first, followed by the production of many similar units, as would happen in constructing a building or machines. The mechanistic model usually results in some arithmetic progression, at best something like 10, 20, 30, 40, 50 . . . . However, biologic growth follows an exponential curve: 1, 2, 4, 8, 16, . . . 128, 256 . . . . Reproduction starts more slowly, often without a blueprint; principles and procedures are adapted and tested, but as the pattern becomes established, the trajectory of growth accelerates (256, 512, 1024, 2048 . . .). Each unit retains autonomy so that it can reproduce nodes for extension, and with these multiple sources of growth, momentum accelerates rapidly. Extension does not go on forever, of course. When the limits in the enabling environment are reached, growth plateaus. Exponential growth in social units has, in the past, come about in unstructured ways. But as growth is understood better, particularly its role in creating truly enabling environments of training and doable ideas, then it is possible to direct the exponential curve of expansion with intentionality.

Healthy Relationships

Development is usually described in economic or mechanistic terms, and the execution of development projects often follows business or engineering thinking. Seeing community development more as a living organism than as a machine or a business, we prefer terminology and metaphors rooted in health and living organisms.

Health was once assessed mainly in terms of disease. Now it is understood to reflect the interaction of complex systems, including nutritional status, spiritual state, stress levels, access to services, educational status, environmental influences, a history of earlier infections, genetics, and the like. Promoting good health requires attention to multiple influences on many levels: cell, organ, whole organism (such as a human body), family, community, nation, and, increasingly, the planet. Excessive physical growth is not necessarily a sign of health; obesity itself can become a health hazard, and excessive economic growth tends to create imbalanced societies. Uncontrolled growth in one part of an organism can become cancerous and endanger the whole organism.

A second feature of healthy growth is that all organs within the organism adjust as the organism grows: legs, lungs, and life processes adapt. Growth is not a linear assembly of artificial development units. It is simultaneous, multiple, readjusting actively as the whole organism changes. A healthy community is one that manages development appropriately according to life stages, and it can survive for millennia by mutually adjusting its parts. A grove of aspen trees is a single organism. Above ground it appears to be a cluster of freestanding trees, some dying while others sprout young shoots, but underground the unit is interconnected and interdependent. Another example, and a remarkable demonstration of enduring progress through the ages, is the city of Rome, which has adjusted its development with remarkable flexibility over two and a half millennia. In a similar way, Thailand has flourished for over two millennia by adjusting its development to forces from the outside world. Healthy biological growth recreates the organism, preparing it for new life stages.

A third parallel between health and development is the precept that prevention is better than cure. The cost savings of prevention escalate with the sophistication of development. When a highly developed item malfunctions, it becomes increasingly expensive to fix, so prevention becomes increasingly valuable. For example, the costs of treating individuals in hospitals are much higher than the costs of removing the causes of disease through prevention in the community.

Viewing development as nurturing healthy communities through a three-way partnership fosters a holistic, time-dependent, and environment-conditioned perspective. Managing development in accordance with health paradigms alters the focus from one of external manipulation (unless one still holds to the outdated view that health depends on doctors rather than on people's behavior) to recognition that development is created by the empowerment of communities with the support of technical skills from experts and an enabling environment from officials.

Tensegrity

Tensegrity is the biological form of building. It works by balancing systems in flexible homeostasis rather than by building in a mechanical way that attaches its components rigidly. Consider the human body. Weight presses on the skeleton's rigid bones, but the bones are not self-supporting like the frame of a house. Bones are loose: they don't even touch one another. Position is held adaptively by soft tissues under tension, muscles and tendons, and regulated by other soft tissues such as circulatory and nervous systems. The bones push out, and skin and muscles pull inward and hold the bones together, constantly adjusting their shape through balances in tension and compression.

As a reader you can experience this dynamic architecture by holding out your arm. Everything feels solid. The considerable physical stability of the extended hand is not achieved by a rigid arm hammered onto your shoulder like a strut for the porch on your house. Your arm is rigid throughout its length because of the inward tension of muscles and tendons pulling in on a compressive outward force of the bones. Nothing is locked; you can break the attachment simply by flexing your arm. This pattern of organization at the organism level is repeated at the cellular level with microtubules and filaments, and on a smaller scale with molecular bodies.[2]

Nature's biological building system of tensegrity has many advantages as a parallel for communities. This is very different from mechanical or military-type thinking. First, the principle of balance in tensegrity allows forms to change shape and move. Push on a cell wall, and accommodation follows throughout the cytoplasm. Flexibility is similarly important in a society. As change bombards communities, the total societal fabric (not just the mayor or the budget) must respond. In this context, it is scarcely surprising that, although the centrally planned former Soviet Union could build steel factories, hospitals, and schools, it could not sustain complex social development, which required flexibility. The command economy was too prescriptively oriented and rigid.

Second, growth occurs in locally specific patterns in accordance with internal conditions. Development follows patterns, which replicate simultaneously, interdependently, and differently according to an organizational pattern adjusted locally to the larger system. Consider the geometric formation of crystals, the iteration of the carbon-nitrogen-oxygen building blocks for the molecules of all life, the dynamic balance of the double helix in DNA, or, with perhaps the most complex but repeating patterns of all, the internal rules that assemble the life tiers of an ecosystem.

This pattern of self-assembly is also the dynamic force of social development. Real development in a community is not driven by a plan from some central bureau; instead, order and organization seem to evolve almost spontaneously throughout the system once it is working, popping up here and there in the manner common to biological patterns. This process of self-assembly seems to be a more precise version of what Adam Smith termed "the invisible hand" when he explained how order appears naturally in the economic marketplace. For self-assembly to occur, it is exceedingly important that there exist an enabling environment for what appears to be locally based growth but in reality is local growth that is occurring because a conducive niche was created in the environment.

A third characteristic of tensegrity is that the whole takes on a different form from that of its member parts. A human body has but a macabre resemblance to its skeleton and possesses considerably more stature than its musculature. Furthermore, although all the components of tensegrity structures may be similar, both the visible appearance and the internal life of each organism or structure are unique. Likewise, each community's distinctive energy, local definition, and mobilization of resources cannot simply arise from a blueprint; they already exist within the organism, and they continue to adapt to changes in circumstances.

A fourth feature of tensegrity is feedback of information. This feedback does not occur in discrete loops as it does in formal top-down management approaches. Rather, it flows on multiple levels through the system. In a society as in the body, pressure on one point, in the dynamic distribution of balance, radiates information throughout the organism to produce adaptive adjustments. Consider how fast news spreads through spontaneous communications in a small town. Such feedback is central to community process.

A fifth advantage of tensegrity is efficiency of construction. All components carry stress, but because the load is distributed among them, individual components do not need to be overbuilt. Just as the cable balances outward stresses on a farmer's silo, on traditional Mongolian yurts, and on the arches of the designer Eero Saarinen, so that the walls become supporting structures and require only half the material mass used in conventional buildings, communities when organized on the principle of mutual dependency require much lighter bureaucracies. The balancing of responsibilities in partnerships creates internal checks and facilitates nonhierarchical organization, delegation of action and authority, and avoids traditional bottlenecks. It avoids the increasingly common top-down bureaucracies created to ensure accountability. In addition to benefiting from the interdependency that creates more efficiency (instead of redundancy), such tensegrity systems can operate at radically reduced costs.

Finally, the interdependence of tensegrity brings accountability. Each component carries responsibilities. Failure to meet these responsibilities produces imbalance. Accountability is different from control. When social systems operate without tensegrity, development continues to reassemble gigantic, redundant bureaucracies that do worse than get in the way—they create a diversionary structure. In tensegrity each member trusts that the other will do his or her job. When this does not occur, the void generated is immediately apparent. People who do not pay their bills do not get credit; people who do not show up at scheduled times live with the consequences.

Tensegrity is the natural organizational process that is already operating in communities—especially those that "feel" wealthy. Implementing it in formal development efforts will not require a social revolution in the communities; it will just require traditional development organizations to adopt a new outlook. Communities do not need to become bureaucratic to develop; rather, bureaucracies need to become sensitive to the complex interdependencies of communities and learn to use these for efficiency, flexibility, and speed of service delivery.

All four approaches described above—blueprint, explosion, additive, and biological—have uses in development depending on particular needs. During a flood or an epidemic, the explosion approach provides rapid mobilization with a narrowly targeted intervention. For pervasive but specific societal needs, such as building a communications infrastructure, a blueprint is probably the best response. For a focused societal need requiring a new model, turning multiple players loose to probe for solutions, the additive approach is probably the best strategy, as occurred in the search for breakthroughs for the Child Survival Revolution (described in Chapter 10). In our view, however, the biological approach has brought the most lasting benefit to communities and entire regions. The biological approach not only seeks solutions adapted to cultural, economic, and ecological realities, but also supports those solutions so that they expand rapidly. It does, however, require changes in behavior that are atypical for most officials, experts, and donors; and an intentional enabling of community empowerment so that people can rise to their new opportunities.

CHAPTER 4

Our Maturing Understanding
of Community Change

Communities today are much more predictably shaping just and lasting futures. But even though a great deal has been learned in the century and a half since his day, Lincoln's focus on strengthening people's capacity still offers valuable lessons with which to begin this review of development thinking.

Faced with enormous and daunting challenges—elected by a minority of voters, with the country fragmented and likely to crumble further—Lincoln responded not by seeking to consolidate his own position but by empowering those around him to learn new, larger, and more effective roles. As commander-in-chief, Lincoln could have told his first series of incompetent generals what to do, thereby moving control of the war to the White House; instead he supported each for as long as their defeats permitted. When members of his Cabinet were trapped by the administrative myopia of their departments, Lincoln fed them information gathered from his community contacts, expanded their vision, and engaged their creativity, encouraging them to strengthen communities rather than their offices. He also worked to foster initiative among ordinary people. To empower Union soldiers, he ignored the military hierarchy and traveled often to the camps, walking among the men and sharing stories, seeking to strengthen both their confidence in their roles and their sense that their sacrifices were appreciated.[1]

Few people will ever face equal challenges. But even for most of us who play minor roles in small communities, Lincoln's leadership style sets an example: faced with calamity, he sought solutions in making his colleagues and his countrymen stronger. In the prosaic places we work in, if our objective is to create stronger communities, we too must empower our partners.

The People's Voice

Around the world today, villages and cities are organizing and building their capacity for positive change. Ordinary citizens now make themselves heard at most international meetings. The activist who led this change was the Brazilian Paolo Freire.

In 1970 Freire had come up from Central America to be a visiting professor at Harvard. One day in April, the day that President Nixon had authorized U.S. forces to bomb Cambodia's villages, several of us remained after his seminar had ended, gathered around a hot-water dispenser to mix up instant coffee. Many of us were upset. A sense of extreme urgency drove our conversation.

Visiting Professor Freire stirred his coffee with a plastic spoon in a plastic cup. "Scratch where the people itch if you want to mobilize that community," he said. "The answer for positive change lies in the people. Each community must begin with its felt needs; then confidence can build. Start with the itch, the issues that irritate . . . Go into the villages and get your hands dirty . . . At most be a midwife to the process; never father it, for then it is bastardized . . . The people can never rise alone; they need help. The role for the outsider is to find the issues that are theirs. Just because you know one community, don't assume you know the next. Each community's concerns are unique."

Freire was adamant that what mattered was not plans, budgets, technical assistance, inputs/outputs, or any form of "logical framework." Global conferences seldom changed things at the community level. Freire's contribution was to drill in the paramount priority of the issues people felt—and to do this all he needed was words, the right words. Freire blessed this insight with the horrible name "conscientization."[2]

Freire was adept at finding the issues people would mobilize behind. He would sit in taverns, homes, and meeting places, listening. When he heard what concerns were mentioned most often, he would teach people to write and read the key words. He painted the words in big letters on walls and put out cyclostyled newsletters. Through literacy drives Freire mobilized entire communities. He was convinced that once people could function in the world of writing and paper, people would organize—and in organizing they would achieve strength. People organized, he believed, when they had hope that they could act upon the issues that mattered in their lives.

A literacy program could begin with just one person—and then each one could teach one. With their own words in front of them, the specific words that mattered to them, people could take collective action. It did not take entrenched leaders long to realize that such action threatened their financial and other interests. As a result, once literacy campaigns had launched such energy, Freire and his followers were usually ejected from a region. Several times we sat with Freirian activists in Central America as they discussed how long it would be until they, the outside experts, would be thrown out of the country and they would start mobilizing people in another place. Conscientized, the people they left would then struggle to carry on, usually clutching at simplistic answers to profound problems.

Despite its connection with revolutionary change, today Freire's thesis that development must start with people's priorities is now almost universally accepted among development professionals and officials regardless of their political views.[3] Almost equally universally, once lip service is paid, the precept is seldom acted upon. Political change was just what Freire wanted, believing that not until corrupt leaders were driven out would space be created to bring in new people-sensitive policies. Figuring out the starting point was what made his impact so significant.

But the history of social change shows that calls for revolution seldom lead to sustained societal progress unless changes in leadership are accompanied by changes within communities. Overthrowing authority usually brings only new forms of authoritarianism, for those who are good at dismembering a system are seldom skilled at building new ones. Sustained change requires transformation of the whole society, building from each community's acute concerns.

The Global Discussion

After World War II, international social development ceased to be led primarily by religious missions and philanthropic foundations. New awareness had grown that action by government could effectively improve the lives of citizens. There was also recognition that improving social conditions also improved national security, both internally and internationally. Therefore, governments, which previously had left social development to other institutions, started major programs.

The success of the Marshall Plan in helping reconstruct Europe generated confidence that with huge infusions of targeted financial aid, newly independent, undeveloped countries could quickly join the ranks of the prosperous. In support of this idea the United Nations rapidly created a cluster of development agencies, the United States expanded its foreign-aid program worldwide, and the World Bank and regional banks were established. As Europe strengthened, it joined the effort. Nongovernmental and philanthropic organizations also expanded their activities. By the 1950s hundreds of development programs were being launched all over the world. Some countries (Costa Rica, Thailand, Brazil, Greece, Singapore) started to show progress.

Soon scholars were analyzing these undertakings to determine the dynamics that made transforming change occur. Among these, Walt Rostow suggested that a definable mix could come together like chemicals in a reaction and create the capacity for a society to "take off."[4] He graphed how societies advanced, with development starting slowly and then expanding exponentially. His analysis built on the capitalist approach and stood in contrast to growing claims that a Marxist approach had proved itself as a universal global model for going to scale with equitable change.

That development could expand exponentially was clear from the astonishing speed with which banking, industry, and transport had spread throughout the world in the first half of the twentieth century. It took a few more decades to realize that such change does not occur in a steady or linear way. Development involves many false starts, real starts, and adjustments that continually synthesize innovations and then produce bursts of progress. The process resembles the changes that occur in physics and biology. An energized electron does not slide gradually from one orbit to another; it jumps into the new orbit. In evolutionary biology, although systematic genetic mutations occur constantly, more significant change occurs when equilibria are punctuated by many almost simultaneous mutations—or when systems cross a negative threshold and then species go extinct en masse.[5]

Global awareness continued to expand as an array of visionary thinkers—people such as Rene Dubos, Gunnar Myrdal, Chou Enlai, Barbara Ward,

Julius Nyerere, Rachel Carson, Ivan Illich, Pete Seeger, Buckminster Fuller—began to place development within larger contexts. From their varying perspectives, they stressed a heretofore overlooked theme: interconnectedness. Perhaps the timing was coincidental, but in those same years human beings first left the Earth in spacecraft and looked back at it, seeing the planet as whole.

Since the 1970s a series of powerful proponents have turned the focus back to people, looking with particular insight at the human dimension within the complex linkages. A handful of studies shifted the paradigm: Alan Schumacher's *Small Is Beautiful;* Mahbub ul Huq's annual series of UN *Human Development Reports;* Jim Grant's annual series of *State of the World's Children Reports;* Gro Harlem Brundtland's *Our Common Future;* Lester Brown's annual *State of the World* reports; David Korten's *When Corporations Rule the World;* Robert Chambers' *Whose Reality Counts? Putting the First Last;* Richard Jolly's *Development with a Human Face;* and Amartya Sen's *Democracy as Freedom.*

Development is viewed in a new way today as a human condition that can be available to people if and when they take the right actions. Expectations have risen, and people have moved to achieve those expectations by focusing on individual incomes and migrating to places of greater personal opportunity. As development has become increasingly synonymous with prosperity, cities around the world have burgeoned in size along with the entrepreneurial spirit.

Agendas of concern have paralleled this expansion. Is the future we are creating one of enduring value? The concerns are being voiced in a wide array of meetings: world religious conferences, international summits and business conventions, sports exchanges, rock megaconcerts, and virtually every transcultural gathering of people. Specialists and officials attend the global discussions and reach remarkable consensus. The agendas of recent major international summits reveal the emerging themes.

In 1972 the Stockholm World Conference on the Environment had issued a statement that all humankind "has the fundamental right to freedom, equality, and adequate conditions of life, in an environment of a quality that permits a life of dignity and well-being."[6] This formal acknowledgment of the growing planetary environmental crisis has since penetrated planning and action on social and economic development.

In 1978 the World Conference on Primary Health Care in Alma Ata, Soviet Kazakhstan, under the leadership of Halfdan Mahler from the World Health Organization, led not to the anticipated proposals for more doctors and hospitals, services that benefited mostly wealthier individuals, but to three precepts that would help people find health everywhere: providing formal health care as close to homes as possible, community participation, and intersectoral involvement. The impact was extraordinary, acknowledging the potential of common people for taking action. Codrafting the basic conference document that brought together evidence from around the world, then watching delegates grow excited as they understood what was now possible, reinforced our understanding that the potential for changes begins in people's homes.[7] Such an obvious conclusion—but how to make it a reality?

Global understanding has matured rapidly, and many parts of the process are coming clearer. Conferences and world summits on other social problems—the environment (in Rio), social development (in Copenhagen), women (in Beijing), population (in Cairo), shelter (in Istanbul), and trade (in many places)—have issued a series of international protocols. The input of nongovernmental agencies at these meetings has shown that a great deal can indeed be done in homes and communities in virtually every sector of development.

Throughout this time scholars have been describing what happens in successful projects.[8] Alongside these formal evaluations there has emerged, to the tune of billions of dollars, an almost incomprehensibly large plethora of project evaluations by professionals hired by donor agencies and nongovernmental organizations. Indeed, evaluating the worldwide development experience has become a huge industry. Professionals seem able to justify virtually any philosophy favored by their clients—or, conversely, to use their skills to undercut a project.

Cynicism has grown along with the field experience and the project evaluations. It has focused on the major dynamic of development: economic growth. What had been viewed as a positive rising tide of prosperity that would lift the many boats of social change is now often seen as a rising global tide in which unregulated corporate interests lift the boats that can navigate the higher waters and make it harder for the small craft that leak. The immunity of corporations to regulation jeopardizes the potential of people (through governments or communities) to direct action to the areas of greatest need.[9] In the increasingly polarized debate, it is hard to see how the sincere, smaller voices of objection will not be worn down.

The search for answers continues, perhaps more urgently than ever before. Earlier theories have been mostly discarded. Six decades of socialist experiments have been condemned as too rigid. Religious movements that built from morality alone have been shown to be idealistic, and those that built from dogma have had their narrowness exposed. The notion, advanced by some NGOs, that rapid, site-specific development could grow outside government structures has not been demonstrated. From the old century, the remaining theoretical system still standing is capitalism. But the flaws in capitalism—rising inequity, environmental decay, and unsustainable economies—are also growing more evident.[10]

In this context community-based action is the major hope. Some large-scale examples of success have been maturing for more than a century. Community-based action does not reside in the naively simplistic notion of bottom-up mobilization—for communities that are at the bottom cannot grow up on their own against all the forces that seek to take advantage of them. Today successful action requires communities to engage pro-actively the forces of globalization, with the same openness to world opportunities that corporate interests have used. Communities, too, can reach beyond their immediate neighbors to forge synergistic relationships with likeminded entities. By learning from one another and mobilizing interdependently through self-assembly, they can withstand, and in many cases use, otherwise overwhelming global forces.

In this quest, mistakes will be frequent. These should not be seen as failures, but as opportunities for self-learning. Don't stop seeking, for the future won't stop coming. Even at moments of apparent failure, make a point of kicking yourself into action, especially when you have partners to support you.

CHAPTER 5

Assuring Accountability
through Better Paperwork

Generally we think of paperwork as a pointless filling out of forms—and indeed, that is one kind of paperwork. But another kind of paperwork assures accountability and both directs and protects the processes of community change. An episode involving our own family brought home the lesson that even basic paper backup can serve as a map to guide discussions when they get out of control and can protect hard work against misinterpretation.

At seven in the morning on Valentine's Day, 1992, the telephone rang in our home in rural West Virginia. "Have you seen this morning's *Washington Post*?" a friend in the nation's capital asked.

"Is the newspaper really that interesting this early in the morning?" Daniel grumbled.

"Well, your story is the whole front page of the second section," she said. "Listen."

As the word spread, from the Corner Shop to the IGA gun counter, to the North Fork Baptist Church, the latest rebellion in this old Civil War campsite broke out . . . When presented with a proposal to lure badly needed state and federal money by making "revolutionary" changes at the community's only high school, 700 townspeople came streaming down the mountainsides to object . . .

Aware of the school's financial problems . . . the Taylor-Ides said they drafted a "revolutionary" proposal that was only what had been called for by [President George] Bush in his State of the Union address . . .

The Taylor-Ides stress that it wasn't a full-blown proposal, but rather a "talking paper" for an alternative school plan.

Nonetheless, after word got around that it had been given cursory approval by Gov. Gaston Caperton after a casual meeting with Daniel Taylor-Ide, fears and tempers were raised so high that sheriff's deputies and state troopers for miles were alerted for possible violence Jan. 21 [at the school board meeting]. That night, a stream of headlights lit the valley as hundreds of cars filed down the windy mountain roads to meet at the Circleville gym.[1]

At the meeting, with rumors flying and hundreds of people asking questions, it was impossible to build the forward-thinking discussion needed for serious planning of school change. Not only did the *Washington Post* pick up the story; a researcher from Harvard University arrived to write this up as an example of how well-intentioned experts can get themselves badly burned.[2]

One key lesson for those of us who were caught in the middle was that we had confused our roles, mixing our positions as members of the community with our expert knowledge of what was succeeding worldwide to improve schools. Without being asked in as experts, we had stepped forward to propose significant changes to the school system, and a newly installed official, the superintendent of schools, had seen that action as an invasion of his territory. Another crucial lesson was that although we had talked with many key individuals in the community, as well as with county and state officials, we had done so in private meetings. When rumors started to fly, most of those individuals fell silent. There was no written record of discussions with the previous school superintendent, the president of the school board, or others, and no truly public meetings to refer to. Seeing the discussions as exploratory, we had not made written records of them, for fear of blocking creative energies.

And then, as so often occurs, one mistake bred additional problems: hard work was misinterpreted, good intentions were viewed as suspect, and words spun out of control. Such domino effects of misinterpretation are especially likely when people overstep their roles. But good paperwork might have contained the crisis. In this instance, the new superintendent knew nothing of the earlier discussions. Written records of communications with his predecessor and of the plan being explored would have rebutted his false statements.

Good paperwork is particularly hard for communities because information and management systems used by governments and large donor institutions are not designed for the skills most ordinary citizens have. Those systems seem to exist as a tangle of paper trails creating a world only the institutions understand. Moreover, through these systems the outsiders usually establish themselves as the gatekeepers and arbiters, imposing top-down controls on the direction and action communities take. To work successfully with these outside systems, communities need skills training and a systematic process that enables them to use outsiders' paperwork to meet their own needs. And those strategies require knowing the kinds of paperwork they must deal with.

Paperwork That Causes Problems

As a method of moving decisions from one desk to another, *files* conveniently bring together the various parts of the decisionmaking process; but when their impact radiates beyond the bureaucracies they are designed to serve, they can reshape a community's future without its knowledge. Files tend to be inaccessible to anyone outside the institution. Ostensibly they are managed by officials, but in fact they are handled mostly by clerks who are accountable to no one. Those inside the bureaucracy add their opinions to the file; those outside, not knowing what is being said about matters vital to their interests, have no opportunity to rebut the comments. Files are probably necessary parking places for perspectives, but genuine partnerships require open sharing of information; otherwise collaboration is impossible. Electronic media offer great potential for easy access to files, wide distribution, and more thoroughly participatory information. Eventually electronic files may serve development partnerships better than their ossified paper counterparts.

External budgets bring order to the distribution of funds, but the ways in which they are created and implemented often subordinate community interests to the donor's. Used in a determinative way to purchase community cooperation, a budget becomes a performance contract.

Budgets conveniently simplify complicated situations, objectives, and schedules by converting them into the shorthand of money. But too often the first question communities ask of potential donors is: "How much money do you have to spend?" Thus dollars, not community inputs of organization and time, become the central commodity of community change. The structure of budgets also stultifies action. Although the narrative accompanying the budget always specifies the goal of the project, that goal can be obscured by concerns about allocations of money to salary, equipment, office rental, and the like. And, of course, the promise of outside money always breeds the risk of corruption. The remedy lies not in more paperwork—the usual response when a new form of corruption is found—but in turning control of the money over to the community and then expecting results.

Success is more likely if communities put aside money matters until the end of the planning. Let the participatory process build as community members engage with one another about their needs, and only then examine how much external funding is needed. This sequence is in fact what the annual work plan (discussed later) achieves.

Requests for proposals (RFPs) are used frequently by donors to solicit ideas for projects to support, but they uniformly undermine community capacity. RFPs compel applicants to try to provide the "right" answer to what the donors want, rather than encouraging internal community agreement on needs and priorities. RFPs raise unrealistic expectations by creating reliance on funding that will not in fact be available indefinitely. They create competition for a limited amount of money among agencies that often should be partners in a common social quest. RFPs commercialize development as though it were a product for sale. They build psychological dependence upon donor direction. And finally, RFPs give the credit for any successes to donors' largesse, not to community action.

Commonly international donors (and increasingly governments) create *outsiders' plans,* sending out a team of experts on a "planning mission" to shape their programs to local conditions. These efforts tend to consume enormous sums of money (much more than would be spent in a SEED-SCALE process), and they almost always halt community momentum. The experts arrive and convene community meetings that immediately make clear who is in control. Since these missions are one-time events, the community never has the chance to enter a balanced partnership.

A larger problem is that the team focuses on outcome, on getting the plan done. This approach short-circuits the community process of finding a vision and using planning to create bridges among factions. In order to get the paperwork completed on schedule, the team often manipulates input and recommendations, and any conclusions it draws from the surveys and community forums it may have used to gather data are almost never shared with the community. The plan is used to set the direction and goals of the project, and the locus of control remains outside the community, indenturing it to others' decisions.

Approved proposals likewise undermine real development. These documents come under many names, such as project documents or grant agreements. They share many of the problems of RFPs and plans prepared by "mission" teams, and in this final stage the outside agency once more establishes its dominance and the community's subservience by prescribing both implementation and outcomes. The donor is protected by clauses that assign liability to the community if objectives are not achieved. As a result, the community never becomes invested, and the project remains an external initiative.

A Better System of Paperwork

In contrast to the paperwork systems described above, we propose an alternative that focuses on the community, creating greater equality among partners and relieving the community from the posture of a mendicant. This system does not eliminate the need to meet the paperwork requirements of outside government or donor agencies—communities that seek outside help in any form will always have to deal with those; but it incorporates that paperwork into a larger, community-centered framework. This system consists of a single primary document and two supporting ones.

The *annual work plan* is the foundation document. It builds from the community's needs but incorporates input from government, experts, and donors. It focuses on the tasks that need to be accomplished that year in the community. Traditional plans move through multiple levels of objectives, situational analyses, inputs, outcomes, and methods of monitoring. By contrast, the annual work plan simply assigns responsibility for who will do what, and when.

The annual work plan brings all partners together. It does not replace the regulations of officials, reports of experts, and national budgets; instead it gives these a foundation in local circumstances so that their formulations gain authenticity. It slides underneath the stack of government and expert paperwork a foundation document, which expresses the priorities and achievements of the people. Government and experts then build upon this because they were also part of its creation. Rather than the paperwork's being controlled from the outside, the outside comes in and supports the creation of a local base on which to anchor all actions.

Because of their locality-specific, independent nature, annual work plans also foster self-assembly and scaling up by communities throughout a region—something that blueprint approaches seldom achieve.

The *contract* is a part of the annual work plan. It specifies the reciprocal expectations and obligations of the community and each outside partner. A contract's transparent give-and-take levels negotiations more effectively than files, external budgets, plans, RFPs, and approved proposals, which move control outside the community. People understand deals, and this is fundamentally what a contract is. A contract may not always be balanced—one side may even be dictating terms; but rather than pretending otherwise, a contract makes the imbalance clear.

Contracts can help prevent mismanagement of money, a frequent source of problems for communities. Typically communities have few problems handling their own money, because members, who each own a share in community ventures, insist on transparency. This same sort of transparency can be provided by contracts that involve outside funds. Outside money is useful to jump-start initiatives that otherwise would start slowly but should not be used to fund tasks that are of low priority for a community but high priority for outside partners.

An *inclusive budget* differs from an external budget in that the former contains all the resources that are required by a work plan, while the latter deals only with monetary resources. External budgets miss the mark when it comes to action because they deal with the outsiders' priorities, not with the problems at hand. Any budget, inclusive or otherwise, must specify how money is to be spent. But it is perhaps more important to tie the money to the tasks that are to be accomplished (and how these will be measured) than it is to state which substance is being paid for at what levels. Second only to the annual work plan in importance, the role of the inclusive budget is much like that of an equipment list on a building project, stating what supplies are necessary to get the job done.

Money is only one component of a budget; an equally important component is time. Time is a sustainable resource. Time is the currency all partners possess and can contribute. Typical budgets categorize time investments as "cost-sharing," "sweat equity," or "partner contributions" suggesting that these contributions are less significant than money. But downplaying the value of the investment of time misses the value of monitoring a project's most important input. To accord time its proper prominence, the work plan must be the first document, specifying the functions that need to be carried out. Then, to bring more clarity to the process, the budget specifies the jobs that need to be done. The ordering here is important: determine functions first, and then list the inputs and contractual obligations of key partners.

Seeking Accountability

An important caveat to this discussion is that regional, national, or even international objectives will sometimes transcend community objectives. For example, a conservation priority may require that communities not develop in ways they wish, national defense priorities may force communities to change earlier decisions, or the threat of natural or human-caused disasters may require communities to increase their levels of protection. The SEED-SCALE system, while focusing intensely on the community level, allows for higher-level input into the work plan and, through the supporting documents of contracts and budgets, provides the means of working out compromises and balancing inputs.

The beauty of SEED-SCALE is that it starts simply and gives communities a voice in conversations that have previously lacked grassroots contributions. SEED-SCALE does not supplant, but rather complements, existing operational and management systems. It recognizes that community development is part of larger social development. Old patterns of paperwork and the alternative that we propose do not conflict. Governments and donors will continue their requirements, but these will make more sense when they are locally grounded.

When conflict arises in the modern age, typically it is resolved through confrontation. Usually the side with most power prevails, often by going to court or in some cases by wielding political influence. Confrontation is expensive, time-consuming, leaves scar tissue, and polarizes parties. Change, which should be forward-looking, instead becomes cautious. SEED-SCALE provides an alternative, positive framework for action that enables communities and the larger players (government and experts) to build a plan for moving forward. Placing one small success upon another, it removes the irritants that itch.

CHAPTER 6

A Crisis Can Become
an Opportunity

*Henry G. Taylor, Carl E. Taylor,
and Daniel Taylor-Ide*

Carl was on the last plane out of Baghdad before the start of the 1991 Gulf War. He and Jonathan Fine, head of the nongovernmental organization Physicians for Human Rights, were evaluating the impact of six months of United Nations sanctions on the health of Iraqi children. They were finalizing their report when word came that bombing would start at midnight. Authorities in Baghdad were so anxious to get the findings to the UN that they secured two seats for them on the last plane to Jordan.

A few evenings before, Carl and Jonathan had been told to be at the door of their hotel lobby at a specific time. Two guards with automatic weapons came through the revolving doors and politely but firmly ushered them into a waiting black limousine. Not knowing more, or even whom they were to see, they were sped through darkened Baghdad streets. Finally the limousine stopped at the gates of a heavily guarded compound. Yasser Arafat waited inside—younger, more relaxed than he now appears, with a clear sense of self-confidence. The conversation moved quickly from the immediate crisis in Iraq to the human crisis in the Middle East. Arafat said, "The United States should realize that this cycle of violence will lead to later cycles of violence. Dropping bombs will not lead to peace; it will create more distrust. Arabs are never defeated; they simply wait and prepare for revenge."

Arafat went on to emphasize that what would most help relations with the

Arabs was not aid or even firm borders and homelands, but respect. He listed the many occasions when Western powers had chosen to punish the Palestinians instead of helping them to develop socially and economically. "This crisis will go away," he said, "when we accept each other's differences."

Arriving in America, Carl immediately went to Jim Grant, head of UNICEF, who went to the UN Director General Boutros Boutros Ghali. They quickly arranged for convoys to bring in urgent medical supplies for children, creating a Corridor of Peace for safe passage even during the bombing. These relief efforts soon became a pawn in efforts to checkmate Saddam Hussein's development of weapons of mass destruction; sanctions were imposed despite numerous reports of severe and rapidly increasing child mortality and malnutrition in Iraq, and within months the convoys ceased. The dramatic and much-acclaimed military response to the invasion of Kuwait subdued but did not defeat the foe, and failed to improve the political situation or to bring peace. And, as always, it was the poor who suffered most from the sanctions.

The Chinese word for crisis, *weiji*, combines the character *wei*, which means danger, and the character *ji*, which means opportunity. Turning a destructive force to good is a very different approach to danger from seeking to overpower and defeat it. Most of the case studies in this book describe communities taking incremental steps to improve their futures. But when crisis strikes, what first looks like danger can be turned into an opportunity. The response can go beyond immediate relief to a restructuring that improves community life and prevents future crises or at least minimizes their devastating effects.

The new century will probably bring more, and more severe, crises. As corporate decisions translocate global economies, thousands of people will be left hunting for new work. Wars, civil uprisings, and ethnic cleansing are likely to increase as greater access to information and communication gives angry people a sense of empowerment and new tools with which to organize. Floods, droughts, typhoons, and ice storms are likely to increase as a result of global warming and disrupted weather patterns. Famine and epidemics will probably accompany greater population density and social disparities. Open land on which to resettle burgeoning and dislocated populations will become scarcer.[1]

Over the decades our family has shared in the despair and chaos of a number of disasters, but also the hope that somewhere in each disaster lies an opportunity. SEED-SCALE offers people a way to look beyond the tragedy, find hope, and break with embedded habits. The first example comes from our home mountains of Appalachia.

Flood in West Virginia

On November 14, 1985, a local newspaper announced:

High waters resulting from five days of steady rain roared down the hollows and valleys of Pendleton County, leaving at least 16 persons dead and hundreds homeless. Turbulent waters killed more people in a single night than any event since the Civil War.

Hundreds of homes were washed away and hundreds more were destroyed as walls of raging water struck with unyielding force. Rivers overflowing their banks cut new channels through farms and skimmed thousands of acres of rich topsoil from bottom land, leaving mountains of rock and sand in its place. Farm machinery, buildings, mobile homes, dead cattle, sheep, and hogs were strewn along the entire length of these once fertile agricultural valleys . . .

The county was isolated from the outside world for three days, with 18 bridges washed out and massive slides blocking roads in all sections of the county. Electricity and telephone service were halted, with utility poles washed out and trees across lines. The only communication out of the county was provided by ham radio operators, who worked 24 hours a day relaying emergency messages.[2]

These communities were as isolated as the Iraqis after Desert Storm bombings. But more support was available in America. Henry Taylor was then a health-center physician in Pendleton County. After a long day as a modern country doctor providing emergency care, he shut the door of the clinic and started to walk the mile toward home. When he reached the south branch of the Potomac River, he found that raging floodwaters had carried the bridge away. Using his radar gun, state trooper Rick Gillespie clocked the speed of debris being carried downriver at seventy-two miles per hour. Henry returned to the clinic to rest, collapsing for several hours on an examining table. The next morning he and two other men who were separated from their families by the still surging water levels attached a long string to a hunting arrow and shot it across the river. By noon, patchwork parts had produced a bucket-and-pulley contraption to carry milk and messages to the other side.

After assuring the safety of their families and loved ones, community members met at John's Pizza Den, which stood on a hill in town. They compiled a list of essentials—twenty-five body bags, injectable morphine, antibiotics, bottled water, radios, and the like—and transmitted it by amateur radio to the State Emergency Operations Center. By the end of the second day relief helicopters arrived from the National Guard. John, a still-traumatized Vietnam vet who owned and ran the Pizza Den, hit the floor every time the helicopters passed overhead, providing teenage witnesses with vivid evidence of the enduring force of terrifying memories.

Neighbors were mobilized in quick order. To control the spread of disease, they collected thousands of dead animals by hand and by tractor scoop and buried them. Hay came in from Ohio for surviving livestock, and mobile housing from Alabama for displaced people. Donated old used cars arrived in convoys from Maryland, and surplus clothing from Pennsylvania.

Local people began to joke about "the second flood," the flood of well-intentioned relief supplies that required more donations (in the form of storage shelters and labor) to manage them. The community relief group wondered how to get the aid to those in greatest need, and indeed to define what "greatest need" was. Was it those who had lost the most, those who would have most difficulty recovering, or those who had been neediest even before the disaster? How could the county use both the actual flood and the flood of immediate response as an opportunity?

Civil War in Bangladesh

Bangladesh offers one of the world's best examples of people learning to turn disaster into a chance for large-scale development. The country has undergone repeated tragedy, including two wars of liberation in one generation: first the chaotic bloodshed between Muslims and Hindus when India was partitioned in 1947, and then a war of independence when Bangladesh split from Pakistan in 1971. But the biggest crisis has come from population growth combined with poverty. At the beginning of the twentieth century the population was perhaps 30 million; by midcentury it was 50 million; by the end of the century, 120 million; and by the middle of the twenty-first century it may be 250 million.

These growing numbers of people are moving onto ever more marginal land. The country sits on the world's largest delta, a reverse funnel for rising waters, a landfall for typhoons off the Bay of Bengal. For nearly half the year much of the land is flooded. Flying over such floods is disorienting: as far as the eye can see, villages appear as scattered islands; the whole countryside seems to have been swallowed up by the ocean, a harbinger of sights to come as seas rise as a result of climate change. Over the years people have learned to cope with the waters by raising their villages on stilts several feet above the flooded paddies. For decades, doomsayers said that the numbers of people and the predictable cycles of flooding gave little chance for progress. But despite repeated crises, the people are managing. Three examples from Bangladesh show differing partner roles and the potentials of nongovernmental organizations to turn crises into development.

After the 1971 Bangladesh war, the Johns Hopkins Department of International Health became involved in relief and recovery efforts, and the new government assigned a team from the Narangwal project (Chapter 10) to Companyganj, a district that still carried the name of the East India Company from two centuries earlier. Under Colin McCord eager young Bengali doctors applied Narangwal lessons to provide integrated and comprehensive community-based health care. A small government hospital was brought to high standards of service. Working through existing government systems, the outsiders quickly retrained local people and achieved high coverage. Great effort went into training villagers, with much testing of options to understand and build on the abilities of both men and women workers.

Then the project abruptly collapsed. The disaster was declared over, the war of independence won, and the familiar, archaic bureaucracy of the British Raj reasserted itself in government services. Knowing from the outset that international donors would terminate relief support as soon as possible, the Companyganj project had tried to integrate innovative substantive change into regular government services. But the mindset inherited from colonial times canceled those efforts at rational change, and innovation was stopped. The team was dispersed throughout other agencies. Lacking critical mass, they could not change existing programs. From this experience we learned a great deal about the need to perpetuate a successful demonstration by transforming it into a SCALE Squared center (see Chapter 22) to help both communities and officials understand and accept innovation.

This experience provided another valuable lesson: that communities and government are more successful when they work together rather than independently of each other. Outside resources and experts provide important leadership in community empowerment. During crises, there is a natural tendency to return to preexisting conditions—to rebuild everything to resemble as closely as possible what was there before (including the problems). To utilize crisis to make life better than before, it is essential to set up demonstrations of the potential of change, providing long-term outside assistance. Where demonstration projects exist, outside experts can work with people over an extended period, testing new ideas and teaching local experts how to adapt and promote better ideas. Where there is no access to outside knowledge, locally based partnerships in research are needed to make conceptual breakthroughs (as discussed in Chapter 10).

Our Johns Hopkins colleague Henry Mosley, working with Susham Bhatia in the mid-1970s, had greater success.[3] From a field research base in Matlab district, they extended tests of cholera vaccines in the 1960s to a series of studies on family planning integrated with health interventions. Establishing an extraordinary database by reliably recording births and deaths in a large and expanding population, they created what is now one of the world's longest-lasting and best demographic laboratories, producing 563 scientific publications by 1990. Matlab's data proved that linking services for family planning with maternal and child health made both more effective.[4] Such studies helped change international understanding and policies at the World Conference on Population and Development in Cairo in 1994. Donor support and national action shifted from promoting only family planning to promoting balanced reproductive health. Since the 1970s the Matlab findings have fed a rapidly growing base of action as more than four thousand nongovernmental organizations in Bangladesh have learned to work more effectively in community-based programs.[5]

The work of one such organization provides a third example of how expert help can create the needed three-way partnership when communities and government programs go to scale. Under the leadership of F. H. Abed, the Bangladesh Rural Advancement Committee (BRAC) became "the largest, non-sectarian, national development agency in the world."[6] Its programs affect life in 50,000 of the country's 86,000 villages providing direct services to 38 million, focusing on the poorest people. Almost 25,000 *shasthya shebikas* (community health volunteers) work at least an hour a day. Each is visited two to three times a month by BRAC supervisors, who are part of a full-time staff of almost 20,000 employees and 34,000 part-time teachers. The *shasthya shebikas* charge small amounts for supplies and drugs. Village committees and women's groups provide leadership for transparency in accounting for local and outside funds. The following statement by Abed and M. R. Chowdhury (the leaders of BRAC) illustrates their philosophy. "Staff must have the authority to experiment and to adapt programmes as they feel best suits their local situations. Our management system actively encourages innovation and flexibility, which are key to learning. Mistakes will occur, but they are the only route to discovering the correct path. Fear of making mistakes prevents many public sector organizations from letting their staff's creativity flower. We use monitoring and field research as an early warning system."[7]

BRAC is best known for a practical approach to empowering the 70 percent of Bangladeshi women who are illiterate. Its national-level impact has been most evident in improving health and reducing illiteracy, but its work extends to microcredit, small agricultural projects, and home-based crafts. Matlab research contributed directly to BRAC's mass programs for health and family planning, helping to implement a variety of interventions to lower child mortality such as treatment for diarrhea, immunizations, and simple, routine care supporting the government distribution of contraception.

Change is spotty nationwide in Bangladesh. In this land of continual crises, there are enduring examples of innovation in using crisis as an opportunity. But overall, government services maintain a culture of stagnation, a culture that is typical of countries in which a top-down hierarchy believes it knows best, a culture that sees the proper role of officials as one of telling communities what to do and that regards experts as troublemakers. Often strong demonstrations (such as Companyganj) cause embarrassment, be-cause they point to changes that are needed in government practice. In this case international pressure (through media, money, and personal influence) prevented the closing of Matlab, enabling it to continue independent research to discover important, practical solutions.

The examples from Bangladesh highlight the contrast between solutions that address an immediate crisis—where the kind of action needed is clear—and solutions that seek to address messy, deep-seated problems. Physical disasters such as a typhoon or a war present obvious points for immediate action; less obvious are the ways to turn relief action into development solutions instead of allowing old patterns to reassert themselves. SEED-SCALE provides a straightforward process to address a development solution and at the same time create a context that will prevent crises from recurring.

Communities' vulnerability to crises can lie latent like a virus, kept alive by unpreparedness as societies ignore the problem in the hope that it will not return, by lack of investment in prevention because other demands seem more pressing, or by quiet but real communal hatred among people that resurfaces when demagogues claim power and incite violence. Wherever and whenever one group has imposed itself on another, less powerful group—Europeans on Native Americans or other colonized peoples, whites on blacks in apartheid South Africa, Russians on Islamic minorities—bitter memories persist, fueling resentment and dreams of revenge.

Seizing the Opportunity in the Middle East

Carl's involvement with the Gulf War did not stop when he got the last plane out of Baghdad. When the massive military action had ended, UNICEF asked him to organize a special program in Kuwait for children who had experi-enced psychological trauma. For instance, some families had been forced to watch their men being tortured; women and children had seen father and brothers left hanging from lampposts in front of their homes. Carl remem-bered his experiences (mentioned in the Prologue) during the partition of India in 1947. At one point he had held in his arms a dead three-year-old girl whose brain had been deeply cut six times with a sword. He had wondered then what had caused such maniacal fury and hatred that her killer could not stop hacking. Later he witnessed similar frenzy in Biafra during the Nigerian civil war, then again in Sri Lanka, Bosnia, and Croatia. Why would normally civilized people take part in the mass psychopathic killing of innocent children just because their parents followed a different religion?

In Kuwait Carl helped plan a pioneering, comprehensive program for psychological rehabilitation of children. Post-traumatic stress disorder (PTSD) was well documented for adults in war, but was this also something that influenced the later development of children? Obviously war and senseless killing must leave deep psychological imprints on them.[8]

A five-component treatment program for children was immediately implemented. First, schools and daycare centers were reopened with a minimum of fuss to show that life was returning to normal, and all children were screened with a quick and simple standard test. Second, children with acute problems were referred to psychiatric care. Third, most children received treatment for PTSD in group therapy sessions at school. They drew pictures, wrote stories, and talked about what they had experienced and what they feared. Fourth, teachers in all classes were trained in basic PTSD preventive therapy to promote positive attitudes. Fifth, and most important, the entire community discussed the special needs of children. Over the radio and in public meetings, health centers, and mothers' groups, people of all ages were encouraged to deal with their terror by talking it out. Children needed to see others dealing with the fear and pain.[9]

The UNICEF initiative in Kuwait was subsequently extended to Bosnia, Sri Lanka, Croatia, and a number of African nations.[10] Remarkable advances were made under the guidance of Magne Raundalen at a center in Norway that specialized in trauma care.[11] Systematic research and large field programs established a quick and effective cluster of treatments for PTSD in children. This cluster also addressed the unhelpful responses of adults. When a child expressed fear or told of nightmares, parents almost automatically said, "Don't talk about the troubles. Forget it. That is over now." Yet often adults themselves could not stop talking about their anger. The result was to leave children's terror undealt with and to overlay it with hatred. The fear and anger would then be buried deep in the psyche, waiting to be activated later. This pattern has prevailed in the Middle East, the Balkans, Asia, and Africa.

Parallel psychological responses have also been demonstrated in children growing up in terror from violence in urban slums in the United States.[12]

Carl witnessed evidence of this pattern of cyclic violence nine years after the Gulf War. In the spring of 2000 he was helping a group of Johns Hopkins alumni plan health services for the hoped-for new state of Palestine. Walking the streets in Gaza, he watched a father making only wooden guns as toys for a group of boys. A few days later, on a morning walk in Ramallah, just north of Jerusalem, he looked down from a hill and saw two groups of boys about eight or ten years of age competing in Stone Age–like warfare. An older teenager was coaching them in how to use slings such as David used against Goliath. When Carl talked about these incidents later with Arab colleagues, they were not surprised and shared a West Bank joke: "The average Palestinian family has eight children. One boy is preparing to take the place of his father when he is killed. One is in the United States sending money to the family, because the economy is controlled in Palestine and there can be no real source of income there. Another is in the Gulf also sending money. The fourth is in jail. And all four girls are preparing to have eight children."

Future Opportunities

With increasing human pressure on fragile ecosystems and more densely packed social systems, natural and man-made disasters will probably increase too. Will communities respond to crises only by coping and simply returning to previous conditions—or will they turn each crisis into an opportunity? Disaster-response planning is most commonly separated into three distinct phases:

Immediate response to prevent loss of life and suffering

Recovery efforts to rebuild and redirect everyday life

Mitigation to reduce the causes of vulnerability and to prevent recurring crisis[13]

Communities, governments, and experts must work together throughout all three phases. Table 6.1 presents examples of the many obstacles to successful problemsolving.

TABLE 6.1   Obstacles to Successful Problemsolving

	Community	Government	Expert
Immediate response	Saving lives and just being neighborly instead of getting organized	Military-style intervention with top-down control instead of partnership	Formulaic protocols for mass application
Recovery and rebuilding	Small groups competing to provide local solutions to common problems	Lack of coordination among multiple agencies rather than education and an operations center	Lack of consultation or research to understand causes of problems and priorities
Mitigation and prevention	Decision to return to the status quo	Lack of funding and early-warning systems for future crises	Lack of monitoring and public discourse to understand events and underlying causes

The SEED-SCALE process offers a practical strategy for communities so that when a crisis strikes people can initiate positive change instead of viewing themselves as victims. Bureaucratic and cultural barriers tend to be surmounted when people cooperate in new ways during an emergency. An outpouring of resources and collaboration can be generated both within and between communities. Historical patterns of discrimination may be forgotten. Because a crisis makes it clear that new realities are operating, it may promote greater willingness to take collective risk. The overwhelming need precipitated by disaster can also create openness to new, more equitable relationships. Since it is impossible during disasters to meet large needs all at once, people may also be more willing to accept systematic planning and incremental, locally initiated change. Change in behavior starts with giving up past practices and conditions that have a negative effect on welfare. The crisis has already destroyed much of the old, and now perhaps people can talk about what might be better while holding on to what was especially treasured.

SEED-SCALE, with its adaptable steps of action, may be useful in helping to organize direction amid the confusion. When people feel that their whole world has collapsed and that they have lost everything, they need to start rebuilding step by step. It is empowering to see that these steps can lead to progress rather than dependency. Since disasters also provide opportunities for selfish profitmaking, sources of outside support must discourage the tendencies of some people to manipulate the crisis situation for their own benefit.

All three partners (community, officials, and experts) are needed. In the urgency of the moment, the differing skills and resources they bring are vital. Officials bring much-needed resources and top-down support. Communities build cohesion and new relationships that allow for new ways of distributing resources. Because crises weaken internal allocation systems, it is easier at such times to make extension of coverage to all, including those in greatest need, a priority.

The role of experts is particularly important. Their outsider perspective and technical skills can convert the emergency responses into a foundation on which to build longer-term change. With help, systems, factions, and policies can be regrouped to support more-just and lasting patterns. One of the most important features of the Bangladesh experience is the demonstration that nongovernmental agencies such as BRAC were able to step in and provide a framework for SCALE Cubed extension when government agencies (whose role it normally is to create the enabling environment) proved unable to do so. In some of the case studies that follow, it becomes clearer how this process can unfold.

A cautionary word is needed. International and national disaster response has become big business—both in raising money and in providing equipment and services. When need is acute, people are willing to part with more money or resources than under normal conditions. Some groups have learned to exploit this fact. A parallel problem is the tendency of relief agencies to address only superficial, immediate needs and then to leave without solving deeper problems or creating essential partnerships. The SEED-SCALE approach creates a partial check on the tendency of particular groups to take control during periods of confusion. This can become a time to balance partnerships, base decision on data rather than on outside sales pitches, and create locally specific work plans instead of relying on outside, boilerplate solutions.

The six criteria of SEED-SCALE are particularly helpful in the deep restructuring that is possible after a crisis. They provide discrete benchmarks by which to measure progress and test whether actions fit local realities so that reasonable, realistic next steps can be shaped.

- Collaboration: Is the whole community involved?
- Equity: Is action helping those in greatest need?
- Sustainability: Is the basis of a better life being built?
- Interdependence: Are actions building trust or dependency?
- Holistic action: Are priorities focused on long-term needs?
- Iterative action: Is monitoring correcting errors, making each trial better?

Attention to the needs of both people and the environment is essential in dealing with crises. A crisis weakens a community's vital resources. The wounds must be properly healed and strength rebuilt for forward progress. Otherwise fracture lines may open up again, with crises breeding further crises. Experience in the Balkans, the Middle East, India/Pakistan, Ireland, and elsewhere has shown clearly that unhealed wounds lead to later violence instead of to real development. And experience in Bangladesh has shown that some vulnerable coastal communities are washed away again and again by typhoons. In rural West Virginia, families cling to their "home place" on a floodplain—or rebuild trailer parks there a few years after the old ones have been washed away. Relocating is both traumatic and expensive. Without the presence of supportive intentionality, after a crisis people tend not to take the opportunity to create a better future.

On the other hand, increasing numbers of examples show that crises can be converted into opportunities. For recovery to build into progress instead of reverting to old, unworkable patterns, a systematic process needs to be set in place. Planned innovation will require help from outside. Not all Balkan countries were caught in the recent rounds of violence. Hindu/Muslim antagonism on the India/Bangladesh border is far less than on the India/Pakistan border. And in Bangladesh many communities, particularly those enjoying innovative support from nongovernmental organizations such as BRAC, are becoming empowered to solve their own problems.

In Pendleton County, West Virginia, a professor from a nearby university came in regularly after the 1985 flood to help counselors at the local mental health center set up a program to manage PTSD. Discussions of personal trials and community adaptation took place throughout the county, in the local media, in churches, and in rescue squads. New bonds were forged and new social structures institutionalized through programs from Henry's clinic in partnership with schools and the community mental health center. Community capacity was measured systematically and encouraged to grow.

In 1998 another major flood struck West Virginia. Henry, now West Virginia's state health officer, saw rapid, effective response by communities, state government, nongovernmental groups, and the Federal Emergency Management Agency. West Virginia had learned some important lessons in thirteen years. River and rain gauges were in place, linked by microwave transmission towers to the State Emergency Operations Center. Improved communication alerted each community to specific threats. More-focused community action effectively mobilized scarce resources. Lives were saved and costs contained.

Countries such as the United States now have great concerns about disasters arising from terrorist activity, particularly from biological and chemical weapons of mass destruction. The panic surrounding Great Britain's hoof and mouth disaster in early 2001 prompted officials, experts, government agencies, and community members to add specific prevention and containment measures to their emergency operations plans. Such systems for responding to overt and covert threats to public health and safety should expand the potential for long-term change as well as relieving immediate needs. Globalization can play an unexpectedly beneficial role if it can promote social as well as economic responsiveness. As one part of the world falls into need, other parts can provide support, acknowledging the interdependence of our collective life on the planet.

PART II

Historical Demonstrations

Ding Xian

The First Example of
Community-Based Development

Go to the People.
Live with the People,
Learn from the People.
Plan with the People,
Work with the People.
Start with what they know,
Build on what they have.
Teach by showing, learn by doing.
Not a showcase, but a pattern.
Not piecemeal, but integrated.
Not odds and ends, but a system.
Not to conform, but to transform.
Not relief, but release.

JIMMY YEN

In the 1930s in Ding Xian (formerly spelled Ting Hsien), a rural county a hundred miles south of Beijing, Jimmy Yen and his colleagues, through systematic research, isolated many of the core components of a practical philosophy of community-based societal development. Today Ding Xian is a quiet expanse of villages and fields in the flat north China countryside. But sixty years ago a series of field experiments brought vividly to life revolutionary ideas that we still are trying to learn how to apply and extend.

Although credit for the discovery of this scientific approach to community development belongs to Jimmy Yen, he clearly drew on simultaneous innovative programs worldwide. In the first decades of the twentieth century hundreds of missionaries and social activists, working among disadvantaged people in almost every poor country, were introducing literacy programs, community health services, and agricultural innovations and promoting the welfare of women and children as part of an effort to combine social and spiritual well-being. Rather than merely establishing institutions such as schools and hospitals, these innovators built services that focused on practical and fundamental changes in lifestyle in ways that fitted the realities of local resources and culture. Although many such creative projects sprang up in China, none was as rigorously monitored, adapted, and expanded as that which occurred in the Ding Xian Experiment.

Jimmy Yen (Yen Yangchu) grew up in a poor but scholarly family in Sichuan. He studied the Confucian classics until age ten, when his father sent him to mission schools. He won a scholarship to Yale University and graduated just as the United States entered World War I. Because of a shortage of laborers, 150,000 Chinese coolies were brought to France to dig trenches, build roads, and work in factories. To supervise these coolies and to interpret for them, the International YMCA recruited Chinese students attending American colleges. Jimmy Yen became responsible for a camp of 5,000 coolies digging trenches on the front lines. In the evenings he found himself working as a scribe, writing letters for his men to send home to China. Each night there were more letters than he could write or read. He started to teach literacy.

Although in China peasants were considered incapable of learning to read and write, Jimmy Yen discovered that coolies were smart and teachable. He worked out a vocabulary of about a thousand Chinese characters based on the words common people used in everyday speech and in the letters he had been writing for them. He selected 40 men and at night taught them to read and write. They in turn taught others. Soon all 5,000 of his men were spending their evenings in literacy groups. The British major in charge of the Chinese coolies on the front was so impressed that he assigned Jimmy Yen to do the same in all the camps. When the armistice was signed, most of the 150,000 were literate.

Jimmy returned to China and started the Mass Education Movement. During the next decade and a half this movement mobilized both private and government literacy campaigns in which sixty million Chinese were taught to read and write. By 1930 the Mass Education Movement had produced so many literate people that its newspaper had the largest circulation in China, and probably in the world.

In 1926, realizing that literacy was only one of many needed changes, Jimmy started the Ding Xian Experiment for Rural Reconstruction to provide rural people with practical and specific tools for improving their lives. These solutions to everyday problems would reach the people through his low-literacy publications. To discover other ways of helping that worked, he persuaded professors from various disciplines to leave their highly prestigious lives as scholars and move to this poor, rural county of about 400,000. The professors and their families shared everyday village living, gathered practical information about people's needs, and systematically tested ways to meet those needs.[1]

This experiment, like the Mass Education Movement, took shape amid increasing conflict among warlord factions. From the overthrow of the Qing dynasty in 1911 until the Communist victory in 1949, China was overwhelmed by struggles among violent and oppressive leaders, brutal invasion by the Japanese in the 1930s, and civil war after World War II. Hundreds of thousands of people died in famines and epidemics, fighting disrupted transport and communications, and corruption among officials was endemic.

In the midst of all this violence and disruption, the Rural Reconstruction Movement matured rapidly, establishing a Fourfold Program of Village Work: literacy, citizenship or community organization, livelihood to improve agriculture and income, and health and family planning. For each subject a "farmer scholar" was selected by the village and trained by the team of project professionals. These farmer scholars tested new methods and ideas through field research. They found what others in such projects have learned subsequently, that good ideas introduced by experts must be adapted locally in order to be accepted. In a two-step process, the farmer scholars first experimented themselves with simple but scientifically based methods throughout Ding Xian villages and then helped others experiment to find out what adaptations would work in each village's circumstances.

The achievements in health illustrate the impact of the program. In the 1920s, life expectancy in China was less than thirty years, general mortality over 40 per 1,000, and infant mortality over 200 per 1,000 live births; that is, one in five children died before their first birthday. In the villages of Ding Xian the chief causes of death were convulsions (presumably neonatal tetanus, the result of unhygienic cutting of the umbilical cord), pneumonia, diarrhea in children, and pulmonary tuberculosis. Parasitic infections were ubiquitous; one teacher in a mission college calculated that the 3.5 million people of Jiangsuo Province carried an ascaris-worm load of over 24,000 metric tons, or an average of fifteen pounds per person.[2]

John B. Grant, professor of public health at Peking Union Medical College, funded by the Rockefeller Foundation, joined the Ding Xian Experiment in 1928. Grant, the son of a medical missionary, had grown up in southern China. He had been in the first class to graduate from the Johns Hopkins School of Hygiene and Public Health, where his perspective had expanded from health care for the individual to health care for the community. To create field training centers in public health at Peking Union Medical College he organized rural and urban demonstration areas for teaching and research. He broadened the range of health professionals beyond physicians, establishing training programs especially for midwives to promote obstetrical care and family planning.[3] In Ding Xian, Grant and his Chinese colleagues went even further, focusing on simplifying procedures that made the greatest difference and training ordinary villagers as farmer-scholar health workers. They evolved eight principles that remain valid today:

1. Good health care depends chiefly on social organization.
2. A vertical health system cannot stand by itself but must be integrated with other social activities.
3. Socioeconomic progress depends on demonstration under local conditions of new methods that are scientific, efficient, economical, and practical.
4. Community use of modern knowledge lags when scientific investigation is detached from society.
5. Effective community demonstration projects promote self-help and encourage a two-way flow of professional and administrative ser-

vices at a financial and technical level appropriate to the local area, with mechanisms for extending the findings.

6. Planning must build from local units of organization rather than imposing central administrative practices on the periphery.
7. Professional training should be in keeping with the needs and resources of the area.
8. Successful social development requires a supportive political and economic framework and equitable distribution.[4]

Grant persuaded one of his former students at Peking Union Medical College, Dr. C. C. Chen (Chen Zhiqian), to join Jimmy Yen and live in Ding Xian. By 1936, when the team was driven from the villages by the Japanese, comprehensive health-care coverage had been extended to almost half a million people. Simple methods that focused on behavior change rather than on curative medicine revolutionized health conditions. Because health services were paid for from local resources, low-cost solutions developed: the annual per-capita cost of care was fifteen U.S. cents.[5]

Chen conducted the first scientific surveys in China to identify the extent of rural health problems. He also trained farmer scholars to record births and deaths, vaccinate for smallpox and other infections, administer simple treatments at home using sixteen essential and safe drugs without displacing traditional practitioners, give talks and demonstrations on health and hygienic behavior, and maintain sanitary wells. Programs were also started for prenatal and perinatal care and for training village midwives in family planning. These village health workers were prototypes for the much-publicized "barefoot doctors" (a political term introduced by the Communists, with no relevance to their actual dress or status) who revolutionized health care in China from the 1950s to the 1970s.[6]

In the 1960s Jimmy Yen, then a wiry, dynamic septuagenarian, periodically took the train from New York City down to Baltimore to talk with us and to explain again the reasons for the Communists' victory in the civil war that followed the end of World War II. He recalled how, as Mao Zedong and Chiang Kai-shek struggled for supremacy, he often argued vehemently with Chiang to build a Nationalist liberation campaign based on the Ding Xian experience. Chiang would tell him: "Calm down, Jimmy. First we'll defeat the Communists and then we'll implement your program." Jimmy would pound the table and say, "If you don't start with the Fourfold Program to get the people behind you, the Communists will defeat you. Mao is building his whole guerrilla movement on these principles. He's setting up people's schools to do rural reconstruction; their graduates are like our farmer scholars. The People's Liberation Army uses slogans such as 'Serve the People' to get the cooperation of the peasants. With the people behind them, the Communists will win."[7]

Of course, Jimmy was right. After the Communist victory in 1950, the impact of the Ding Xian Experiment expanded in three very different political contexts: China, Taiwan, and the Philippines.

China under Mao

The Ding Xian Experiment provided much of the basis for Communist China's rural transformation. Although Jimmy left China, his youngest son stayed to work with the new Communist government, and his two older sons returned after completing studies in the United States.

Principles from Ding Xian and demonstrations by other pioneers who came to China from around the world to help (Rewi Alley from New Zealand, Norman Bethune from Canada, Kotnis from India, and George Hatem from the United States) were used in the 1950s to create village schools and cooperatives as the new government consolidated its control over the Chinese countryside. Principles from the Mass Education Movement were used to extend literacy throughout China. Through the use of barefoot doctors, health services became nearly universal in three decades for almost one-quarter of the world's population.

Communist leaders showed an extraordinary willingness to experiment with social change. Programs decreed by officials in Beijing were implemented and paid for at the local level. Radical shifts in leadership and policy (especially regarding economic and industrial development) led to chaotic shifts in direction, but in health and education policies remained more consistent, building from the proven system of Ding Xian. Results were clearly so superior to ancient patterns that people cooperated. After the cataclysmic Cultural Revolution, government priorities shifted from social development to the Deng Xiaoping economic reforms, and the funding mechanism for commune-based social services collapsed. But in the 1980s the Model Counties project (described in Chapter 19) revived concepts from the Ding Xian Experiment and adapted them to new economic realities.

Taiwan

When Chiang Kai-shek retreated to Taiwan in 1950, the Nationalist Chinese took control of the island and its indigenous people, who had suffered greatly under Japanese occupation. Official development policy, with large infusions of aid from the United States, focused on the cities, where the mainland Chinese settled. But many leaders from Ding Xian also went to Taiwan and moved into the rural areas, where they used a comprehensive, people-based program to foster development among the indigenous people. They studied local needs and adapted the Fourfold Program of Village Work, which rapidly improved literacy, health, agriculture, and the economy.[8] They focused on home-based health-care initiatives and on improving the supply and variety of food. To eliminate poverty among the rural poor, the Rural Reconstruction Movement also developed an export economy, based on mushrooms and exotic foods grown in village homes. The Taiwanese government supported the rural development policies and financed islandwide education, health, and technological improvement. A broad-based economic revival grew from initial expansion of agricultural production to rural high-tech industry. This holistic approach and the growth of an educated workforce contributed to Taiwan's emergence as one of the Asian economic tigers.

The Philippines

From China, Jimmy Yen went to the Philippines and launched the Philippine Rural Reconstruction Movement in Nueva Encija Province, where a local Communist movement was resisting control by the national government. Successful development in that province led Jimmy to establish the International Institute of Rural Reconstruction in Cavite, near Manila. The institute became extremely influential as a learning and innovation center, extending his concepts worldwide. It continues to the present as a classic example of a SCALE Squared center.

Over the next fifty years Jimmy Yen and his disciple Juan Flavier continued to experiment with the fourfold approach to community-based social development.[9] Many organizations started demonstration programs in various parts of the Philippines and around the world. Because of the uncertain political environment in the Philippines, few of the local programs went to scale nationally. Government attempts to promote top-down development "blueprints" in the very different islands failed to create local partnerships and empowerment. As funding for national development shrank, the government devolved authority, financing, and responsibility for social activities to municipal or district levels. An unexpected result was an increase in local exploitation and inequity; in the view of village people, having corrupt officials nearby was worse than having them far away in Manila. Lacking an enabling environment, both government and nongovernment programs in the Philippines failed to scale up as effectively as expected.

Lessons from Scaling Up the Ding Xian Experiment

The Ding Xian initiative had its greatest and largest-scale impact in mainland China, where it began. In one generation the disciplined communal system achieved community-based revolutions in education and health that made modern China's development possible. With the erosion in recent decades of motivation for local service, the achievements of Ding Xian have been largely forgotten. It is easy now also to forget the extreme poverty, ignorance, and isolation that dominated life in China during the first half of the twentieth century. Ding Xian was a pioneering breakthrough in modern China's transition.

In Taiwan, the Rural Reconstruction Movement also was important in the early stages of the island's modernization. The Fourfold Program helped build capacity among the rural indigenous people in basic health care, literacy, civic capacity, and agricultural innovation, creating a platform for government expansion of development.

In the Philippines today there are many projects, some of the world's best experts in community development, and successful demonstrations. However, government efforts to take control in prescriptive expansion of successful projects have undermined local flexibility and self-reliance. Nongovernmental organizations have tried to assume an enabling role in building partnerships to go to scale, but they lack authority to create legal frameworks and conduct oversight. Thus programs continue to struggle against obstacles that would be easily overcome if each member of a three-way partnership was performing the role best suited to it.

Many who have strong biases in favor of grassroots action believe that communities can develop best when governments get out of the way, and in countries where government is not providing an enabling environment, many nongovernmental agencies and experts make a point of avoiding links with government. But nongovernmental agencies cannot replace government; they cannot pass laws, establish the systems or institutions, or enforce legal responsibility. The experience in China and the Philippines demonstrates clearly the vital role of the right kind of government partnership. In China, government support of local action brought nationwide provision of education and health care; when such support ceased during the Cultural Revolution, the forward momentum abruptly stopped. China is at increasing risk today because national policies coast on the social-development foundation of an earlier generation; the country's economic momentum increases inequity and undermines the national social foundation. In the Philippines, despite a cavalcade of good pilot projects, without appropriate government support development has had little success in going to scale.

Jimmy Yen's decades of experimentation have shown that community capacity and self-reliance are fragile but essential components of development. When participants ignore or forget the basic principles, community leadership can all too easily become community manipulation. Jimmy Yen's poem at the beginning of this chapter makes clear that the process requires mutual cooperation year after year, trying and then improving what works best at the community level. As in the villages of Ding Xian, development can start small and grow to huge scale when an iterative process is sustained.

Kerala

Development without Wealth

For several decades development scholars have been mystified why some places, such as the Indian state of Kerala, achieved the mortality, fertility, and educational levels of wealthy societies but without parallel economic development. When its success was first noticed in the 1960s, Kerala had the best health and education indicators and the highest political participation in India, but it was also the poorest state in the country. Today Kerala is advancing economically as well as socially. Kerala's experience demonstrates that when development is just it can also be sustainable.

Most analyses of Kerala's success have focused on events since Indian independence, when increasing amounts of data showed statistical associations among variables such as infant mortality and health facilities or literacy and schools.[1] Our own review confirms a growing awareness that traces the reasons for success to events in Kerala a century before independence.

Origins of Social Development in Kerala

The state of Kerala was created in 1956 from three much older political units, each with a distinct character: the two independent princely states of Travancore and Cochin, and the Malabar Coast, which had been under British administration for a century. This southwestern tip of India was known as "the spice coast." Here traders had maintained contact with both West and East, traveling as far as the Roman and Chinese empires, for a thousand years.

The independent princely state of Travancore appears to have led the trend to innovation. In the early nineteenth century, Travancore was among the most orthodox and rigid centers of Hindu culture: when a high-caste person walked along a path, people of lower castes had to step aside to let the twice-born pass. But at least four factors were also present that catalyzed change. One was farsighted leadership by the rulers of Travancore. A second was the very strong and unusual matrilineal tradition of the Nairs, a Hindu high caste. A third factor was the Church of St. Thomas, founded in the first century by the Apostle Thomas, whose teachings eventually converted one-fifth of the people of Kerala to Christianity; conversions of many in the high castes reinforced progressive thinking among the elite. The final, and perhaps most important, factor was a progressive people's movement that pushed for social reforms, cash-crop-based agriculture, active links to outside forces of change, and enlightened leadership.

In 1817 Rani Laxmi Bayi, the wife of the maharaja of Travancore, issued a proclamation supporting general education for women and presided over the opening of the first Christian mission school for girls. In 1865 her son, opening the Trivandrum General Hospital, announced that one of his chief ambitions was to make good medical care available to all his subjects.[2] Until Indian independence in 1949, this royal family supported education for girls and the construction of schools and hospitals. Although the family remained orthodox Hindus, an interesting cooperation evolved between newly arriving Christian missions and the government. Perhaps concern over the increasing number of Christian converts persuaded the royal family to incorporate mission schools and hospitals in its already progressive programs. Adding to the expansion of religious tolerance was the respect enjoyed by the large, low-caste Esheva community, one of whom, the religious reformer Narayana Guru, had influenced the opening of Hindu temples to all castes.

This forward-looking social base made possible the emergence of a progressive people's movement in the late nineteenth century, initially launched to fight caste-based oppression within Hinduism. Over time it expanded to address broader social-justice issues, with peasants and city workers joining in its campaigns. In 1957 the 65,000-member organization formally constituted itself the Kerala People's Science Movement. Since then its members have been popularizing the use of science and making people aware of environmental issues. In successful efforts in land reform, the Kerala People's Science Movement helped to reduce the size and scope of some of the larger spice, coffee, tea, and rubber plantations. It also became the backbone of the state's highly successful total-literacy campaign.

Since 1949 the people of Kerala have been increasingly involved in politics, occasionally electing Communist governments with a distinctively independent local stamp. Communist party leaders in Kerala enjoy a reputation for relative honesty and for a commitment to a more just society.[3]

All these factors exert continuing pressure for social equity. Civic commitment and political engagement are high. In part because Kerala has by far the highest per-capita readership of daily newspapers of any state, people monitor the performance of public servants closely and report laxness to higher officials. Kerala offers the most advanced opportunities in India for women in education and professional roles. The rate of population growth is one of the lowest in the country. The people have come to expect a better way of life, and they express those expectations to one another and to their leaders.

Parallel Promotion of Social Development in India

Early in the twentieth century events elsewhere in India also affected Kerala. Leaders in many parts of the country were creating powerful visions of the potential for community-based, comprehensive, social development. Perhaps the most influential of these pioneers was the poet, novelist, painter, philosopher, and social reformer Rabindranath Tagore, who received the Nobel Prize for literature in 1913. Tagore grew up the son of a landowner in Bengal, and his development philosophy grew out of practical programs he devised for villagers on his family's land. In 1901 he started a rural university at Shantiniketan, in West Bengal, which became a magnet for Indian nationalists. He also started a major training center for development at Sriniketan, an institution that grew in parallel with his rural university. His ideas directly influenced Mahatma Gandhi's "experiments with truth," which were taught in many ashrams (spiritual and community study centers).

Missionaries also provided important leadership in community-development efforts. For example, in the 1920s Charlotte and Bill Wiser found themselves sitting on the running board of their Model T Ford outside the village of Karimpur, in the United Provinces, wondering how they would get behind the mud walls. They put up their tents and developed trust and friendship with neighbors. Doors opened first when Charlotte, who had taken a three-month course in simple medical care, was asked to see the sick child of a village headman; her success led to the opening of a simple clinic. Bill, who had been a concert violinist before becoming a missionary, took out his violin to join village wedding processions. Their India Village Service in model villages in Etah district led directly to the nearby Etawah project, which became for a time a SCALE Squared center of action learning and experimentation. This demonstration district served as the model for Jawaharlal Nehru's Community Development Movement in the 1950s, with its national system of community-development blocks.[4]

In a parallel, third stream of influential programs, some British civil servants added village development to their administrative duties. One of these was F. L. Brayne, district commissioner of Gurgaon, in the Punjab, whose incentives for improved practices among farmers seemed at first to revolutionize village welfare. His success led to statewide promotion of the program, but when he left Gurgaon the incentives ceased, and the program fell apart, illustrating how easy it is to confuse real social changes with only apparent ones. Another member of the Indian Civil Service, Malcolm Darling, initiated a program of village banks and cooperatives to combat ancient systems of village usury. In northeast India the participatory, site-sensitive approach implemented by Verrier Elwin, an Oxford anthropologist and civil administrator, helped protect minority tribes. His approach of first discovering and then building from local realities greatly informed our SEED-SCALE methodology.[5]

Dynamics of Social Development

Definitive analyses of the Kerala experience by T. N. Krishnan, P.G.R. Panikar, and others at the Trivandrum Centre for Development Studies document the magnitude of changes achieved and contrast these with social change in the rest of India. According to 1991 census data, rural infant mortality in Kerala was one-fifth that of the rest of India (17 per 1,000 live births as compared with 86 per 1,000 in the rest of India and 61 per 1,000 in the Punjab, the state with the highest per-capita income). The birth rate in Kerala was 18 per 1,000 as compared with the all-India rate of 31 per 1,000. Kerala is the only state in

India in which there is no preference for male babies: in 1991 the gender ratio was 1,036 females to 1,000 males, compared with 927 females to 1,000 males for India as a whole. Life expectancy for females was 74 years in Kerala, 65 years in the Punjab, and 59 years in India as a whole. Literacy among females was 87 percent as compared with 39 percent for India.[6]

In another study, Moni Nag compared Kerala with West Bengal, a state with a similar history of education, cultural leadership, and long periods of Communist control of the government. The contrast in health indicators is telling. Infant mortality was lower in West Bengal than in Kerala until the 1940s, but after independence Kerala's infant mortality dropped to about half the West Bengal rate. Utilization of health services in Kerala is approximately twice that in West Bengal, as is the availability of education for women. Such differences seem surprising, given that West Bengal has always been both more industrialized and urbanized than Kerala, two factors that are usually associated with improved socioeconomic indicators. Nag concluded that after 1949, West Bengal focused on economic development whereas Kerala focused on social development, and that the latter produced the long-term benefits.[7]

The analyses show clearly that mortality reduction, literacy promotion, and political activity are strongly associated with the presence of health facilities and the early introduction of modern schools, especially for girls. However, they also show that other factors (such as reduced rigidity in caste and religious affiliation) helped create a unique climate of social expectation in which people identified specific and attainable social priorities on which action could focus.

Kerala's social indicators are remarkable in themselves, but they are even more striking when compared with its economic indicators. Social development in Kerala occurred before economic growth. Although Kerala's 1991 per-capita domestic product was 4,618 rupees as compared with 9,643 in the Punjab and 5,586 for all of India, the share of Keralans living below the poverty line had declined from 60 percent in 1973 to 32 percent in 1987.[8] The current increases in per-capita income arise not primarily from local economic development but from infusions of revenue from large numbers of educated Keralans working in the Gulf countries, other parts of India, and

North America. Today this reinvestment in Kerala is syncrgistically fueling a boom in economic activity as well as continued improvement in social indicators.

The Three Phases of Kerala's Going to Scale

The Kerala experience demonstrates the three-phase development described in this book. In fact our decades of observation of the Kerala experience greatly clarified our thinking about the dimensions of development. In Kerala the evolution was serendipitous, but now it may be possible to implement the process intentionally.

Phase One: Successes Rise to Attention

The princely states of Travancore and Cochin were extremely orthodox Hindu centers, and, as in most such communities, their rulers and elites resisted change. However, in Travancore the combination of external and internal influences described above led to significant expansion of education and health care.

By the end of the nineteenth century, Travancore's evident progress was inspiring Cochin's leaders to follow. There, too, essential three-way partnerships evolved as outside experts introduced schools and hospitals, local rulers implemented supportive policies, and community-based groups encouraged progressive action. As education and health services expanded into rural areas, and as communities came to realize that a better life was possible, their confidence in change grew. By the end of World War I, large reform movements had emerged in Travancore and Cochin that would not be seen in colonial areas of India until more than a generation later.

Such an enabling environment was not found in the Malabar Coast, which was under British colonial administration during the century of this remarkable social transformation. The British agenda was to serve economic interests back home, extracting natural and any other resources to benefit the empire. Development initiatives were concentrated in administration, buildings, railways, roads, and communications to promote the growth of rubber, tea, coffee, and spice plantations. The focus on economic prosperity instead of social development increasingly separated elite society into the developed and the traditional as a new economic class of well-educated, privileged Indians evolved.

Phase Two: Adapting and Adopting

From World War I to 1956, Travancore and Cochin systematically extended their earlier scattered demonstration projects by promoting larger enabling frameworks. Education and health-care coverage increased and improved dramatically. During this period missionaries played an important role. One of these was Spencer Hatch, who during the 1920s and 1930s expanded a program for village workers in Martandam into a SCALE Squared training center. Another was Dr. Howard Somerville, who in 1922 and 1924 achieved fame as one of the early highest climbers on Mount Everest. He fell in love with the mountains of India and moved his medical practice from England to the hills of the Western Ghats, where he became internationally known for doing more gastric resections than any other surgeon up to that time and then went on to make major contributions in medical education.

Other help became available from outside institutions. In 1928 the maharaja of Travancore requested help from the Rockefeller Foundation to improve health care. The foundation sent W. P. Jacocks to work in Travancore, Cochin, and Sri Lanka. (During this period the foundation was also supporting John Grant in China and his work with Jimmy Yen.) In 1931 Jacocks started a system of health services based on primary health centers. These community-based centers extended rapidly through Travancore and Cochin as well as Sri Lanka, providing accessible care to villagers while collecting vital statistics, doing health surveys, organizing communicable disease control, training public health nurses and maternal and child health workers, improving sanitation, and emphasizing community action linked to the identification of specific behavior changes necessary for improved health. This network of health centers and women's greater access to education probably worked synergistically to produce a dramatic decline in infant mortality, from 220 per 1,000 live births in 1921 to 120 per 1,000 in 1956.[9] The parallel extension of health centers and village schools spearheaded the expansion of social services from the cities and larger towns into the countryside.

Phase Three: Going to Scale

The momentum of development in Travancore and Cochin was challenged in 1956, when the two states were amalgamated with the Malabar Coast to form the new state of Kerala. Now two socially empowered blocks were joined with an entity whose priority had been the extraction of resources to benefit a distant foreign empire, and which had neglected social development. Instead of leaving the new state developmentally segmented, the new Communist government immediately started scaling up education and health services to total coverage of Kerala. Using the experience of Spencer Hatch's Martandam, Jacocks's health centers, mission schools, and government health centers as SCALE Squared centers, the state government created an enabling environment for extending community-based services into Malabar as well as the remotest areas of the two former princely states. Although outsiders played a role in starting this process, it is unlikely that the penetration would have been so complete without input from the Kerala People's Science Movement, which allied itself with the robust political left. A well-educated and politically aware populace ensured that the alternating Communist and Congress regimes kept delivering social services.

Kerala's focus on universal social development contrasted with Nehru's priorities of industrial and agricultural development in much of the rest of the country. Its achievements were impressive. From 1956 to 1966 infant mortality was cut from 120 to 68 per 1,000 live births; over the next decade it fell further, to 55 per 1,000; and by 1992 it had declined to 17 per 1,000.[10] In the late 1980s, Ernakulam became the first district in India to achieve universal literacy. A process that had taken a century in Travancore and Cochin was accomplished in thirty-five years in Malabar.

During the extension from Travancore and Cochin to Malabar, Kerala's government consistently demonstrated flexible responsiveness to community concerns and created integrated services. Its extension of family planning illustrates this commitment to community. Through the 1960s and 1970s, while Indian national policy was separating basic health services from family planning, Kerala maintained linkages between them in rural centers and hospitals alike by using trained midwives and community-based workers.

One result was widespread acceptance of family planning; fertility became the lowest in India. Another result was an increase in the share of births delivered by trained midwives, from 26 percent in 1973 to 91 percent in 1991.[11] During this same period, in response to pressure from international population-control enthusiasts, India's national government separated family planning from health care and instituted sterilization camps. The results included not only a setback in family planning but also the temporary fall of Indira Gandhi's government.

Kerala is one of the few places in India where a pristine environment can still be found. The verdant Western Ghats of Kerala are one of the country's two large centers of biodiversity, offering an extensive stretch of montane forest. These rugged hills resisted early exploitation largely through historical accident: people were concentrated in the plains along the coast, the maharaja of Travancore owned private estates in these hills and protected the area generally, and some of the large valleys there are sacred to orthodox Hindus. More recently, largely through efforts by the Kerala People's Science Movement, popular will has mobilized not just to preserve this treasure but also to heighten public awareness about sustainable development.

Lessons from Kerala

Kerala's long path to progress, now extending over almost two centuries, brought significant social development without requiring wealth. Much of that progress was serendipitous, especially at the beginning, but it need not be unique. Many of the factors promoting Kerala's success can be replicated in other places.

Four factors played key roles early on in Kerala's transformation: the evolution of remarkable tolerance among religious groups; the encouragement of female literacy, which directly affected family well-being, especially the health of children and acceptance of family planning; the influence of ideas and help from outsiders; and enlightened political control of development.

Progress in Kerala has not been steady or linear; community capacity built slowly through isolated demonstration projects centered largely on schools and hospitals, then consolidated and accelerated into key achievements in gaining political influence, new gender roles, and the like. Through informal learning centers practical lessons from these demonstrations radiated outward to broader populations. Some groups took hold of the new ideas early and advanced rapidly while others were scarcely beginning. Helping to keep the momentum of change in balance was an enlightened societal framework of leaders and political parties that required accountability, ensured that services were integrated, and with remarkable prescience filled in the gaps.

All three principles defined in this book were present. Crucial to the early formation of a three-way partnership was the Travancore royal family's willingness to take risks. Top-down leadership joined with expert assistance from missionaries to support community decisionmaking. The expert role was later greatly augmented by an unusually effective progressive people's movement, which mobilized communities to put pressure on the political system. Because both Jacocks and the Kerala People's Science Movement based local decisionmaking on real data, local health centers successfully adapted outreach programs to local circumstances, changing behavior and creating a healthier environment.

Development spans the three dimensions of SCALE. First, local models grew for almost a century, setting a standard and systematically building community-based momentum. In Travancore and Cochin schools and health centers became local, hands-on demonstrations and then steadily expanded their coverage far beyond the elite. This human-centered change promoted increased political participation, which in turn put pressure on the administrative system to continue expanding services. The social capacity thus fostered in the two princely states became the platform for launching development throughout the new state and overcoming Malabar's legacy of dependency and social disempowerment. Throughout this expansion, first regal and then democratic Indian leadership focused on nurturing people's capabilities.

Kerala's experience reveals all six criteria of sustainable social development. Early experiments in comprehensive development (by Hatch, Jacocks, and many missionaries) promoted a holistic approach instead of a focus on economic prosperity. Year after year new ideas were adapted, creating an iterative momentum over a surprisingly long time. The left-wing political bloc kept a premium on equity and extending services. Interdependence and collaboration among diverse people and communities grew ever stronger as factions and political parties learned to compromise. As Keralans working in the Gulf countries, North America, Britain, and other parts of India become more conscious of environmental issues, they are awakening public concern back home to protect Kerala's development successes and to preserve its remarkably intact natural systems. This consciousness may be coming just in time.

In the words of Bill McKibben, in its development achievements "Kerala supplies no new technology. Its gift is more precious: a new fuel for our imaginations."[12] For millions of poor around the world who do not have the option of basing their development upon wealth, Kerala offers a refreshingly different, and sustainable, alternative key to the future.

CHAPTER 9

The Adirondacks

An Evolving Balance between People and Nature

Around the world many people know the Adirondacks chiefly as home to the Lake Placid Winter Olympics in 1932 and 1980. Most are unaware that these attention-catching events with their intensive human impact took place inside a unique nature preserve.

The Adirondack State Park of New York is America's best-tested model for integrating people and nature. It is also the most successful at encouraging diverse sustainable human uses. Established in 1885, ten years after Yellowstone, the six-million-acre Adirondack Park embodies a profoundly different alternative to the land-conservation strategy of the better-known U.S. national park system. The Adirondack Park is the largest in America outside Alaska, greater in size than the combined areas of Glacier, Olympic, Yellowstone, and Grand Canyon National Parks. The park continues to grow—and one reason it can do so is that its operating costs are less than one-third those of the national park model.

The park encompasses the whole ecosystem of the upper New York plateau. Its size allows it to absorb a considerable human impact. A geographic area as large as Belgium accommodates a human population of 130,000 year-round residents, 200,000 seasonal residents, and 3 million annual visitors, balancing multiple objectives, economic bases, leadership agencies, and landowners. The park is far from perfect; a recent article described its management system as "a mess."[1] Yet that remarkable—perhaps unique—system has compelled zealous proponents of private rights and equally zealous advocates of public conservation to work out their differing priorities together.

Most land preserves in the world separate people from wilderness. In the

Adirondack system, large numbers of people live and work inside the park; in fact half of the park land is privately owned. The Adirondack approach brings together government and private landowners, using citizens as participants in management rather than just as visitors to be managed. Adirondack management is unruly, to be sure—almost every group involved believes it knows a better way to manage the park. But given the park's operating costs, its size, its ability to accommodate people, its promotion of sustainable livelihoods, and its record of conservation protection, which matches or surpasses that of any other park in America, it is hard not to conclude that the management approach is a success.

Living within such a conservation framework restricts people's freedoms to exploit the land. It reminds them that our natural heritage is a legacy from earlier generations and one to be passed on, not a product to be consumed by those who happen to live on the land today. The people who live inside the park are aware that conservation is inconvenient; by forcing a longer perspective on the consequences of actions it slows the drive toward immediate profit. For 117 years public interests and private desires have tugged and pushed in creative struggle. Neither side wins, and that fact frustrates both.

Although the United States has other important and successful people-based, centuries-old examples of environmental stewardship (the Menominee tribe and the Coon Creek watershed in Wisconsin, multigenerational farms in Appalachia, and the Amish communities of highly productive farms), no other formally constituted conservation entity allows so many sustainable uses for the land or achieves conservation at so little cost. Although there are several other large multiuse conservation efforts in the nation (including some recent innovations on National Forest lands, New Jersey's Pine Barrens Preserve, the Lake Tahoe Regional Plan, and some greenway projects), none equals the Adirondack Park in size or in advancing the well-being of people while preserving the environment.

In 1885 Americans were traveling by horse or railroad, the Wild West was being opened, and, in the East, fields stretched almost continuously from Maine to Florida. In the East the woodland elk, bison, and wolves were gone, never to return, and the white-tailed deer, wild turkey, and foxes had been driven into the few small remaining pockets of what had been the world's most extensive temperate forest.[2] Alarmed by similar threats to the environment in the West, the federal government had established the national parks of Yellowstone and Yosemite. In New York State, the Adirondack montane plateau remained as a small island of forests surrounded by farms, providing an important source of water for the Hudson River transportation system, including the then newly constructed Erie and Mohawk River canals. This watershed-protection rationale was used by wealthy people in New York City, who were starting to vacation in the Adirondacks, to pressure the legislature to create the Adirondack State Park.

The central feature of the park is that the state government owns approximately half the land and private citizens own the other half. Protection of the government land is stricter than in any other preserve in America (and perhaps the world). Article 14 of the New York constitution designates state land within the Adirondack Park as "forever wild"; to change a boundary within this designation requires two separate votes of the state legislature in successive election periods. While the state pursues a program of land acquisition by buying sites that are ecologically sensitive and therefore best never developed—wetlands, areas of old-growth forest, and areas at high elevation—it also takes the view that private land is a fundamental part of the park that adds cost efficiencies and contributes in important ways to the special lifestyle there. Since the park's inception the state government has incrementally shaped a zonal land-use plan that specifies what uses are permitted on the government-owned, forever wild land. A separate agency, composed of citizens, administers a set of regulations that keeps private land uses and the larger conservation priorities in balance.

Innovations in Management

No visionary founding master plan created this innovation of public/private partnership, nor have its efforts to meet the needs of both people and environment been adequately recognized as a model. Expediency and circumstance backed the park into its revolutionary management paradigm.

Two separate agencies oversee the two different types of land within the park. Some see this arrangement as dysfunctional, or at best as a half-baked compromise; we view it as a positive system of checks and balances. New York's Department of Environmental Conservation administers the land that belongs to the state. The Adirondack Park Agency, an independent, appointed commission consisting of private citizens, sets guidelines for private land use and in regular public meetings reviews petitions, case by case, for local adjustment; but the Park Agency does not own the land, nor can it tell people what they must do.

The result is a system in dynamic tension. The government land is to be forever wild; that much is clear. But with half the land in private ownership and seven major types of land use allowed, diverse economic forces are constantly challenging the land-management guidelines with requests for exceptions. The guidelines specify that shorelines of the 2,800 lakes must be buffered with trees at least 100 feet back; road building is restricted to current levels; timbering must not damage the streams or cause soil erosion; towns cannot expand beyond existing limits. Billboards are not allowed anywhere in the park, and lighted signs are permitted only on buildings. Even so, decades of decisions about ecospecific needs and human hopes have produced a patchwork map of land uses.

A second innovative feature is the park's low operating cost—noteworthy in an era when nature preserves worldwide are under financial stress. Whether constituted at a national or state level, a traditional park of significant size is expensive. It requires its own infrastructures of transport systems and communications networks, and a small army of rangers and administrators to oversee not only the systems within the park but also compensation systems to people displaced by the entity. Costs attend both the creation of the new entity and the elimination of the old as people are displaced from their lands and former economic activities. Some of these costs are intangible, but the process is always both socially disruptive and hugely expensive.

In the Adirondacks costs remain low because systems already in place were not dismantled and the new administrative layer is thin. Local people are employed in a variety of jobs. Citizens living inside the park monitor and report on regulation compliance, eliminating much of the need for wardens and their attendant administrative system. Whether based on number of visitors or number of acres, our calculations indicate that this park's operating costs are approximately one-third those of the U.S. national parks. Piggybacking conservation onto existing systems has resulted in economic efficiency.

The third innovation of the Adirondack Park is the diversity of its economic base. Many nature preserves allow sustainable harvesting of resources (limited hunting, collection of medicinal plants, selective timber cutting), and increasingly they are providing employment opportunities, typically in connection with ecotourism. The Adirondack Park, by having people inside it who are always figuring out new options, has built up an uncommon array of seven kinds of activity that create an exceptionally diverse, resilient, and durable economic base.

Natural resource harvesting: Four natural resources have been or are being extracted from the park: trees (for both pulp and timber), minerals, energy (through hydroelectric generation), and animals (through fishing, trapping, and hunting).

Nonharvest natural resource uses: New ways to use the wilderness are evolving all the time. Current activities include, in the spring, whitewater rafting, canoeing, hiking, and wildflower trips; in the summer, camping, lake canoeing, biking, climbing, birding, and hiking; in the autumn, foliage viewing and hunting; and in the winter, ice climbing, snowshoeing, and every sport in the Winter Olympic repertoire.

Education: Public schools are both primary and secondary; private education supports four schools, two colleges, a training campus for winter sports, and a variety of educational programs in wilderness education.

Health and retirement: A century ago, sanatoria drew tuberculosis patients to the clean environment. Now the pattern is for people to move into the park to retire. As support facilities inside the park have matured over the last fifty years, medical research and long-term medical-care centers have been added.

Penal correction: Five state prisons inside the park provide well-paid year-round employment to people lacking higher education. Siting penitentiaries inside a wilderness area reduces incentives for escape for predominantly urban inmates.

Economic incubation: As communications, education, and health facilities have grown and the variety of residents increased, so has the attractiveness of the Adirondacks as a base for professionals, writers, and innovative companies.

Government sector: Whereas in most parks government jobs account for most or even all employment, in the Adirondacks the share is only 40 percent. When jobs in schools, prisons, and the Olympic facilities are subtracted from this figure, government and park-related jobs account for only 20 percent of employment.[3] This low percentage prevents formation of the government culture of prescriptive management that has blocked innovation in parks such as Yellowstone.[4]

The presence of people inside the park fosters local ownership of business. Many people start out working for someone else and then launch their own small enterprises and make them grow. In some cases people start out as guides, gradually take in a few clients as boarders, and eventually establish bed-and-breakfasts. A consortium of locally owned businesses supports such entrepreneurship and makes it difficult for large corporations to open franchises—such as the recent attempt by Wal-Mart to open a store in Lake Placid. Local ownership of businesses fosters an entrepreneurial spirit: proprietors are on-site, thinking and experimenting, and hence continually expanding economic niches.

The Adirondack experience suggests that people are willing to experience a measure of economic hardship to live in an environmentally pleasing area. Seasonal unemployment in the Adirondacks is double that in the state as a whole, yet people who could move away to "better" jobs elsewhere choose to stay. Such dedication creates economic resilience. A measure of economic hardship appears to be offset by other rewards.[5]

Operation of the Principles

Partnerships

A singular feature of the Adirondack Park is the absence of a formal central leader or hierarchy. Some experts consider this a handicap; indeed, an important recent review cited it as the park's primary problem.[6] But in our view this leadership void is a strength.

In fact, in the Adirondacks there are plenty of leaders; there is simply not a single person or agency in control. The traditional role of park superintendent is filled by multiple agencies. New York's Department of Environmental Conservation administers the state land, and the Adirondack Park Agency defines the uses of the private land. These are supported by a huge mosaic of state institutions none of which is under the control of another: the Department of Transportation fashions the travel corridors, the Department of Economic Development promotes economic well-being in the area, and other departments such as Health and Education have parallel authority. In this mix, 105 autonomous townships also vie for position, as do a rising number of energetic and sometimes well-financed nongovernmental groups with specific agendas, the International Olympics Commission, and many civic groups.

No person or agency, but rather an operational framework supports a dynamic balance of power. To place one agency in control would weaken the vibrant momentum of constant experimentation and risk overly narrow judgments with dangerous consequences.[7] Under the existing system, each sector must daily balance its priorities with the needs of other sectors, and each decision is examined and justified on its own merits.

Experience with the timber industry illustrates how in the Adirondacks usually hostile bedfellows have come to be partners. Since government forests are not available for harvest, tree cutting can occur only on private land. Environmental groups, which prefer to see forests selectively harvested rather than obliterated by housing development, work with timber companies to get favorable timber tax rates. However, in this protected area other priorities also play a role—one large priority being public relations. Thus the timber companies, though eligible for lower taxes, often pay higher commercial rates so that communities will view them favorably and will continue other timber-friendly policies. To recoup the added tax costs, the companies create hunting camps, which they rent out at high prices because the park's conservation practices improve hunting. The hunting, in turn, promotes economic activity in towns, intensifying the synergy among communities, conservation interests, and corporations.

Data-Based Management

In 1885 the park was created with a twofold objective, based on the best information then at hand: to protect as much territory as possible as forever wild, and to deal in the least alienating way with private landowners. Separate management along these dual tracks continued for eighty years. On the private lands there was virtually no regulation, and when the government believed that conservation management was needed in certain areas, it simply tried to purchase the land. Such practices, involving rigid separation of conservation and development, are common in many parts of the world. But by the 1960s, with sixty million people within one day's drive of the park, use patterns started to change. For hundreds of thousands of people seeking to escape urban and suburban life, the Adirondacks offered a gigantic base for second-home development. Private landowners began reaping huge profits by subdividing their holdings around the lakes into small lots. A dialogue arose among citizens, experts, and officials—and these various parties went to Governor Nelson Rockefeller. He created a commission.

The Temporary Study Commission worked through the mid-1960s. More than most commissions of that era, which tended to hold hearings and then draft plans based on solicited opinions, the Temporary Study Commission built from data, gathering information on the rate of second-home development and on the ability of the land to support it. The commission considered alternative management approaches such as making all the Adirondacks into a national park or having the state buy all the private land.

The commission produced two sets of proposals. One recommended expanding the preserve's boundaries to approximate those of the whole ecosystem; this topic was not particularly controversial. A second set of proposals suggested regulation of private lands, a topic that fueled controversy and resentment that continue today.

Over the past thirty years, the increasing use of data by each side in the controversy has led to greater understanding of the issues at stake, to a measure of compromise, and to arrangements that people have found they can live with. The acrimonious crossfires of accusations and opinions that marked hearings in the first decade have subsided as each side has learned that it is more likely to succeed when it bases its arguments on facts rather than pure rhetoric.

Changing Behaviors

In most conservation efforts involving government and people, changing practice tends to be a one-way process; officials simply tell people: "Your land is going to be taken away, and you'll have to figure out for yourself new ways of living." But in the Adirondacks, new behaviors evolved instead of being prescribed. The Adirondack Park Agency first tried to impose top-down conservation as government officials usually do. But when the people pointed out that the body did not have such authority, the agency changed. Neither side could enforce its will on the other; both had to change. For the people, regulation of private land initially reduced opportunities, but they learned to work within them, and now economic opportunity is broadening. The Park Agency found it could not just make regulations, but had to incorporate people's priorities.

The model works. It does not eliminate conflict, but establishes a mechanism by which conflicting parties are forced into a dialogue. It is the dialogue, not the structure, that is key. This pattern of reciprocal adaptation has now extended outside the park. In 1938, to protect dwindling marshland bird habitat in St. Lawrence County, just north of the Adirondack Park, the U.S. Fish and Wildlife Service established the 7,200-acre Montezuma National Wildlife Refuge. Fifty years later it was clear that the area was too small and not adequately varied. Moreover, development pressure was threatening the larger wetland habitat outside the preserve. The government's initial decision, supported by most environmental groups, was to enlarge the preserve boundaries to include the full 46,000-acre ecosystem.

That decision threatened multigenerational farms and other lifestyles. Local residents rose up in fury. Populist anger and local organization rendered expansion out of the question; furthermore, the government did not have enough money to fund the project. The refuge manager, Gene Hocutt, began to talk with citizens, exploring alternative options. The nearby Adirondack model, in this case functioning as a SCALE Squared center, had shown that public land could be integrated with private holdings to create a larger preserved area. Government and people collaborated in a decision to try this approach.

The government land was designated the core area. The core zone would be supported by a buffer zone of private land where owners retained their uses but adjusted their behavior. Hocutt started to build wildlife ponds on these farms to make them friendlier to wildfowl and helped rechannel drainage ditches to expand wetland areas. State agencies and groups such as

Ducks Unlimited, the Nature Conservancy, and the National Audubon Society joined the effort. Initially some of the private groups bought people's land outright, but in time they turned to obtaining easements and use restrictions and providing incentives when landowners restored habitat. Farmers learned how to adjust their dairy operations to be compatible with avian habitat. Local entrepreneurs discovered business opportunities from tourism. A success in one place prompted neighbors to copy it. After Hocutt's retirement, the process continued under the leadership of Sheila Sleggs. Partnerships in the Montezuma area strengthened as Fish and Wildlife Service officials realized that invested participants from the community were assets, not adversaries.

A few facts demonstrate the success of the arrangement. The larger, 46,000-acre Montezuma National Wildlife Refuge was the first site in the eastern United States to reintroduce bald eagles into a breeding habitat; by 1999 three nesting sites were established. In the late 1980s, osprey had only one nesting site in the biome; today there are nine. Sightings have increased for other nesting birds, and the numbers of many migratory species are also increasing.

The Six Criteria Create Checks and Balances

During the Adirondack Park's first half-century, its people were ignored, with no statutory role in park administration and no compensation for resources to which they had lost access.[8] However, 105 towns and 100,000 people cannot be ignored when they organize. Over time, town councils made their voices heard at the state level. Special interests organized through nongovernment organizations and learned how to help draft and change policy, using economic leverage to influence decisions. People's involvement changed the pattern of two parallel land-use systems to the current more integrated approach.[9] Today all six criteria of genuine development are operating.

Equity. The Adirondacks community was once divided into two classes: the visiting rich, who came in from New York City especially for hunting and fishing vacations; and those who worked for them. There was a firm class line between those with money and those who needed it. Today, with a rapidly growing middle class, the line is not so sharp. The regulatory commissioners of the Park Agency come from a diversity of backgrounds and represent a broad range of perspectives. Park residents now talk about the opportunities the system offers them, not about the restrictions it imposes.

Sustainability. The Adirondack Park is America's largest and longest running formally constituted demonstration, outside the Native American communities, of people living inside a preservation area. The environment grows biologically healthier each year; natural resources are better protected today than at any time since the mid-1800s. Boundaries have expanded and new agencies created as understanding has grown about the complexity of the biome and about what environmentally responsible living involves.

Although the Adirondack biome is large, environmental awareness among those who love the park is even larger. The partners in the system realize that there is a connection between industrial pollution in America's Midwest and acid rains that threaten the survival of their forests. They realize that setting land apart as forever wild is no longer enough; to achieve sustainability many more people must change the way they behave. The Adirondacks is becoming a center for regional action on environmental concerns.

Interdependence. The Adirondacks are clearly dependent on the larger region, and even on European sources, for revenue, whether that revenue comes from selling sustainably produced timber (as is now being done by the innovative Paul Smith's College) or from marketing the park to tourists and sports enthusiasts. But dependency works the other way, too; in establishing the park the larger region has acknowledged its dependency on preserved natural resources. In a similar sense, within the park interdependence between private landowners and stricter governmental protection creates a greater conservation potential.

Holism. The Adirondack experience shows that nature conservation can be a means of diversifying economic activity. When conservation was organized to bring in a diversity of jobs, livelihoods in the park expanded to include tourism, sports, education, retirement communities, small businesses, and even prisons.

Collaboration. People in the park espouse conflicting viewpoints with a passion often bordering on religious zeal, but they keep talking to one another. Perhaps the lack of a single authority encourages diverse opinions to converge. Perhaps knowing that they share something special builds commonality. Whatever the reason may be, uncommon collaboration marks Adirondack meetings. People regularly stand up and speak either "as a resident of the park" or "on behalf of the local people." Into the 1970s, meetings, proposals, and all decisions originated in the state capital, Albany; now they come increasingly from inside the park.

Iteration. The Adirondacks experience has evolved incrementally over more than a century. Economic diversity, the interdependence of interests inside and outside the park, collaboration among factions in the community, the three-way partnership of community, officials, and experts, and the accumulation of data on the biome all took time, and the iterative growth inevitably caused frustration among the participants, since everyone would have preferred to prevail rather than compromise. Now, consciousness of what they are achieving is growing, and, as in a healthy ecosystem, diversity keeps any one species from dominating. So the process feels its way, correcting itself when it overextends. This repetitive growth is management by iteration. Most of the solutions that seemed right a century ago have now gone through many changes in a continuing quest for greater success.

Lessons from the Adirondacks

The forces that created the Adirondacks were unique to their time and political circumstance. By the early 1880s the eastern United States was nearing deforestation. Two and a half centuries of settlement had taken a drastic toll; although the human population then was much smaller, there was less wilderness in the region than there is today. From the 1830s on, adventurers increasingly sought out the wilderness—and to find it they had to go to northern New York State. But as outsiders discovered the Adirondacks, timber companies also moved in, cutting first the tall white pines, then the spruce, then the hardwoods for furniture and pulpwood. After these came the charcoal burners. Lacking any long-standing precedents for parks, lacking clearly defined models of conservation, concerned people nevertheless established the park.

As the need for conservation efforts intensifies, the Adirondack experience provides a useful model for expansion to other conservation initiatives in the American landscape. The Adirondacks itself cannot be replicated, but the process can, perhaps in the Virginia Barrier Islands or old coal-producing areas within a hundred miles of Washington, D.C.; perhaps in a Northern Woods Initiative, extending east from the Adirondacks into Maine; perhaps with a restructuring of American national parks to create buffer zones around their strictly managed cores, as is now being contemplated for the greater Yellowstone ecosystem.

When the New York legislature mandated the park in 1885, it aimed to protect land by setting aside a major tract to be forever wild, reclaiming land that had been cut over and identifying key watersheds for preservation. As the focus of the park changed to recreation, the state bought more land. From the beginning, most conservationists have lamented that the legislature did not establish a clear intent to acquire all the land—or at least to impose tight control over the land remaining in private hands. But by failing to exclude private landowners from the park and by giving them remarkable latitude, the legislature inadvertently fostered an extraordinary model whose relevance has grown over time. By allowing—and later actively encouraging—people to work within a mandate for nature protection, the New York legislature created an enabling environment that is evolving into a globally relevant model of a just and sustainable future. Few places demonstrate so well that people can learn to integrate environmental protection with the way they live.

CHAPTER 10

Narangwal

The Role of Conceptual and Cultural Breakthroughs

In 1969 we were two years into a field experiment to improve the survival and nutrition of children in a cluster of villages in Ludhiana district, in northern India. Several family health workers (FHWs) from our project were being trained how to diagnose childhood pneumonia in the pediatric wards of the Ludhiana Christian Medical College teaching hospital.[1]

In the area around Narangwal village pneumonia was the second-largest cause of death among children under three years of age, as it had been for children through the centuries around the world. It was then killing more than four million children worldwide each year. To prevent deaths from pneumonia, diagnosis and treatment had to be quick, since when infants developed pneumonia they died within two or three days. The only effective cure at the time was penicillin, but its use required early diagnosis in village homes. Diagnosis was difficult, because most village children had chronic coughs and runny noses. To know whether penicillin was needed, the health workers had to have a simple technique to distinguish between pneumonia and a common cold. In a pediatric ward a professor was showing the FHWs lung X rays and explaining the signs and symptoms physicians looked for. The FHWs were having great trouble learning how to use stethoscopes—not surprisingly, since even skilled clinicians have difficulty hearing faint changes in breath sounds in babies.

In frustration, an FHW said, "Why do you want us to learn to use these instruments? We have talked this over among ourselves and we have found a better way: *just watch the babies breathe!*"

The doctors stopped teaching and observed. It was true. The babies with pneumonia were breathing differently from normal babies. Respirations were rapid, labored, and frequently grunting. Those with most consolidation of lungs had visible retraction under and between the ribs. Systematic trials followed, checked by X rays, and they showed that persons trained in direct observation could make diagnoses as accurately as pediatricians with their stethoscopes.

Once it was shown that family health workers could diagnose pneumonia, the obvious question was whether they could safely use penicillin injections for treatment. The government reluctantly gave permission for well-supervised FHWs to administer these injections if they then referred babies when there was no improvement. One year later, pneumonia mortality in study villages had dropped by 45 percent as compared with control villages.[2] This was the first published demonstration of what became the World Health Organization's case-management method for childhood pneumonia.

A few years later workers in New Guinea standardized the observational methods by counting respirations.[3] This effort led to the current guidelines: if a baby less than two months old is breathing more than sixty times a minute, it should promptly be treated for pneumonia; between two and twelve months, the threshold is fifty times a minute; and at more than one year, forty times a minute. UNICEF produced rugged battery-operated timers that beep after thirty seconds to help in counting respirations accurately. Procedures were simplified even more with the safe, broad-spectrum oral antibiotic cotrimoxazole, costing only twenty-five cents for a full treatment.[4] As a result, pneumonia death rates in children are dropping significantly worldwide.

The Importance of Conceptual Breakthroughs

Creating a more just and sustainable future requires periodic conceptual breakthroughs such as the one described above. Each sector of development (agriculture, health, schooling, transport, and the like) will have its own cluster of breakthroughs. Usually these occur spontaneously and unpredictably. But in recent years they have been increasingly stimulated by deliberate experimentation at field research centers, usually focusing on a particular set of priority problems. The role of the Narangwal research center in the conceptual breakthrough on childhood pneumonia is one example.

Field-based research centers have fueled intentional breakthroughs in health as they did the Green Revolution (discussed in Chapter 2 and the Conclusion). In public health as in agriculture, progress in one place has stimulated trials at other sites. During the 1960s and 1970s a network of field-based health laboratories around the world experimented with alternative interventions, building on one another's discoveries and systematically developing new approaches.

The International Center for Diarrheal Disease Research, in Dhaka, Bangladesh, is one of the oldest and best-known of the worldwide web of centers. Its field center in Matlab district was established by Henry Mosley (as mentioned in Chapter 6) to test cholera vaccine. Its most important innovation was a simple system of data collection to get total monthly counts of births, deaths, migration, and other population figures. With this continually updated database, field trials took rigorous testing of new vaccines beyond the laboratory and into large populations for clinical trials and promoted integrated health-care interventions that led to still more breakthroughs. Matlab confirmed Narangwal findings (described later in the chapter) that women more readily adopted modern family planning when it was integrated with basic maternal and child care. Its database was also used for definitive field experiments showing that oral rehydration therapy could control death by diarrhea, the number-one killer of children worldwide.

Another important center in this informal world network was the Johns Hopkins Center for Tropical Medicine Research and Training, in Calcutta, which worked with the Bangladesh and Narangwal centers to develop mass methods applying this simple, low-cost cure for diarrhea. In 1976 an editorial in the eminent medical journal *Lancet* declared this cure to be "the most important medical discovery of the twentieth century."[5]

Another center making key discoveries was the Institute for Nutrition in Central America and Panama, in Guatemala, where Nevin Scrimshaw and his colleagues provided clear evidence of a synergism between malnutrition and infections. They followed up this conceptual breakthrough by showing how low-cost and adequately balanced nutrition could be achieved in large populations.[6]

These are only four of the better-known centers worldwide. Other pioneering activities had been under way for at least a century, most significantly among medical missionaries, who despite tight financial constraints had experimented constantly to evolve effective but low-cost innovations in their isolated settings. Some of their innovations were picked up, refined, and then publicized by the research centers.

Many of these threads were drawn together by Halfdan Mahler, the director general of the World Health Organization in the 1970s. With a worldwide mandate for improving health, and recognizing that most countries could never afford services that depended mostly on specialty clinics and physician-based care, Mahler persuaded the World Health Assembly in 1974 to make primary health care a priority by bringing services as close as possible to families and changing the health practices of people in their homes and communities. In the mid-1970s UNICEF added to this momentum through its child-health efforts. In 1978 the World Conference on Primary Health Care in Alma Ata, Soviet Kazakhstan, endorsed this new approach based on practical, community-based strategies. One major reason for this widespread acceptance was the research centers' presentation of solid, quantitative evidence that breakthroughs had made implementation possible.

Narangwal is a village in the Indian Punjab where we did health research from 1961 to 1974. The field studies demonstrated the feasibility of using simple new interventions to reduce quickly the four main causes of child death: diarrhea, pneumonia, protein-energy malnutrition, and neonatal tetanus. The research also showed that it is more practical and cost-effective to integrate family planning and maternal and child health than to provide separate services.[7]

The Narangwal team of research workers and field staff lived and worked in multiple clusters of villages according to a controlled experimental design so that it was possible to compare the efficacy of different packages of interventions. The project tested hypotheses under field conditions that partially replicated the controls used in laboratory experiments. The area covered three community-development blocks (the term officially used in India) with a total population of 260,000. The main village clusters comprised a total of twenty-six villages with a combined population of 35,000. The research was conducted jointly by the Indian Council of Medical Research and Johns Hopkins University's Department of International Health and was reported in six books and more than a hundred journal articles.

The field studies focused on the major causes of death and helped provide the conceptual basis of the Child Survival Revolution in developing countries. In the fall of 1973, six years before he became the executive director of UNICEF, Jim Grant gave his annual lecture at Johns Hopkins University. After his lecture we showed him data from the community-based research at Narangwal, where, in controlled village trials, child mortality had been cut in half by a package of interventions carried out by village women guided by family health workers at a total cost of just over two dollars per person per year. As we walked down the hall afterward he stopped and exclaimed, "Carl, we can start to talk about a Child Survival Revolution!" This was the first time I heard him use what became one of his favorite terms. By the 1990s he was able to claim that child survival had improved more in the previous four decades than in all prior human history.[8]

Diarrhea in Babies: Cutting Mortality by Half

Throughout human history, diarrhea has been the number-one cause of death. In the mid-twentieth century there were more than five million diarrheal deaths each year. Diarrhea was so common in young children that in many villages it was considered a normal part of childhood.

In the heat of a Punjab summer, babies died in two or three days when diarrhea drained away their bodily fluids. Simple interventions were needed for immediate care. The presence of diarrhea was obvious, but the most urgent need was for mothers to recognize early signs that the baby was about to die from dehydration. These signs were sunken eyes, skin that stayed puckered when pinched, and, in infants, sunken fontanelles. We first trained family health workers to recognize the signs of acute dehydration and then to refer the babies to a special ward at the health center, where they were lined up on cots to receive intravenous drips into scalp veins.

Colleagues at the Johns Hopkins Center for Tropical Medicine Research and Training had already shown in a refugee camp that oral rehydration therapy would correct fluid loss from cholera and quickly save lives.[9] The question then followed, could oral rehydration therapy be an effective home treatment for common diarrhea? Narangwal, working in parallel with the Calcutta and Bangladesh centers, had FHWs use little plastic bags of a carefully measured mixture of salts and glucose dissolved in a liter of water. The solution was fed to the dehydrated infant by spoon. A year later there was no improvement in mortality. Investigation showed that the family health workers still thought intravenous therapy at the health center was more scientific, so they were referring patients instead of starting the oral therapy. The babies were dying before they arrived at the ward. We closed down the special intravenous ward and issued new standing orders: whenever FHWs saw a case of diarrhea with dehydration, they were to stop whatever else they had scheduled, prepare the solution, and give it themselves until the mother could continue the care. After a few dramatic demonstrations of child recovery, mothers began to use the technique spontaneously when diarrhea started, and the diarrheal death rate in study villages fell by almost half.[10] Parallel data came from Bangladesh and elsewhere.[11] Since then the procedure has been further simplified with the use of even safer and more-effective cereal-based oral rehydration solutions: mothers or health workers simply add salt to whatever cereal flour is available in the home and mix it with water. A rehydration solution made from roasted barley flour has been especially effective in Tibet (Chapter 18), requiring no outside resources.

Protein-Energy Malnutrition: Marasmus

Although pneumonia and diarrhea are often the direct causes of death in young children, a synergism between malnutrition and common infections is commonly the underlying cause of death. We had already defined an association between diarrhea and malnutrition in the 1950s, in a project in Khanna, just twenty-six miles from Narangwal.[12] The breakthrough in understanding causation came when all the factors were put together: a child weakened by poverty, ignorance, lack of appropriate food, and/or natural catastrophe would develop a simple infection such as diarrhea, and that event would precipitate a downward spiral. The infection would make the malnutrition worse, which in turn would lower resistance to other infections.[13]

Marasmus results when both protein and calorie deficiencies are present. This condition could be easily corrected by nutrition supplements, but in the Narangwal villages it was the third leading cause of death. It was much more common among girl than boy babies, who were given preferential care. The difference was obvious from observations of children who should have been the same size. At three years of age, girls were on average two centimeters shorter and one pound lighter than boys, and caste differences widened the gap: the average low-caste three-year-old girl from a control village that did not have our nutritional supplements was six centimeters shorter and weighed five and a half pounds less than a high-caste boy from a nutrition care village.[14]

Control of the problem required sensitivity to traditional beliefs and feeding practices. The local name for the condition was *sokha,* which means "drying or shriveling up," a term that described a baby half normal size with the face of an old man. Traditionally when marasmus became severe, the village wise man or faith healer was called in. If he diagnosed *sokha,* death was believed to be inevitable; the baby's body had been taken over by the shadow of a *parchawan,* or evil spirit. The baby was then kept in a dark room so that the shadow could not move to other children. Marasmic babies who received supplemental feedings, however, responded dramatically, with almost daily catchup in growth and vitality.

Most cases of marasmus were in the lower-caste sectors of villages. Village elders agreed to locate feeding centers in areas where the need was concentrated and to provide the necessary supplies. Volunteers visited homes and gave out supplements of grain and milk. Families learned to use appropriate weaning foods, and the condition rapidly disappeared. These results led to open questioning of the power of faith healers, a factor that was also important in dealing with neonatal tetanus.

Neonatal Tetanus

The fourth major cause of childhood death in northern India (as in many traditional villages around the world) was neonatal tetanus. We realized its importance in the Khanna project, where the first year's data showed that many babies were dying at the end of the first week of life. The symptoms suggested tetanus, although the local people called the condition *artwhan,* meaning "eighth," because babies became sick and died around the eighth day of life.[15] When we reported the frequency of neonatal tetanus, officials challenged our findings, because the condition was never seen in the hospitals. The next year we had the answer: the people had told us, "There is no point in taking these babies to doctors, because they all die anyway"—which was true.

Later in the Narangwal project, we showed that as with cases of marasmus, people believed that a *parchawan* (also called a *bhoot*) was responsible; a shadow of an evil spirit had entered the baby at birth. To prevent shadows, traditional midwives usually delivered babies in darkened rooms with mud floors so that the placenta (considered a major source of spirit pollution) could be buried promptly. The umbilical cord was commonly cut with any sharp farm instrument such as a sickle, and the stump was tied with an old piece of string. The floor on which all this occurred was commonly plastered with sacred cow dung, which was heavily infected with tetanus bacilli.

We did not directly challenge people's beliefs in evil spirits. Instead we told them that science had determined that the evil spirit came from the tetanus germ, which grew in polluted soil and especially dung. We then introduced two parallel actions: FHWs gave midwives simple sterilized packets consisting of a razor blade, cord tie, and antiseptic dressing, and they also arranged for mothers to receive an injection of tetanus toxoid. The latter practice accorded with local beliefs in the value of increasing positive forces that were transmitted to the baby.

The breakthrough here consisted in using both clinical and anthropological data to incorporate scientific understanding with traditional beliefs. People changed their behavior when they were helped to reinterpret their values. This was one of the first population-based studies to show that tetanus toxoid immunization could eliminate neonatal tetanus. The tetanus deaths totally disappeared in two years.[16] The experience also shows that it is often better to use a demonstration to change practices rather than struggle to change people's beliefs first.

Integration of Maternal and Child Health with Family Planning

The Narangwal field trial sought to prove that family planning would be more accepted if it was integrated with a child-survival program so that people recognized there was now less need for additional children.[17] This family planning research grew directly from the work of John Gordon and John Wyon at Khanna.

A breakthrough was needed to get villagers to adopt family planning. Simply giving families modern inexpensive contraception and telling them how to use it would not be enough. We tested whether people's desires for children were motivated by a complex set of values and expectations, and if so, by which ones. We collected anthropological data on the assumption that before parents adopted smaller family sizes they needed some assurance that their desired number of children would survive to carry on the family's place in society. The project at Narangwal measured the specific components of health care that most directly increased family-planning use. Five clusters of villages received different combinations of family planning, maternal care, and child care, and these were compared with a control group that had only the government's separate health and family-planning services.

We found that combining family planning with children's preventive services almost tripled contraceptive rates among couples who had not been using modern family planning. When curative services for women and children were added, the practice of family planning almost doubled. Integration also promoted measurable movement from less-effective to more-effective family-planning methods. Combining health and family-planning services was two to three times more cost-effective overall than simply promoting family planning. The integrated service package of all services cost about U.S. $2.20 per individual per year (at 1970 exchange rates), with about 90 percent of services provided by family health workers. When the project started, 21 percent of high-caste couples practiced family planning, compared with 13 percent of low-caste couples. After three years of services, about 46 percent of both caste groups practiced family planning. Similar reduction of caste disparities occurred in utilization of both preventive and curative health care.[18]

It took two decades for this breakthrough in understanding the importance of integrating family planning with maternal and child health to be accepted. Not until the Cairo World Population Conference in 1994 had sufficient evidence accumulated in repeated studies around the world for international leadership opinion to change about how family planning should be promoted, integrating services under the term "reproductive health."

The twofold lesson here is not limited to family planning. First, we emphasize throughout this book the necessity for integrated services, because people in the real world do not live in just one category of need (such as health, or, more narrowly, family planning, or, even more broadly, health and economics). They do not like to make repeated visits for services that could be provided all at the same time. Moreover, promoting separate services to meet people's priorities is both ineffective and inefficient, since it requires duplication of infrastructure and support services. There are not enough skilled personnel—and certainly not enough funding—available at the local level to implement the number of parallel activities required. Moreover, the integration of services creates a mutually reinforcing synergism.

A second lesson in promoting family planning is the necessity for community participation in decisionmaking that so profoundly affects daily life. Family planning was separated from integrated health services not because this was what communities wanted, but because international donors were controlling funding of efforts to reduce world population growth rates. Their insistence on quick results led to a worldwide campaign focusing only on family planning and orchestrated by fundraisers and administrators thousands of miles—and light-years of understanding—away from the people whose lives their decisions were affecting. Not until decades later did the Cairo Conference consolidate the realization that a complex problem such as world population growth does not have a simple solution even though the contraception itself may seem simple. Bringing together the dynamics for a just and lasting future is even more complex.

The Roles of Private Enterprise and Traditional Practitioners

An early question we asked ourselves at Narangwal was whether traditional village practitioners could be integrated into community-based management of primary health care. In the mid-1960s the project's Indian anthropologists were doing comparative studies of Ayurvedic (traditional Hindu medicine) practices in seven parts of India.[19] One of them, Jagdish Bhatia, was filling out detailed checklists of care routines used by traditional practitioners in the Narangwal area. One evening, dismounting from his bicycle, he told us, laughing, "You'll never guess what I saw today. A *vaidya* [a fully trained

Hindu medical practitioner] gave a patient some capsules, and when I asked what they were, he said he didn't know English, so would I read the label for him. Isn't that funny?"

It turned out that the capsules were an antibiotic called Chloromycetin, which we didn't use even in hospitals without carefully checking blood tests. We urged Bhatia to find out how the man had gotten it and how he had learned to use it. Bhatia returned and said that the Punjabi words *bukhar da laye,* meaning "for fever," had been written across the bottle's label.

Further research by Bhatia uncovered an underground system of drug distribution and medical education. Urban pharmacists in Ludhiana had an informal teaching arrangement in which they supported a network of traditional practitioners. The practitioners, both Ayurvedic and former hospital orderlies, came in periodically and asked questions such as "I'm seeing a lot of eye infections. What do you have that's new?" The pharmacist would reply, "The detail man from [any of the big drug companies] was in last week, and he says these ointments are good." The most important criteria for these practitioners in their do-it-yourself trials were how quickly the drugs would take effect and which yielded the greatest profits. To hold their network together, the pharmacists had organized a district association of traditional practitioners and paid for monthly meetings providing good food and drink along with drug sales pitches. Bhatia joined the association with no trouble and got the details of its operations. This trend was confirmed by a national commission for health-care reform, which found that pharmaceutical corporations were profiting hugely from a relatively uncontrolled drug market.

The magnitude of this problem has grown until now, thirty years later, the commercial sale of medicines through unregulated channels of freewheeling privatization accounts for the dominant share of health-care-delivery costs worldwide. The flood of modern drugs, promoted as part of global privatization by the drug companies and by the United States, the World Trade Organization, the World Bank, and other international groups, is undermining five decades of intensive worldwide effort to promote rational primary health care using safe, low-cost medicines. Rather than being enabled to become more self-reliant and to create healthier lives, people are having dependency imposed on them, often with high-risk side effects.

Fully government-funded health care is expensive—too expensive for

most countries. Unregulated privatization of health care is not the only remaining option. Community-based care is a third possibility that aims at
preventing diseases instead of trying to cure them with dangerous drugs—
and is far less expensive. Community-based care also leads to other changes
besides improved health. Managed in a holistic way it can change the future
of groups of people, not just of a few individuals. Since government resources
are increasingly strained by conflicting demands (such as campaigns for the
eradication of specific illnesses and expensive hospitals for the elite), the best
hope for communities is to organize and balance their own priorities.

Our fieldwork in the decades since the Narangwal research, work in
China, Nepal, and many other countries, shows that most health workers,
even those providing government, supposedly free, services, are devoting
more and more time and activity to selling drugs and giving injections. Greed
is driving what is mostly only symptomatic treatment. And often these health
workers administer injections or intravenous solutions with minimally sterilized or unsterilized equipment, increasing the potential for transmission of
viral infections such as hepatitis and HIV/AIDS on a truly calamitous scale.
Creating a new balance of top-down control and community-based organization seems the only plausible, effective response to these vast and imminent
dangers. Without it, the problem of inappropriate acute care will grow more
urgent daily.

The Dynamic of Conceptual Breakthroughs:
The Simple-Complex-Simple Axiom

The Narangwal experience contributed a vitally important insight to our
thinking about the SEED-SCALE process. Problems in the real world are
complex, yet solutions through community action have to be simple enough
for all the people involved to understand so they can cooperate. To navigate
complex realities, new breakthrough pathways are essential. Finding simplified solutions was not simple. The change from complex, hospital-based
intravenous drips into the scalp to homemade rehydration therapy seems an
obvious move after it is made. But to get there required repeated trials and
complex analysis that examined the relative effectiveness of a sequence of
ideas and always pressed to find simpler possible alternatives. The science

required to discover what worked in homes was as complex as the systems for hospital interventions. Finding the simple solutions required sophisticated science—and the economic returns to health providers were far smaller.

In the economics of simplicity lies the explanation for why research so seldom seeks simple solutions. Unless great quantities of a simple item can be sold, it is not profitable to invest the complex research required. Hospital-based care makes more money than home-based, even though home care brings better health. Those making the larger profits do not want to give them up.

Once again we return to the importance of partnership. The community-based efficacy that comes from simplified solutions depends on officials' providing an environment that overrides the focus on profit that keeps solutions complex. However, financing and policies are not enough either; in order to achieve the conceptual breakthroughs to simplicity, the experts must do the research.

SEED-SCALE is a system that moves action toward simplicity because it keeps the focus on community. It accommodates the simple-complex-simple progression by promoting the framework that creates feedback loops from community need to officials and experts. With official support and financing a few excellent research-oriented centers can make the conceptual break-throughs. To keep the experts in touch with realities, these centers must be field based, such as those at Narangwal and Dhaka, not academic laboratories. Networks of SCALE Squared centers can then adapt the break-throughs to local culture, ecology, and economics. The enabling environment of SCALE Cubed then supports extension of the lessons throughout the region.

The examples described throughout this book demonstrate the need for caution in adopting overly technical, complex interventions. In the urgent search for breakthroughs, experts, officials, and business interests can easily ignore the larger social good for their own benefit in the form of money, prestige, or career advancement. Research and business derive little profit from low-cost mass interventions suitable for scaling up in community-based programs. Over 90 percent of all health-research funding is focused on the chronic problems of the world's affluent people.[20] But when a single intervention receives international endorsement, as occurred in a series of international oral-rehydration conferences, then almost automatically those interests promote it as a "silver bullet" in mass campaigns. Gravitating to these dramatic interventions and promoting them vigorously misses the real leverage that they offer. Saving millions of babies from death by diarrhea may seem to be a huge success. However, it is not nearly as helpful (or as lasting) as integrating the treatment into a larger program of community change. The confidence and community achieved by mothers incorporating such breakthroughs as tools within larger community action will lead to holistic change—and one feature of holistic change is that it continues to pay its own costs, unlike the mass international campaigns that expend their budgets and then move on.

Experience in some environmental programs also illustrates how the search for conceptual breakthroughs often remains stuck in complex solutions, with little likelihood of becoming a real part of the simple lives of people. For example, experts employ complex technology to catalogue treetop insects in jungle canopies, in the evenings they sit down at dining tables laden with food flown in from afar, and then they work in research tents with sophisticated equipment whose manipulation justifies their salaries. But outside these tree-top stations, local people cut down the trees to provide themselves and their families with a means of living. The scientific knowledge obtained by the researchers is unlikely ever to reach the local people, whose lives would benefit from practical findings, and generations of local knowledge about the environment never find their way to the researchers to provide a basis for partnership and participation.

When people find a way to bridge the gap between basic and applied science, they engage the dynamics that drive our collective future. At Narangwal researchers lived among the people in the villages they were studying. They learned what was relevant in their data through talking with their neighbors, through watching the babies breathe. Villagers improved their lives by gaining access to outside ideas and working with outsiders to find ever simpler and more-affordable solutions. SEED-SCALE works because its annual cycle keeps bringing research action back into touch with local reality.

PART III

Evidence from the Community Level

CHAPTER 11

Curitiba, Brazil

A Better Pattern for Cities

Evolving patterns of just and sustainable living in cities is a central challenge for our future. Nearly 60 percent of the people of the world now live in urban settings, and within another two decades the share may exceed 70 percent. By 2010 at least 500 cities will have more than a million people, and 26 of these will have more than ten million. As world population doubles in the next four decades, two-thirds of this increase will settle in cities.[1]

Cities grow because that is where people find hope and jobs. Despite poor conditions in what we call urban slums, studies around the world show that even in the worst of these, access to services and the possibilities of economic opportunity and higher education result in lower mortality rates and greater food security than in the poor rural areas from which the urban migrants come.[2] The impetus for urbanization will therefore continue, but it is hard to imagine how services will be able to keep up with demand, let alone cope with squalor and social instability.

A dynamic interface of growth exists in cities. Constant in-migration requires both newcomers and established residents to adjust. This circumstance creates a zone of opportunity, at least for some, and their success gives hope to others. Cities that are effective expand development opportunities even faster than their population. With their higher levels of entrepreneurial spirit and greater access, they provide a number of powerful development tools. One example is urban agriculture (described in Chapter 16), which creates jobs for newly arrived citizens and contributes to civic stability and healthier lives.

Curitiba, Brazil, stands as a concrete demonstration of how innovative urban planning created a ripple effect of people-focused development. Curitiba, a state capital at the southern tip of Brazil, grew tenfold, from 180,000 to 1.8 million, in the years 1950–2000. Disparities between rich and poor persist there as elsewhere in Brazil; people continue to rebuild shantytowns along the river after floods, even after fifty years of efforts to dissuade them. Infant mortality is 41 per 1,000, considerably higher than global averages suggest it should be for a city with an average per-capita income of $8,000.[3] Curitiba has by no means overcome all the challenges of modern development; yet an unusual approach to urban planning has expanded opportunities for both the established well-to-do and recent arrivals from rural areas. Today Curitiba has a hundred times more parkland than in 1950, significantly less pollution, reduced danger from flooding, and, most important, a feeling among its people that the quality of life will continue to improve. Social indicators such as health statistics, education rates, movement out of poverty, and a lower crime rate are better than in other Brazilian cities. A sense of community pride is almost palpable. All these improvements occurred within the constraints of Third World politics and economics.[4]

Most of this success has derived from Curitiba's pattern of growth. In most Third World cities growth radiates outward in ameba-like squatter settlements, with a large floating population seeking shelter by night and work by day, increasing traffic congestion, insufficient plumbing and electricity, clogged social services, and the constant risk of civic instability. In contrast, Curitiba expanded in a planned manner through a process that in Chapter 3 we discussed as self-assembly, one of the features of tensegrity. The city achieved this orderly expansion without access to exceptional sources of money or other special resources.

Transport is a determining feature of the character of any city. In most modern cities, automobiles, buses, taxis, and trucks rapidly displace carts, bicycles, and pedestrians, with inevitable increases in congestion and air and noise pollution. In the 1960s officials planning the rapidly growing city of Curitiba recognized the importance of transport, and the mayor sponsored a contest for a new urban master plan. The best ideas were presented for public debate, and a team of young architects incorporated the collective input into an integrated set of solutions. One of these architects was Jaime Lerner, who later became mayor and accelerated the use of thoughtful planning. The guiding principle of the master plan was that patterns of mobility and land-use planning should function synergistically.

The resulting transport network was quite different from conventional patterns of sprawl and congestion. Both subways and buses keep space-consuming private cars out of cities. Most urban transport designs assume that a subway system is the optimal method, since it can carry greater numbers of people than buses and can move on an array of networks underground. Subways, with their dedicated rails and shorter stops to let people on and off, are indeed faster than buses. But Curitiba could not afford a subway system. So the planners took subway ideas and implemented them above ground, with the same benefits but at only 5 percent of a subway's cost.

Curitiba has five major arteries radiating outward from the center, a common enough design in cities. But in Curitiba each of these arteries has three lanes going each way, and each is dedicated to a specific form of transport. Along the inmost lane in each direction, three-unit articulated express buses with a capacity of 270 people speed along just as a subway would do below ground. Flanking these are a high-capacity lane for cars and, on the outside, a lane for local access. From each of the five spokelike arteries a network of secondary bus routes links commercial and residential areas, rich and poor, throughout the city. More than 12,500 bus trips are made each day.[5] Traffic patterns are prioritized to maximize ecological and public efficiency.

Another efficiency came from reducing the amount of time express buses were stopped. Buses are slow, the planning team realized, chiefly because they stop more often than subways, because their doors remain open longer to allow people to climb and descend the entry steps, and because paying fares to drivers creates a bottleneck. So in Curitiba people board buses on the level, from elevated easy-access loading platforms, where they pay their fares before the bus comes.

The system's efficiency is proven by the fact that nearly a quarter of Curitiba's population, from every socioeconomic group, uses public transport. Although the city has the second-highest per-capita share of private transport in Brazil (600,000 private cars), per-capita fuel consumption is 25 percent lower than in comparable Brazilian cities because of the popularity of the buses. With people using their cars less, taking them chiefly when buses will not get them where they want to go, traffic congestion and urban air pollution are the lowest in Brazil. Public transport has become the city's primary mode of travel, fostering a greater sense of community.[6]

The transport system also stimulates economic activity. Since buses are not city owned but leased to private enterprises, a number of private transport companies compete to improve efficiencies. The city pays companies according to the distances they drive rather than according to the number of passengers they carry. This arrangement removes the incentive that favors high-traffic routes and supports extension of geographic coverage. Thorough coverage and short travel times reinforce high ridership, which makes the transport system self-financing. Thus Curitiba avoids the heavy public-transportation subsidies that burden most cities.

Curitiba's experience provides a robust lesson in the value of an enabling framework of genuine partnerships, and specifically in putting people to work in the roles they are best equipped to perform. In the 1960s, when a mayor saw the problems arising from rapid urban growth, he spontaneously created a three-way partnership among city officials, experts, and the community: experts (in this case, architects) brought in new ideas, citizens critiqued them, and officials pressed toward total city coverage. In this process roles remained clearly defined: officials did not try also to be experts, and they sincerely sought participation from citizens. When one of the technical experts later became mayor, and other experts also assumed positions in government, it would have been easy for them to exclude experts from outside, but instead the partnership has continued. In keeping roles separately defined, officials also shunned the actual running of services and telling local people what to do. This avoidance of taking on inappropriate roles is a vitally important feature of Curitiba's successful partnership. Recognizing that some functions were more effectively implemented by nongovernment entities, the government contracted out tasks to the private sector, where competition has produced efficiency and promoted job growth. The operation of buses by private companies is only one example of such arrangements in many sectors, and in all cases service contracts are self-supporting rather than publicly funded. The result is an uncommonly light administrative and services superstructure.

Curitiba's transport system is the most visible sign of its alternative approach to development, but the fundamental shift seems to have begun with concern about urban flooding. In the 1950s, when Curitiba started to grow, urban migrants pressed into marginal floodplains, building along streams, even on top of streams, filling in low depressions, and digging trenches to drain wet banks. Periodic floods regularly swept away these precarious toeholds of the poor, eroding both hope and land for ever-growing numbers of migrants. Pressure to build houses along the streams continues today, but the government, understanding the larger issues at stake, works hard to keep this land open by providing alternatives.

A policy begun a generation ago has made a major difference. The usual solution to urban flooding is to build concrete raceways to carry water out of the city as fast as possible. To address this problem in the 1950s and 1960s, the mayor adopted a "design with nature" approach. The architects who collaborated in developing the master plan arranged for unoccupied strips of land along each side of the existing waterways to be protected. New construction was prohibited. Older construction was incrementally replaced with trees and parklands. Artificial lakes were created to absorb the sudden surges of streams in flood. Low areas in possible floodplains were set aside as sports and leisure facilities for nonresidential use. Land-use planning that started as flood-control prevention increased per-capita public green space from half a square meter in 1970 to fifty square meters twenty years later—a hundredfold increase while the population grew fivefold. Curitiba had started with just one park; today the whole city feels parklike.[7]

The green spaces do not look like customary parks, a scattering of square blocks or oases that separate communities. Curitiba's parks are green strips that run aesthetically through the urbanscape. The creation of these green corridors has reoriented the ways people live. They serve as places where people walk and meet—like the buses that encourage people contact. They tie neighborhoods together instead of isolating them. A concern for an outside danger, in this case flooding, strengthened community. People responded to a danger not by opposing the threat but by removing it.

Architects can do more than devise spatially creative solutions for transport and flood control. In Curitiba their spatial approach also addressed the problem of poverty. Poverty is a phenomenon that communities usually try to hide. But Curitiba brought poverty into the open. As the city planned its growth and as new neighborhoods were laid out, low-income housing was incorporated into each area, and poor people were given easier access to transportation and industrial nodes. This planning encouraged job growth and strengthened the community by moving people out of dependency.

Garbage collection was another area of innovation. City officials looked at garbage not as a nuisance but as a resource that created opportunities for the poor. Curitiba started a waste recycling program that employed disfranchised people, recent immigrants to the city and the homeless, as crews on privately contracted garbage trucks. In 1989 an outbreak of rat-borne leptospirosis created a crisis: the city's garbage trucks could not navigate in the slums where the disease was harbored. City officials calculated what it would cost to create a subsystem to haul the waste out, and they added that amount to Curitiba's budget for garbage removal. But instead of simply paying the money to subcontractors, they arranged for people in the slums to bring their trash out to the trucks and receive food in exchange. It was the poorest families who benefited most: garbage went out, food came in, and farmers outside the city, who in the past had moved into the city when times were hard, and thus exacerbated the problem of in-migration, now had a larger and more regular market.[8]

Another innovation in Curitiba, prompted largely by city leaders' wives, is a cluster of programs addressing the needs of children. In the mid-1980s, before the programs began, more than five hundred children were adrift on the streets without parents or parental support. Today Curitiba spends 40 percent of its budget on child services, recognizing them as a cost-effective way to break the cycle of poverty. The city provides daycare centers for preschoolers for up to eleven hours a day and adds to funds from national sources to improve the schools. Although Curitiba lacks resources to operate schools for more than half a day, for children lacking home support the city sponsors music, sports, and other activities during the rest of the day. Children who turn in nonbiodegradable trash, such as batteries and toothpaste tubes, are given pictures of their heroes. Children and adolescents may create personal gardens on open land under adult instruction and supervision and may eat or sell what they grow; the program teaches them skills and gives rise to organized support networks. (For more ideas on urban agriculture, see Chapter 16.) In all, the city has established thirteen support houses offering practical job training. Over the years the number of children adrift on the streets has declined by 60 percent.[9]

Almost every city has its "lighthouse" programs, services that stand out and guide others. But Curitiba's lighthouse programs are remarkable in several ways. First, there are more of them than in most cities, and their sheer number creates a critical mass of hope that strengthens the momentum of development and creates a self-regulatory feedback loop. Second, the programs have been improved and expanded steadily every year for four decades despite changes in political leadership. Third, one outstanding idea has frequently generated or linked up with other new ideas, and this self-assembly of new initiatives automatically prompts critiques of older ones. Fourth, awareness that the city is part of a larger natural environment is reflected in Curitiba's extensive parklands, millions of trees, and urban gardening, all of which make the city healthier. Citywide there is confidence that Curitiba can solve its own problems. By effectively supporting genuine development, officials have gained wider influence, trust, and credibility.

Many cities became centers of progress by taking resources from colonies, from the profits of trade, and/or from the produce of rural or wilderness areas. Curitiba is developing by drawing on the resources within it; its people are rethinking and reorganizing city life to meet their own priorities.

Curitiba has become a SCALE Squared center, a model for other cities around the world. Cape Town is patterning its growth directly on Curitiba's. Prague, New York, Montreal, Paris, and Moscow are adapting aspects of the Curitiba approach to their own needs and goals.[10] Curitiba has not solved all its problems, but it is demonstrating a different path to urban development. In the process it is shaping its own future.

Bill McKibben, whose writings have done much to bring Curitiba to the world's attention, puts it this way: "Curitiba is among the world's great cities. Not for its physical location: there are no beaches, no broad bridge-spanned rivers. Not in terms of culture or glamour: it's a fairly provincial place. But measured for 'livability'—a weak coinage expressing some optimum mix of pleasures provided and drawbacks avoided—I have never been any place like it. In a recent survey, 60 percent of New Yorkers wanted to leave their rich cosmopolitan city; 99 percent of Curitibans told pollsters they were happy with their town; and 70 percent of [Sao] Paulistas, residents of the mobbed megalopolis to the north, said they thought life would be better in Curitiba."[11]

CHAPTER 12

Jamkhed, India

The Evolution of a World Training Center

Mabelle and Raj Arole

*I am a Dalit [below-caste] widow. As an outcaste I used to think I was a
nobody. I lived in constant fear because I was treated worse than an
animal. My son died when he was less than three years old, and I was
blamed for it and sent away by my husband. My parents made me
marry an old man who had tuberculosis; then he died. I returned to my
village in shame. I lived in darkness. To support myself I swept and
cleaned the village and did hard manual labor. I received a pittance.
Even dogs were welcome in the houses, but I, as a Dalit, was not. Then,
along with many other women, I decided not to accept this anymore.*

LALANBAI KADAM

As young doctors, we made a commitment to each other that we would
devote our lives to improving the health of the poorest of the poor in rural
India. After graduating from Vellore Christian Medical College in 1959, we
worked in a rural mission hospital. The hospital flourished and expanded.
From this base we went out into the villages and held village clinics.

To our dismay we found that our hospital and our village work were
having little impact on the health of the people. Infant mortality continued to
be high. Most diseases we encountered were preventable. Many women had

problems such as obstructed labor and then came in too late. We started questioning the top-down, doctor- and hospital-centered health-care approach. Learning from the collective wisdom of many pioneers with similar concerns, we planned a program that would involve communities.

Beginnings

In 1970 we were looking around for an area where people were interested in starting such a health program; an enlightened political leader in Jamkhed, a community-development block 5,500 square kilometers in area with 110,000 people, in Ahmednagar district, in the state of Maharashtra, invited us to visit. Local officials wanted to start a hospital to take care of obstetric and other emergencies and in general provide relief from pain and suffering. We explained our intention of working with the people to improve health through preventive programs. The leaders were not impressed. However, lacking other candidates willing to help, they emptied a veterinary dispensary in the middle of a cattle market and provided a couple of sheds to start the "hospital."

Soon a woman was brought in with a ruptured uterus, and we had to operate on her to save her life. We followed up by developing direct links with her and other patients' home villages. Using curative services as an entry point, we came into contact with more and more people. Gradually we expanded to other villages. It soon became evident that poor people were interested chiefly in relief from unbearable pain; illnesses that were not painful were mere irritations. When pain was gone they were aware of other pressing needs. "We need water; we need jobs so that we can buy food to kill the hunger pangs, and then we won't have to migrate to cut sugarcane." "You ask us to wash hands, to use soap. Where is the water? Do you know the cost of soap?" they challenged us.

We had to redefine what we considered to be the scope of our work. As a medical team we had to think about the effects of poverty on health care. So we decided to live on forty-five rupees (about seven U.S. dollars) per month, the prevailing average wage at that time. We were in for many surprises: soap cost almost two days' wages, and in that desert area the amount of water needed to flush a toilet just once cost more than a month's wages. But the biggest shock to us was that, living at that basic level, we considered our needs for food and water to be more urgent than our needs for health interventions.

Temporarily setting aside our health agenda, we focused on getting safe drinking water. We found an interested group and obtained their assistance in drilling tube wells in thirty villages in the Jamkhed area. The Dalit, or below-caste, villagers were concerned that they would not have access to the water if the wells were located in the upper-caste parts of the villages. We took a water diviner into our confidence and asked him to walk through each village, but to divine water only in the Dalit section. More than 150 tube wells were drilled in these areas. Rich and poor, people of all castes, came to the wells.

In providing this lifegiving service and making it accessible to the neediest people, we established a success to build from. But we know that to carry out our project, we needed more than support from government officials and help from nongovernmental organizations. Larger systems had to change. Health improvement required communitywide action to protect the physical environment and to stop harmful social practices. Religion, caste, and politics divided rich people from poor. Starvation and undernutrition resulted more from rigid social attitudes toward women and children than from an actual shortage of food. To start momentum it was vital to create partnerships, and to sustain that momentum it was important to prevent confrontations.

We started informal volleyball games, which brought people from all groups in the villages together. After the games, both onlookers and players stood around and talked. These informal groups were then organized into farmers' clubs, which included not only farmers but also the landless poor. With government extension workers acting as partners, they offered seminars and training in dry-land farming and primary veterinary care. At that point people were more interested in the health of farm animals than in their health or their children's. Then, as their larger life needs were addressed, people became interested in human health.

Assessment, Analysis, and Community Action

In 1974 the farmers' club members and teams from the hospital project started conducting a health survey of the villages. The collection of data transcended local factions. One villager recalled: "We saw the survey as for our own good, so we did an accurate survey. Each of us took one area of the village and filled in all the information. No family was left out. There were questions about immunization of children and whether they had been ill in the past two weeks. We reported any child's death in the past twelve months and details of how the child had died. We assessed the nutritional status of children by measuring their arm circumference. To our surprise, many children we thought had severe illness turned out just to lack adequate food! There were questions on pregnancy and family planning. We knew who was missing at the time of the survey, so we went back and questioned them later."

With the data providing a solid starting point, we engaged the villagers in a survey analysis to help them understand the causes and effects of disease. Armed with this knowledge, the villagers began taking action. At a public meeting afterward one villager reported: "We had believed that children did not thrive because of a curse from God. When we looked at our surveys we understood that the problem was lack of food and preventive care. So we organized a community kitchen. We monitored the growth of our children by weighing them every month and plotting their weight on a 'road to health' card."

Improving the environment grew as a priority. Many villagers experienced repeated attacks of fever and chills associated with malaria. Diarrhea was common. These and other conditions led people to understand the need for better sanitation. In the words of one villager, "Our data became more powerful as people gathered more facts and learned to use them. Eighty percent of our families in the year before had had at least three episodes of fever with chills. We learned that if we got rid of the puddles made by wastewater and composted our rubbish, we could drastically reduce the breeding of mosquitoes and flies. Previously we had spent close to ten rupees every time we got these fevers. The more we talked, the more we agreed: why not clean up the village? Farmers' club members dug soak pits that drained away standing water, and the owners provided the filling of sand, broken bricks, and a plank to place over them."

Women, Health, and Social Change

The farmers' clubs demanded that women be trained as village health workers (VHWs). "Educators or professionals from the city speak an educated language," they reasoned. "Our women will accept someone from their own community whom they trust."

The connection between the status of women and village health became more apparent. One VHW, Sarubai, described her experience: "I was married when still a child, got pregnant at fourteen, and, as is the custom, came to my mother's house in Rajuri for delivery. I was in labor for three days. Finally a *dai* [traditional midwife] arrived and said the baby was too big and I would not be able to deliver normally. The only way to save my life was to remove the baby from inside me piecemeal. I remained weak and ill for months. During that time I never heard from my husband. Later he sent word that he did not want a woman who could not produce a living child. I became an outcaste, unwanted, uncared for, living on the charity of my brother. I was too young to bear a child—only fourteen, a piece of property. I was thrown off by my husband."

Another VHW replied, "At least you lost your baby. My daughter has two healthy children. She needed a caesarean operation, and now her husband has sent her away, fearing that she won't be able to do hard manual labor and carry heavy loads because of the operation."

When our work began, women from different castes were not permitted to socialize. They were viewed as the keepers of tradition. Centuries of subservience had made them accept their place; they were trained to suffer in silence. How could lone village health workers change these attitudes? The VHWs began to meet with women for a couple of hours every week or two. In the beginning, only eight or ten women from a village came to the meetings, never sure whether their husbands' families would allow them to continue.

Sarubai told how she organized women in her village. "In the beginning I convinced seven women to get together. We gathered in one woman's home, sang songs, and listened to each other. In between, I taught child care." More and more women joined these informal groups in different villages. As they began to take their gatherings seriously, they decided to call their groups *mahila vikas mandals,* or women's development associations. Discussions of health and social conditions soon gave way to talk about the need for money. Young children needed food or medicines; older children needed books and school uniforms.

Traditionally when village women needed financing each woman contributed a small sum to build a fund, and at the end of a given period a name was drawn, and that person received the pooled contributions. Eventually every woman had her turn. The *mahila vikas mandals* modified this system so that instead of being based on a lottery, the money went to the woman who needed it most in descending order of need. Often the money bought food or treatment for a sick child. Others used the money to improve a vegetable plot or produce poultry, market vegetables, or dried fish.

As membership increased, women realized that they had greater power as a group than as individuals. Health workers introduced social issues, especially the problems of women and girl children. They asked why daughters were treated differently from sons, or why girls were not fed properly or sent to school like their brothers. They talked about alcoholism, wife-beating, the harsh treatment of unwed mothers, and how these problems could be solved. Sarubai described the women's involvement in her village: "We divided the village into four sections, with one *mahila vikas mandal* member responsible for the health of her section. She ensures that all children are immunized and all the pregnant women receive prenatal care. We also trained three women to be in charge of deliveries when I am not around. Every year we repeat the house-to-house survey. It helps us plan our programs and understand what to emphasize."

The *mahila vikas mandals* have "keep the village clean" drives. They got rid of allergenic weeds, constructed drainage pits, and encouraged the use of toilets. They help the village health worker follow up patients with tuberculosis and leprosy and assist in the rehabilitation of these patients and their families. In many villages the farmers' clubs turned over most of the health responsibilities to the *mandals* while the men concentrated on projects such as planting thousands of trees and building small dams to reduce the frequency of drought and thus the need to leave the villages to find work.

Most village women had never attended school or been involved in decisionmaking or control of their time. The *mahila vikas mandals* became their schools and gave them a structure in which to organize. By 1978, thirty-one villages had associations. Caste differences became much less important, and women found it increasingly easy to work together.

Previously women had feared government functionaries and avoided entering courts, police stations, or other government offices. Now in their meetings they adopted strategies to remove these fears by practicing meeting high-level police and revenue officials, local judges, bankers, and others. Then they went out and did so. They found these officials cordial and genuinely interested in their work and welfare. Women grew confident.

Bank officials, accustomed to providing credit to rich businessmen or farmers, at first treated women condescendingly. The paperwork for small loans to scores of women was for them a bother. However, the government had a special program for credit at low interest rates to women and marginalized people. The women had read the rules and were sure they had met the criteria. At first the bankers refused, offering many excuses: the women had no property, no collateral, were illiterate, and so on. But the women did not give up. They sat in the banks until the bankers made a decision either to grant the loan or to explain their refusal in writing.

The first women to obtain small loans triumphantly shared their stories with other villages. They used the loans to enhance incomes. They bought chickens and goats for breeding. They started small businesses, buying and selling bangles, dried fish, or vegetables. Some dug wells for irrigation, bought a pump, or acquired bullocks to help in farming. One woman bought a small canopy, loudspeaker, microphone, and record player, which she rented for weddings, elections, and the numerous festivals in the village; she repaid her loan in six months. The Dalit widow Lalanbai Kadam, whose previous situation opens this chapter, leased government-owned fruit trees growing by the roadside. Now she sells the fruit and makes a yearly profit of 10,000 to 30,000 rupees.

Access to credit made being part of the *mahila vikas mandals* popular. More than three thousand women who had never had a hope of getting out of poverty now took out loans. Their performance attracted the attention of higher bank officials at the state headquarters, who invited the women to share their experiences with bankers in other parts of the state.

Expansion

As outside physicians who had pledged to help, we were catalysts for development activities. With the health center functioning as an organization independent of both community and government, we introduced ideas, supported new behavior, and encouraged and forged three-way partnerships among increasingly unified communities, officials from many departments and levels of government, and ourselves as experts. As communities came to feel more empowered, capable of standing on their own feet, we were no longer the only catalysts.

The project had begun in thirty villages. As villagers contacted their relatives and friends about the changes taking place, the program expanded to cover a region of 250,000 people. As people became more self-reliant, more than three hundred volunteers went to remote villages to start new programs. In their turn, those village people became facilitators for change in what has become a growing people's movement.

Although it started with health care, the program expanded into many other aspects of development. Through frequent seminars and meetings, government personnel joined with the poorest of the poor in providing services. In the mid-1970s villages began cooperating with the state's forestry department in developing plant nurseries and promoting reforestation; in 1987 they won the highest national award for planting of trees in their area of India. Expanding linkages among sectors, they joined with nongovernmental organizations and with government in watershed-management programs.

The cumulative statistics are gratifying. Over a period of twenty-five years, 250,000 marginalized men and women improved their own lives and those of the people around them. Infant mortality (a sensitive indicator of overall health) fell from over 175 per 1,000 births to 18 per 1,000. Although more people now live longer, the rate of population growth is moving toward stabilization; the birth rate has declined from over 40 per 1,000 to 17 per 1,000 and continues downward. Small families have become an accepted social norm, with 70 percent of couples using family planning. A desert area that people were deserting is now increasingly fertile, with check dams that feed the soil, with grass that can support cattle, and, most important, with people who are trying one idea after another to improve their lives.

Becoming a Learning Center

When we had worked in the villages of Jamkhed for twenty years, some of the VHWs came to us with the suggestion that it was time for us to go somewhere else. "We can look after ourselves now," they said. "Many other places in India have greater needs than we. You can start similar projects in other places." In 1989 we received a grant to return to Johns Hopkins University (where we had originally been trained in public health) for two years to write a book about our experiences.[1] The time seemed to have come to start over. Before we left Jamkhed we identified a new area about two hundred kilometers away, at Bhandaradara, where 60,000 tribal people had been displaced several years earlier from their tribal forest heritage to create space for a dam that would irrigate large sugarcane plantations.

As we began writing the book behind desks in the United States, it was hard to recall the early days at Jamkhed; we kept focusing then on what we were going to do next. After a year, Raj went back to Jamkhed to get tape recordings of our early partners talking about what had been important to them in those days of great uncertainty. Upon arrival the first thing he learned was that the new project at Bhandaradara had already been established. Groups of VHWs had bought bus tickets to Bhandaradara, moved into village homes for a week at a time, and trained local VHWs, creating a new model of extension. Without going through our approach of slowly developing village contacts and trust through volleyball games and tube wells, they had directly translated the entire package of locally relevant interventions based on village dialogue.

In Baltimore, as we finished writing our book, we realized that an opportunity had emerged to change our orientation from demonstration to training. Instead of starting one more project, we could train people so they could start their own projects. Jamkhed could become a learning center, a SCALE Squared center. Churches and other donors provided funds for dormitories and classrooms for groups of about twenty-five students at a time. The first course started in 1994. In the first four years nine groups of students, 180 participants from sixteen Indian states and sixteen countries, completed diploma courses.[2]

The diploma program began with three months of intensive training. Students accompanied VHWs who explained their routine tasks and how they had learned what worked. They talked about why different villages were doing the same activities in different ways and how procedures had evolved. These demonstrations prompted intensive discussion about conditions in the students' regions and countries and how Jamkhed ideas could be adapted there. Classroom sessions were divided into modules according to group interests, focused on both theoretical implications and practical applications.

In the final module students developed their own projects, then returned to their own job environments for six months to implement them. During this time Jamkhed faculty visited each project at least once to monitor progress. Finally, the students returned to Jamkhed for two weeks of intensive evaluation. During this final period they explored the behavior changes needed in themselves, their colleagues, and their spouses at home (principle three of the SEED-SCALE approach) to create a cooperative environment for the new projects.

In addition to the diploma courses, demand grew for short courses, most of them lasting one to two weeks. In the first four years 1,135 people, most of them from nongovernmental organizations, participated in ninety-seven such courses. Thirty-two of these were international courses given by and for experts from eighteen countries. The remainder served Indian participants from seventeen states, including twenty-eight courses for Maharashtra and four all-India courses.

In the early 1990s the Methodist Mission Board in New York hired Mabelle to run workshops in Latin America and Africa describing what we had learned at Jamkhed. She then joined the UNICEF regional office in Kathmandu to run training workshops throughout Southeast Asia. Trainers came to Jamkhed from Pakistan, Bangladesh, and Nepal to take courses. In 1998 Mabelle returned to Jamkhed to teach full-time. Since 1996, Raj has provided special orientation courses for candidates from India's elite government cadre, the Indian Administrative Service, in community health care, conducting seven-to-ten-day sessions at the IAS academy and fieldwork at Jamkhed. The Jamkhed approach to health services has extended to several other states.

Lessons from Jamkhed

Jamkhed's scaling up began slowly. The first ten years involved a progressive expansion of SCALE One, with a distinctly bottom-up emphasis on community empowerment. In an extremely poor and rigid social structure, village-to-village extension of social development permeated and revolutionized the traditional culture. As people became aware of their own potential, they developed new attitudes, behaviors, and strategies to meet their own desperate needs for a better life.

Blueprint extension of the Jamkhed model, tried by the Indian government, met with little success. Once local projects were made part of a national program, bureaucratic rules distorted the community base. Primary-health-center doctors, made responsible for local training of community health workers, failed to involve village women selected by village people as someone they would trust.

Jamkhed became a SCALE Squared center by carefully designed training that serves multiple needs, bringing together communities, officials, and experts. Now, operating as a SCALE Squared center, Jamkhed advises officials around the world about the elements needed to create the enabling environment for communities to go to SCALE Cubed. Notwithstanding this influence, Jamkhed still speaks with the unassuming voice of village people; the Jamkhed Center and the quarter-million people active as global trainers make no pretense at having left the village behind.

In the words of one Jamkhed woman: "People are like wick lamps—simple, inexpensive, and unattractive. But unlike the expensive chandeliers (which professionals are), the wick lamp has a tremendous energy. It is capable of lighting another lamp and another and another to cover the whole planet."

Gadchiroli, India

Addiction as a Barrier to Development

Abhay and Rani Bang

Communities afflicted by a collective addiction are blocked from social progress as energies focus on supporting the addiction.

Addiction, as we use the term, involves more than chemical dependency. In cases of physical addiction, chemical adjustments reorient bodily functions. The process is analogous for a community addiction: collective systems are reoriented, and collective behaviors focus on satisfying the compulsion. Societal addictions range from widespread substance abuse—dependence on opium, peyote, or other chemicals—to behavioral addictions such as an all-consuming cultural practice, value, or anything else that blocks community energy from seeking balance in life. Societal addictions are increasingly manipulated by outside economic interests; large corporations make huge profits from mass obsessions.

Moving communities away from addictions is difficult. Even when the negative impact is obvious, communities can seldom break out of addiction on their own, for in many cases their own leaders own or in some way benefit from the dependency, thereby strengthening their position. But outside experts and concerned officials can create awareness and stimulate community-based change. In Gadchiroli, India, the people used group activities to overcome a communitywide barrier to social progress.

Step One: Building Capacity

Gadchiroli is the least-developed district in the Indian state of Maharashtra. Most of its inhabitants are tribal people who lived in the area millennia before the now-dominant Indian castes moved in. Eighty percent of the people live below the poverty line, literacy is only 22 percent, roads are poor, and health care is rudimentary. In 1986 we founded a voluntary organization, SEARCH (Society for Education, Action, and Research in Community Health), to provide community care and conduct research on the health of women and children.

We began with a misstep. Earlier research had persuaded us that sickle-cell disease was an urgent problem among the tribal people of Gadchiroli. The government had recognized our research with a special award, and the state health ministry funded a special research center in Gadchiroli district. But the people had not participated in the collection or analysis of the information and didn't have a sense of ownership; sickle-cell disease was not a felt problem for them. Our initial efforts to address it went nowhere.

When we began to organize gatherings of rural women and young people to discuss common health problems, at all the meetings women described how their lives had been ruined by alcohol addiction. They claimed it was nearly universal among husbands, fathers, brothers, and sons. Men got drunk, didn't go to work, failed to support their families, beat their wives, quarreled, and even killed each other. Some women wept as they told their stories. Young people angrily charged that their male elders were failing in their responsibility to care for their children. Adult men who attended the meetings did not disagree. But although community conviction against the drinking was strong, it had not been strong enough to lead to action. The first step was to help people understand how alcohol operated in their lives, to gather objective data that outlined the scope of the problem.

- At a two-day workshop, 150 men and women from thirty villages took part in focus-group discussions to review their experiences over the past forty years. There was general agreement that alcohol consumption, from both licensed and illegal sources, had greatly increased.

- A group of teachers collected data on annual liquor sales from licensed shops and on the regulations governing the shops.
- In evening meetings villagers estimated the amount of money spent on alcohol.
- In 104 villages forty-three village health workers conducted a survey on the number of people drinking, frequency of drinking, expenditure on liquor, common symptoms, and deaths attributed to alcoholism.
- Working with the community, we obtained official documents relating to government policy and guidelines on the sale and consumption of liquor.

The surveys showed that about 100,000 males in the district drank frequently, about 8,000 seemed to be addicted, and a surprisingly high number died of alcohol-related consequences. In addition, people blamed high intake of liquor for chronic abdominal pain, loss of appetite, vomiting (including vomiting of blood), swelling of feet and abdomen, jaundice, progressive weakness, impotence, accidents, injuries, loss of income, poor employer relations, family disruption, and even mental derangement. An average village spent about 200,000 rupees on alcohol each year.

Notwithstanding a commitment in India's constitution to prohibit both the sale and consumption of alcohol, as well as a specific recommendation by the national government that alcohol not be sold in tribal areas, the state had licensed fifty-seven shops in the district and in addition had issued permits to 2,000 individuals to purchase up to twelve bottles at a time. In effect, these permit holders acted as subagents for selling liquor in the villages. Annual sales in the district amounted to 200 million rupees (over 5 million U.S. dollars), while the government's total annual support for all district development programs was 140 million rupees.

Step Two: Choosing a Direction

Large numbers of people conducted this research. Teams of social activists, political leaders, ordinary citizens, government officials, and experts from SEARCH took the results back to the people, visiting hundreds of villages throughout the region to give each community an objective self-portrait. In meetings they discussed both the problem and possible solutions. During these discussions people often recalled a tribal folktale as a helpful way to objectify the problem instead of blaming themselves:

> In ancient times the tribal people were all healthy and happy, for they lived deep in the forests—it was the time before outsiders came to cut those forests. One day the devil mixed the blood of a parrot, a jackal, a tiger, and a pig and offered it to the people, a wonderful drink he called "liquor." Anybody who drank it became first talkative like a parrot, then cunning and a cheat like a jackal, then loud and aggressive like a tiger, and eventually a human pig rolling in the gutter.

As awareness grew, boys from two especially well-organized and highly committed villages pressed their communities to start acting. They cooperated with village health workers to organize a ban on liquor. Stores selling alcohol were closed. Bottles were broken. The streets were patrolled at night to prevent alcohol from being brought in, and drunks were fined. Such action worked in these villages, but it was not a strategy that could readily extend to others.

After further discussions a collective movement started to emerge. Groups of women and young people in 349 villages passed resolutions to ban all liquor. Marches were organized and subdistrict-level conferences convened at four places. In November 1988 more than three thousand delegates from more than 400 villages attended a district-level conference against alcohol. Even very poor people gave money to defray the costs of the conference. Present at the meeting were the district magistrate, the police chief, and other officials who wanted to be seen as standing up for the public interest. People were blunt as they presented their data and described how the officials gave cover to the illicit sales.

From this meeting and from smaller discussions, a consensus emerged that action must strike both at village interdiction and at government policies. Tasks were assigned to every village as people felt empowered to act for their own protection. SEARCH and other experts, supported by newly strengthened community groups, began presenting their demands at higher government levels.

Step Three: Taking Action

A district *darumukti sangthana* (organization for liberation from liquor) was formed, and more resolutions were passed. Two hundred villages enacted bans on the sale and consumption of alcohol. Women in one village locked up drunken men overnight and publicly disgraced them in the morning. This strategy was widely publicized. A deputation visited a village where the ban was being defied and warned that a boycott would be imposed in the absence of compliance. A day later the village fell into line.

Alcohol trade at the village level was stopped, but sales in towns continued in shops licensed by the government. These shops were invariably owned by local politicians, receiving official patronage and protection. The state asserted that its substantial revenues from the sale of alcohol were necessary for welfare programs. The people retorted that they could take better care of themselves and their families if they retained more of their money, and that government had no right to sell addiction. Under such public pressure three members of the state legislative assembly elected from Gadchiroli submitted a memorandum to the chief minister of the state of Maharashtra demanding the closure of licensed shops and the transfer to local villages of authority over the use of alcohol. The chief minister agreed, but no action followed.

The people decided they could no longer depend on the government to control alcohol. On October 2, 1992, the anniversary of the birth of Mahatma Gandhi, People's Liberation from Alcohol was announced in the presence of 10,000 delegates assembled from more than six hundred villages. Again every leader there—including a member of the national parliament and a minister of the state cabinet—publicly declared support for the people's resolution. The conference authorized villages throughout the district to assume responsibility for controlling alcohol. Throughout the discussions the speakers returned again and again to the data they had themselves gathered and fully memorized. They interspersed the data with personal stories of problems in their communities. The most common theme was that this one problem of addiction was the most important barrier to all other development.

The October 2 conference was a high point of participatory democracy in the nonviolent tradition of Gandhi. It became a powerful symbol of a shift in the locus of authority from government to a partnership of people, experts, and officials bold enough to stick their necks out (though they sometimes later pulled them back in). The bureaucrats stalled, but the coalition did not go away. In 1996 the state government finally banned the sale of alcohol in Gadchiroli, closed all fifty-seven liquor shops, and canceled the individual permits.

Two followup surveys over the next two years showed that alcohol consumption was 60 percent less than it had been before the ban. However, a political solution alone cannot cure a social problem; in fact, burying an addiction beneath laws may sometimes make it more pernicious by allowing denial of the problem. Long-term education and continuing organization are essential to truly reduce the problem and to keep it from returning. In the Gadchiroli case, however, making alcoholism illegal did have the immediate positive benefit of enabling families to save money for their own needs. Social pressures and changed norms also made drinking a much more private activity, and brawls and beatings dramatically decreased.

The Gadchiroli story was told all over the state. A nucleus of activists from the district lobbied the state assembly and gained passage of legislation that guaranteed closure of liquor shops in any village where 51 percent of women voters passed a resolution to do so. The task is far from over. In Gadchiroli the challenges will be to sustain community participation, to keep updating the data, and to expand real and lasting behavioral change throughout the district.

Lessons from Gadchiroli

To combat Gadchiroli's collective addiction required real partnership among local people, officials, and experts. On their own, citizens could not have gathered data systematically, sustained pressure against entrenched interests, and achieved the legislative results.

The community approach to gathering data, identifying the nature and scope of the problem, and finding solutions was crucial to success. Participatory research created a common focus that transcended earlier differences and produced a large social force with irresistible leverage in pressing for legal changes. With removal of this major barrier to development, other activities could begin—in health, income generation, food security, and the like.

Customary medical or epidemiological research done by professionals would not have been nearly as effective, either politically or socially. Participatory research should not be more sophisticated than local needs require, and its implementation should not require skills that local people don't have. If community-based action addresses a need that the people themselves have identified as a priority, they will join forces with well-intended outsiders who have come to help. Only then will the resulting partnerships have the potential to form a base for just and sustainable development.

CHAPTER 14

Kakamega, Kenya

A Promising Start Derailed

Miriam K. Were

Many of us who were starry-eyed with optimism when most of Africa gained independence in the 1950s and 1960s are now dazed by the realization that more than half of our people remain stuck in subsistence living below the poverty line. Prosperity has passed us by.

In the 1970s it seemed that Kenya, along with the rest of Africa, was firmly established on the development road. National leaders, having just won independence, knew that their power derived ultimately from the people. But projects that first seemed full of promise failed to mobilize public energy on a large enough scale. In this era, Cold War polarities were forcing African governments to choose sides, and macroeconomic forces (such as the falling price of oil, export of minerals or other natural resources, and large loans from international banks) were deflecting governments' attention from communities and accountability to them. Two decades were lost, trickle-down development failed, and today Africa's optimism has withered. We need to rediscover the confidence that came with believing (and acting upon the belief) that destiny was in the people's own hands, when our communities were partners with our experts and our governments—both showing accountability to the people for whose benefit they serve.

The Kakamega project on community-based health care, lasting from 1974 to 1982, achieved great improvements in environmental sanitation, clean drinking water, basic primary health care, immunization of children, use of family planning, and many other health and economic indicators. Perhaps most important were qualitative changes that increased self-reliance, mutual support, confidence—a sense of empowerment that came as people worked together. Communities organized their own structures to link with the formal health system. They established community bank accounts from which most activities were financed. By 1980, things were going very well indeed.[1]

The Kakamega project demonstrates a very typical development problem: an extraordinary project gets started—and in this case achieved worldwide recognition—but then the momentum stalls. The central problem at Kakamega was that a true three-way partnership was never created. Community and experts worked well together, and as the project evolved, officials at the national level leadership lent support. But after the project was publicized as a dramatic success story at the Alma Ata World Conference on Primary Health Care in 1978, the Ministry of Health, using international donor money, took over the project with good intentions but no understanding of how to work with the community base on which a successful partnership must be built. The result was that over time the other two partners (community and experts) were disempowered.

Origins of the Kakamega Project

After graduating from the University of Nairobi's Faculty of Medicine in 1974, I proposed a comprehensive community-based primary health demonstration in Kenya. My professional friends along with officials at the Ministry of Health were incredulous and dismissive. Many asked: "How can you think of abandoning direct delivery of health care to the people?" I explained that people were already looking after themselves, since coverage from the health system was less than 30 percent at the time. The challenge was to find ways to strengthen their capacities. They dubbed it "second-class medicine." Because I had graduated as the best all-round medical student, two years later I was awarded a Population Council fellowship to study at Hopkins School. I returned to Kenya to do two years of fieldwork for my doctoral dissertation. The Ministry of Health lent support by creating a pilot project to explore whether communities could serve as the basic units of the health-care system in the context of a national primary-health-care strategy.

The project covered two divisions of Kakamega district in Kenya's Western Province: Tiriki, consisting of fifty-three communities, and South Kabras, consisting of thirty-nine communities, with a total population of 134,200. In each district the only outsiders were a team of facilitators that included a community nurse from the Ministry of Health, a community-development assistant from the Ministry of Social Services, and a data expert from the district statistical office. Both teams were trained in participatory learning techniques. To provide official involvement at the local level, a medical assistant/clinical officer supervised each team. I could join them only on weekends.

Collecting Data and Building Capacity

Activities started in each location with a *baraza,* an open public meeting traditionally used by chiefs to communicate with the people. Since we had heard conflicting definitions of community boundaries, we first asked for the people's guidance in defining local community units for organizing project services. After intense argument, the people agreed that a geographically discrete unit of neighborhoods and hamlets was best so that "no one would eat twice and no one would be left out." The next task was to identify action priorities. The two teams of facilitators went through their areas asking the people what they considered their most important problems, taking care not to push people in their answers. Ninety percent of the ninety-two communities identified some health issue as their number-one problem, with malaria, diarrhea, and other childhood illness taking the first three slots. Other frequently identified problems were poverty, food shortage, and shelter.

Once communities had identified their problems, they discussed possible solutions with the teams, then formed community health committees made up of three women, three men, and the community health worker. Ninety-eight percent of the communities chose a man as the chairperson, and all the communities chose a woman as treasurer, "because women will not steal the little money we collect." Selection criteria included literacy in the local language, respectability in the community, and a "good heart." The method of selection became a big issue. The people wanted us outsiders to make the choice, explaining: "If we don't choose the chief's relative, he will beat on our heads forever, but you can go away." Finally we settled on a compromise. At a *baraza* on a day publicly announced in each local area, and after extensive discussion, those interested in the position lined up. Then, in what they called "deciding in the daylight," all the people lined up behind their choice. The three people with the longest lines from each community were then assessed for literacy and knowledge by an examination set by the university faculty, and a final choice was made on that basis. Ninety-nine percent of those selected to be community health workers were women.

As soon as talks on community action began, the issue of money came up. Most communities expected money to come from outside. At a meeting of the community health committee, the team of facilitators explained that the money would have to come from the people themselves. "We may have to become a little poorer in order to become richer later on," one old man explained.

The people decided that if the project was to be truly their own, it was important for them to give something to their community health worker. They established a household levy as well as a minimum fee for services to start their community fund. As the money accumulated, the people could hardly believe that "this much money could come from us, ourselves." In addition to the monthly payment to the community health worker, withdrawals were made to purchase cement for protecting springs and to cover expenses for clinic and community activities. Gifts made at harvest time were sold and the money added to the account. Fears that the money would be misused proved unfounded; each community insisted on a level of transparency that allowed them to "watch each other like open-eyed hawks."

Systematic data collection was an early priority. When the people decided to have household levies they realized they had to have complete household counts. The first household surveys collected information on the number of people in each family and the home environment. The "right-hand men" of the local chief served as liaisons between the teams and each family. The response was so good that people began annual surveys of vital statistics. This survey was expanded to nine questionnaires covering demography, preventable diseases, use of preventive measures, agriculture, income and expenditure, dairy cattle, cash crops, distance to facilities, and family planning. Each year the people became increasingly proud of and fascinated by the data about themselves.

Evolving Partnerships

Any community-based project gets strength not only from the community but also from outside support services. For a health project, the balance between village and secondary care is especially important; a community-level worker cannot handle every medical need. To strengthen community-based capacity it was essential to increase support provided by the clinics in town to the villages. Community health workers were taught that they must refer to their district health center women in obstructed labor, children with very high temperatures who had convulsed even once, and all cases of moderate dehydration. The plan that evolved was for the committee to organize the patient's transportation while the community health worker stayed with the patient. Transportation took various forms, including bicycles, homemade stretchers carried by people, and private cars.

When it became clear after several demonstrations that women in obstructed labor could be saved if transported to the district hospital in time, linkages grew between health needs and social needs. For example, several communities that had lacked roads began to improve tracks to motorable status through their own organized labor. But there were rivers to be crossed, and the people didn't know how to put up bridges. In a meeting the people agreed: "We must go to the district headquarters in Kakamega to talk to the district road engineer. He is not there just for town roads." And so they went. The bridges were built. Taking control of their health services led to action on roads and bridges.

Expansion of Women's Roles

Improvements in overall village life benefited women's self-perception. Although people found it acceptable for women to participate as treasurers of the community funds and as workers, initially many criticized the project for "looking up" to women or publicly praising their contributions in other tasks.

Sometimes I had to be direct and personal when making points about women's roles. Quite often this involved reminding people, especially the men, that I was a wife and mother just like their own wives. Highlighting this common status broke down barriers. A frequent comment was that women had to be kept in their place because otherwise they would start to speak "rudely" to men. At one meeting I asked the men: "Do you think my life has dignity in the eyes of my husband?"

"Yes, obviously. You are a doctor," the men responded.

"You have seen my husband come to some of these events with me. Do you think because he is courteous to me I talk rudely to him?"

There were some embarrassed grunts. Then someone said, "You are different! You are a special woman."

"Are you telling me my husband did a better job of choosing a wife than you did?"

Silence.

Then I would add, "I don't think so! I think your choice of wives was excellent!"

Silence.

Finally someone said, "Well, this is the way our people have *always* acted!"

It became clear that women, who were in most need of a "breathing space," would at first find it only through involvement in activities that were generally approved of by husbands, fathers, and even brothers. In many places such as tradition-bound Africa, complete gender parity remains a long road on which women have been allowed to take only a few small steps. But bit by bit in our villages, relations between women and men expanded. The more mobilized communities became, the more their larger vision of development was endorsed; women took part in improving environmental sanitation, protecting springs, developing kitchen gardens, building latrines, paying for first-contact health services provided by the community health workers, and organizing immunization days once a month. On these occasions all young children in the community were taken to the health center as a group event. The youngsters were carried by men and women alike, each taking turns to make the town trip. Eventually community-based daycare centers were established, supervised by adults, an approach that replaced the practice of leaving babies in the care of children. Eventually, too, discussion moved to spacing the births of children, and the communities endorsed modern contraceptive methods. Over the years, both women and men became increasingly active in political matters. This was not one of the project objectives any more than constructing roads and bridges was. But it became clear that when people feel confident and empowered, they start to participate in the important issues of life and will not be kept on the fringe of decisions.

By 1980 people were experiencing a sense of "we can do it" empowerment that stood in stark contrast to the sense of being trapped that had dominated the opening talks in 1974. As the activities moved ahead, the teams of facilitators reduced their involvement by reducing the frequency of visits, from weekly, then to fortnightly for three months, then monthly for three months, and finally quarterly. In the first *barazas* a major issue was to decide the sequence of extension from community to community. After much debate it was agreed that the poorest and most remote communities would be first because their needs were greatest. The use of data was crucial both to these decisions about which activities to undertake and to the communal sense of achievement. People could see the results firsthand and talk through what they meant. Data were not kept in government offices but taken to the communities. As people planned their lives, it made sense to them also to plan their families. With the advent of active national family-planning programs, the birth rate dropped sharply.

Transition: 1980–1982

In 1978 Kenya presented the Kakamega project at the World Conference on Primary Health Care in Alma Ata, Soviet Kazakhstan, as a demonstration of the proposed new approach for the global primary-health-care movement. In the same year UNICEF recognized Kakamega with its prestigious Maurice Pate Award for outstanding contributions to the development of primary health care in Kenya. In 1979 UNICEF organized a global senior staff seminar in Kenya so that officers from all UNICEF country programs could closely observe the process and accomplishments. In 1980 the Ministry of Health decided that this national pilot project had proved itself and took direct control. The teams that had been leading the project were reabsorbed back into their regular jobs. Only the field supervisor, who had been assigned to the provincial primary-health-care division in Kakamega town, was still in a position to make periodic visits. After the Alma Ata Conference, international donor agencies poured in huge amounts of money in ways that undermined the community-based management, transferring the locus of control to the donor groups and reorienting work objectives from community to outside priorities. The focus shifted from communities working for what they wanted to individuals working—and being paid—for what donors wanted.

A parallel distraction came from visitors. During the pilot stage of the project, a decision had been made to limit inputs to what was available from local resources; no volunteers from outside had been accepted. International recognition of the project's success brought a flood of enthusiastic visitors eager "to help." The visitors asked a lot of questions, expected precise answers about matters still under discussion, and tried to move activities forward in their own shorter, less-inclusive time frames. Remembering colonial days, villagers inevitably felt that visiting foreigners were making judgments about whether their answers were "good" or "bad," and that they were being tested by questions such as "What is the purpose of the Kakamega project?" This questioning added to the anxiety people already felt about the uncertain process they had started. The people said, "When a seedling is planted, it is not pulled up every day to see if the roots are taking."

While the Kakamega project was developing, other community-based projects sprouted up all over Kenya, with an especially large number initiated by missionaries. Notable among these was the Kenafya project, sponsored by the government of Kenya and funded by aid from Finland, which extended the Kakamega approach to other parts of Kakamega district and Western Province. Other projects supported by other groups concurrently expanded care in Nyanza, Eastern, and Coast Provinces. Elsewhere in Kenya the Aga Khan Foundation supported parallel projects, while the Ministry of Health encouraged church groups and small NGOs to expand community-based care, especially out of mission hospitals. The formation of a very active coordinating committee at the national level made it easy for communities to get international support for village-based work. On the surface this international support appeared to be a good thing, but the methods of organization, sense of urgency, and outside priorities brought to the task all had a strong tendency to undermine community capacity. As outsiders' development objectives displaced community-based objectives, in many places the well-intended donors embraced their projects into helplessness.

After 1982

In 1982 Kenya's Ministry of Health created the Community-Based Health Care Unit at its headquarters in Nairobi. The consequence was to institutionalize a people's process. Those who had served as key staff in the successful demonstration were given no role in the larger implementation. Instead of providing supportive supervision through teams of facilitators holding dialogues with communities, the ministry issued top-down directives, behaving as they had been taught officials should behave. Back at the university, however loudly I explained the basis for the success, key officials were uninterested in the "time-wasting tactics."

The Kakamega project continued to receive visits from top government officials bringing high-powered teams from UNICEF, the World Bank, and many other donors. Easily observed differences in the project sites were used as testimonials to the positive achievements. But the publicity now focused on results, and this focus deflected attention from the process. Given the sums of money now coming from the donors, it was easy to believe that programs were becoming stronger. Officials and international experts could not understand that the successes had arisen from the process, not from the setting of performance targets, and that the forward momentum had been generated from within the community and not from external financing. They assumed that by adding their version of support—more stringent management directives and considerable outside funding—they could make things happen faster and go to larger scale. They had never acquired the fundamental faith in a three-way partnership that used local data instead of outside prescriptions to change behavior and that accepted the limitations of each partner's roles. They were uncomfortable with the need for humility and the necessity of learning to set aside their own culture (bureaucratic or ethnic) and to delegate authority and responsibility so that they could mature in the hands of their new owners. Delegation is not remote control.

What most drastically undermined the process was the arrogant, simplistic assumption that getting "community participation" merely involved "telling the village people to clean up and do a few things." Community-based action is more than "just common sense." Central to the change of orientation was the focus on results pushed by money. Money allowed outsiders to introduce their priorities. Seeking to systemize the increasing cash flow, the ministry established a framework of oversight and mechanisms for conveying outside contributions to communities. There followed cycles of periodic "overfeed" and "drought." Overfeed occurred when, following the 1978 Alma Ata Conference, many agencies adopted the new development fashion in short-term projects, then abandoned communities in order to pursue other interests. Both the national government and the donors failed to understand that communities were sensitive to the need for stable services, and thus to steady funding. The droughts took the form of periodic drying up of local inventories of essential drugs. Because the donors now controlled the distribution of medicines, communities no longer had their women watching like open-eyed hawks over each local fund and medicine cabinet. Many aspects of health care may need outside support, but paying for medicines is a cost that people, even poor people, are almost always willing to assume. At the most they need help getting lower-cost drugs, not free medicines.

The Kakamega project was formally disbanded in 1982. Nevertheless, nearly two decades later the experience continues to have an impact. Both in the communities and in the Ministry of Health people recall the successes of the Kakamega project, when the villages were taking action in their own behalf. And indeed the villages themselves, though now lacking their enabling partnership, continue to make progress, albeit with greater confusion.

Even more encouraging than continued progress in the original villages is that other communities have learned from the Kakamega experience. Those lessons are not what they could have been had the process been sustained through enabling partnerships, but these other communities are repeating parts of the projects and (one hopes) not the errors. There are flickers of hope in the lives of people in many places despite recent major disasters of disease, flooding, and war that have caught larger attention. Some communities are changing, understanding continues to grow, and hope persists that these continuing small successes can ignite into larger mobilization throughout Africa.

The White Mountain Apache,
United States

Reclaiming Self-Determination

Few strategies to promote development have differed so starkly as those of the U.S. government directed toward Americans of European origin and those directed toward Native American peoples: on the one hand, expansion of communications, education, health, transportation, and financial institutions; and on the other, confiscations of land, "assimilation" policies that involved removing children from their families and otherwise undermined traditional ways of life, and, finally, "support" programs that promoted dependency instead of self-reliance. This latter history shows all too clearly how government actions that are controlling instead of enabling (even if well-intended) can do profound and lasting damage.

Today the Cibecue community of the White Mountain Apache is pursuing parallel pathways in education and health care in an effort to regain control over its own future. As a result of federal legislation over the past few decades, the tribal government is evolving increasingly effective community-based approaches in partnership with Washington and with independent experts of many sorts.

The two thousand Apache of the Cibecue Valley, in eastern Arizona, are the most isolated members of the White Mountain tribe. A high percentage of the people still speak the Apache tongue, and they try to keep older ways alive. Older residents tell of idyllic childhoods spent in the forests with deer and other wildlife as neighbors, when Cibecue Creek still abounded with trout and beaver. They tell of times when women spent their days collecting plants for food and medicines while men and children spent their days on their horses. Young people are encouraged to learn traditional stories, dances, and handicrafts and to take an active part in rituals that strengthen tribal identity and values.[1]

The Cibecue area remained little disturbed by outside intrusion until just after World War I, when the U.S. government came in with policies that changed both habitat and lifestyles. The first move was to sell grazing rights on Apache lands to non-Indians. The sale of too many permits resulted in severe overgrazing and extensive damage to the land.[2] From the 1930s to the 1960s the government tried to turn the Apaches into cattle ranchers, worsening the damage. By the 1960s the adverse impact was clear, and the government decided to reengineer the landscape and, with it, the ecology. The Bureau of Indian Affairs introduced "vegetation modifications." Native junipers and beargrass were uprooted and exotic grass species introduced. At the same time, reservation waters were tapped to meet needs downstream in the rapidly modernizing state of Arizona. To enhance the volume of the Salt River before it left the reservation, cottonwood trees along the streams were girdled and chemically poisoned. To speed up their flow, the rivers were "straightened" with bulldozers, a practice that continued into the 1980s.[3]

To jump-start economic growth the federal government in the 1960s promoted creation of a local timber industry. The Bureau of Indian Affairs went through the paperwork and had a sawmill operating in Cibecue by the end of the decade. With a significant facility to justify, the BIA recommended timber harvesting at rates that exceeded regrowth (in marked contrast to the harvesting practices of the Menominee Indians in Wisconsin, who resisted outside direction and have maintained one of the world's most sustainable forest-management programs for over a century). For a long time, however, the Apache derived little benefit from these major timber operations; white contractors made the only significant money until, in the 1980s, the tribe took over control of the timber contracts and the mill.

When we began to work in Cibecue in 1996 we found that residents viewed the preceding decades of mostly well-intended actions as disrupting both to the environment and to the social fabric of Apache life. But the adverse outcomes were not all the government's fault; Apache leaders, themselves unsure about the best course to follow, had generally gone along with government recommendations. There had been no enabling partnership to systematically build local confidence and capacity. Almost all projects had been driven by government paperwork and funding rather than by community work plans and a balancing of resources.

Building Capacity and Education

In the 1930s traditional Apache tribal government was abolished, and with it the old pattern of holding chiefs responsible for their community's well-being. In the mid-1970s, supported by passage of the Indian Self-Determination and Education Act (P.L. 638), an energetic Indian tribal council took a number of forceful actions to regain some control in shaping their own lives. By the late 1980s the balance of power between government and the Apache tribe had shifted to more-inclusive decisionmaking by outside experts and tribal members. Using paperwork knowledgeably to acquire and wield power, they devised significant new policies that created opportunity for locally based solutions in watershed management, improved access to communications and information, and new economic alternatives that included a ski area, world-class hunts for their exceptionally large elk, tourist trout fishing, and a gambling casino. Although none of these endeavors alone is hugely profitable, together they substantially diversify the economic base of the tribe, much as multiple tourist-based initiatives did in the Adirondacks. These varied activities have also systematically moved the locus of power into the community.

At Cibecue the people decided, under the new policies, to take control of their school, previously managed by the Bureau of Indian Affairs. Not only did they choose community control rather than federal management; they also calculated that with money coming directly to them they could expand from eight grades to a full high school. They reasoned that to have a local school would reduce dropout rates by eliminating a long bus ride across the reservation, and that having a local athletic team would help strengthen community pride.

As part of this effort, the Cibecue community hired an imaginative and well-trained new principal and reorganized the school committee. Then a surprising resource appeared. A loyal bookkeeper who had handled the school's accounts for many years had been quietly investing the yearly surplus from the Bureau of Indian Affairs budget in one of several savings accounts around the state. With the end of each accounting year, he had reassigned the unspent balances to future needs. Together these various accounts had been quietly accumulating interest and now added up to a significant sum—large enough to help pay for a new school building and to fund the expanded enterprise well into the future.

Self-Evaluation and Environmental Action

We walked into this context in 1996 in response to a request by the Indian Health Services to evaluate the Cibecue Health Center. Although the Indian Health Service would have preferred a more traditional evaluation by a management group, key tribal leaders had preferred the community-based approach and asked for us. At a time when we were implementing the SEED-SCALE process in large prospective trials in the Third World, we saw this as an opportunity to learn how it might work in the United States.

After organizing meetings with tribal leaders, health center staff, the Cibecue school committee, and the tribal planning department, we held a community meeting at the school gymnasium to get public input about Cibecue's needs. Hundreds of people attended. At this meeting the new principal ingeniously modified a Participatory Rural Appraisal technique of community mapping: instead of trying to promote participation by asking the traditionally laconic Apache to talk through their ideas, he distributed Lego blocks (he had bought a large quantity at yard sales over the years).

Neighborhood groups clustered around tables scattered through the gym. Each group was asked to build a model of what it would like Cibecue to look like. The people in these groups somehow communicated while saying little. Energy was palpable as they fitted together visual statements of their ideal community with the little plastic blocks. Every group included a Laundromat, and all but one showed a swimming hole or pond in the creek. Their models were limited to the town area, possibly because the square plastic Lego blocks facilitate building towns and not forests and streams or possibly because the instructions in Apache had limited the scope of the vision to the town. Both the Laundromat and the swimming hole would have brought important health benefits, but neither directly fitted with the expectations of the Indian Health Service, which had hired us only to find out whether it should enlarge its clinic building.

At the end of the exercise, we asked the people to describe their vision. We had been calling the Cibecue project Healthy Communities. But the people came up with their own way of describing a healthy community. They decided that health was not a matter just of freedom from sickness but rather of *dish chi be kho bil na zel*, "our Cibecue community walking forward together."

With this start, the project launched more systematic data collection, hiring high school students under a federal summer program. One group was to do a household survey to determine health needs; another was to assess ecological conditions along Cibecue Creek. The high school and the watershed program of the tribe's planning council took responsibility for the environmental data-gathering. The students doing the health survey became frustrated and stopped halfway through; they felt that the other survey group's work was more interesting, and they also felt some discomfort at entering people's homes to ask private, sickness-related questions. We realized that as outside experts we had made several mistakes. For one thing, the health questionnaire was too elaborate. For another, since health services had been provided by the government, community members had no sense of real involvement in decisionmaking on these matters. Finally, it seemed that in this situation young people were the wrong interviewers; their mothers would have been more effective in gathering this kind of information.

In contrast, the environmental survey prompted immediate action. The tribal planning department hired local people to efforts to restore Cibecue Creek. Volunteers from the school—students, teachers, administrators—fenced off access to the stream to reduce soil erosion, removed sediment to reopen the channel, and cleaned up a historically important spring to provide a source of safe drinking water. Some of the students involved in this action learning and service have gone on to study environmental subjects in college and to take jobs in this field.[4]

The Experience in Health

Following our difficulties with a standardized health survey, and lacking support from the Indian Health Service to conduct a full SEED assessment, we shifted to gathering health data through in-depth interviews with four groups: twenty Apache officials and Cibecue residents, seventeen Apache health workers, eighteen non-Apache health workers, and four non-Apache officials living on the reservation. We also organized several focus groups of older and younger people. The extensively computerized health information system on the reservation provided an abundance of data to support a major shift in orientation.

Census data for 1990 confirmed the community's poor general health and economic status. The figures showed a median annual income of $4,400 for males, $2,800 for females, and $9,200 for families; more than 50 percent of households were below the national poverty line. Infant mortality was 14.3 per 1,000 live births, about twice the figure for Arizona and the United States. The main causes of death were cardiovascular disease (20 percent), diabetes (10 percent), motor vehicle injuries (8 percent), alcoholism (7 percent), and homicide and suicide (7 percent). Death rates were twice as high for men as for women. Prenatal care coverage seemed good, but there were high rates of teenage pregnancy (19 percent) and unmarried motherhood (57 percent), as well as high rates of alcohol and tobacco use during pregnancy, with low-birth-weight babies, and anemia and diabetes among mothers.[5] According to tribal estimates, alcoholism affected 40 to 60 percent of the people; 43 percent of hospital admissions and 42 percent of deaths between ages twenty-one and seventy-four were alcohol related. In a survey of students aged nine to eighteen about 30 percent reported weekly use of alcohol or drugs as well as alcohol and drug addiction among their parents. Forty percent of students aged ten to seventeen did not live with their parents, nor did an even higher proportion of the more than 50 percent of youth not in school.[6]

The interviews revealed that the dominant health problems arose not from infections but from a sedentary lifestyle largely promoted by government welfare programs, from consumption of high-fat, high-salt, sugary "white man's" food, and from easy access to alcohol. These health problems were very different from the ones being addressed by the good clinical treatment provided at the health center.

The sharp dichotomy between the statistics and the services provided demonstrates the importance of gathering community-based data before decisions on new initiatives are made. A more conventional evaluation would have limited analysis to conditions at the clinic and focused mostly on issues of acute illness and infection control. The new data showed that chronic diseases in the community stemmed from social factors that might not be considered directly health related: the breakdown in relations between elders and youth, the lack of communication between men and women, the decline of family gardening. Those problems could be corrected only by behavior change, not by new clinics.

The health center was providing good medical care in routine clinical services. The knowledge and performance of health center personnel were adequate and in some cases very commendable. The equipment and facilities, though old, were functional and used appropriately. People's conventional health needs were being competently served. But looked at from a larger perspective, the community's health problems were not being addressed at all. During interviews a senior official explained: "Acute care is the first priority, and it uses all our resources. If we put money into diabetes prevention, people would no longer receive adequate acute care, and then they would not trust the prevention program." This official perspective had not looked into the lifestyles prevailing in the homes beyond the clinic walls.

In the Cibecue community it was clear that many people were eager for change but were worried about what their role would be. In 1995 the U.S. government, recognizing that its welfare programs had promoted dependency among the poor nationwide, abruptly swept away support services that had evolved over several decades. These changes did not take into account the specific needs of Native Americans. In the Apache context, the new welfare-to-work options were rightly recognized as impracticable, since almost all opportunities for jobs on and around the reservation had been destroyed by earlier policies.

Meanwhile the Indian Health Service remained interested in a larger clinic building that would be more convenient for both staff and patients. We supported that project but recommended that the new building also house facilities for programs that focused on prevention and wellness. Even more important, we proposed action that would go far beyond acute care: the creation of a health-care delivery network that would promote community self-reliance (an ancient Apache value).

Not surprisingly, our proposals prompted robust discussions with the Indian Health Service and at all levels in the community. At the time, all sources of funding were tightly confined to the government's separate categorical programs. Our recommendations required a new approach, one that did not fit comfortably with established government practices, which make it hard for crossover action to occur among health, education, and environmental sectors even when solid research has made linkages clear. The Indian Health Service did, however, expand the Cibecue Health Center by constructing an adjacent Wellness Center and providing more prevention services.

Ideas once planted sometimes sprout and bear fruit later. In 2000 a task force consisting of local residents and health-care providers used our earlier data and report as a starting point and held regular public meetings in an effort to promote real partnership between health services and communities throughout the reservation. The task force decided to use a reservationwide SEED type of assessment to collect information. It created, pilot-tested, and implemented a simple data-gathering system. Community meetings are focusing on defining health priorities and actions. They hope to collect data annually to help communities revise their own health plans.

Lessons from Cibecue

The first, difficult steps toward empowerment have been taken. Ultimately, of course, the tentative new linkages among the energized community school, the increasingly outward-looking health services, and expanding environmental projects need to be made sustainable. Doing so will require the creation of new economic opportunities and the promotion of deeper value changes.

These experiences, though clearly specific to the Apache situation, show how top-down development assistance interferes with building community capacity—even when done unintentionally to compensate for earlier exploitation. Services and subsidies usually undermine self-reliance. Local people need to strengthen their own capacities if they are to become real partners with government and experts in setting and implementing their priorities. To do these things all three partners need a systematic, regularly updated process and a commitment to cooperate.

PART IV

Large-Scale Applications

CHAPTER 16

Urban Agriculture

A Powerful Engine for Sustainable Cities

Jac Smit

People around the world are returning to farming in cities. As a Ford Foundation urban adviser in 1968 I found that people in Calcutta were producing one-quarter of the fish and vegetables being consumed there, using wastewater and solid waste. In many places today urban agriculture supplies between one-quarter and one-half of city dwellers' total food needs. In the 1980s a compilation of thirty-two studies from twenty-five countries showed that urban agriculture had taken hold in hot and cold climates and in command and open economies alike.[1]

Urban agriculture does not specialize in cattle or cereal crops but in a diverse range of perishable food—vegetables, fruit, fish, poultry, small mammals—all high in vitamins, minerals, and proteins. Urban agriculture is typically intensive, producing three to fifteen times more per hectare than do common rural methods. It uses recycled urban waste as a major input, not because of idealism, but because urban waste is abundant and available. The urban farmer's labor-intensive methods use far less water and chemical fertilizer per unit of production than does industrial agriculture.

Urban agriculture offers much more than a greater array of food sources and better food quality. Urban agriculture is a development entry point for cities. It increases civic stability, reduces traffic congestion and overall energy consumption, improves air quality, and gives the enterprising, unskilled poor a way to start making money.

Bringing farming into cities reduces their ecological footprint. Today greater London requires 125 times its actual area to provide the food it consumes. This footprint reaches to the farthest corners of the Earth, with tea coming from China, shrimp from the Bay of Bengal, and flowers from Kenya. Urban areas cover 3 percent of the planet's surface but import two-thirds of the natural resources people consume—and most of that is converted into polluting waste.

In Valparaiso, Chile, Theodora Luna rises early in the morning and feeds her quail and guinea pigs the leftovers from her family's and a neighbor's meals. Before preparing breakfast, she inspects the fence of the one-tenth-acre (0.04 hectare) home plot for damage from the community's free-ranging goats. At the end of the day she tends her raised beds of vegetables, trellises of cucumber and zucchini vines, and flats of hydroponic lettuce on her roof. This small city farm produces one-third of the food and two-thirds of the protein and micronutrient needs of Luna's family of five. In addition to giving her family a healthy diet Luna raises culinary and medicinal herbs that are sold on a consignment basis by a grocer near her husband's place of work. She generates her own fertilizer by composting her family's and neighbor's wastes and uses the gray water from their kitchens and baths for irrigation. Her small plot is green from boundary to boundary, and the space is cleaner and cooler than the many brown plots in the neighborhood. Her children are healthier than the average child in the neighborhood.

Stoitcho Ainarov lives in Viongradetz, a suburb of Sofia, Bulgaria. Around his house is a thirty-by-forty-meter orchard of fruit and nut trees. Most Bulgarian suburbanites have similar orchards. Ainarov receives monthly pension worth thirty-five U.S. dollars, and he lives well. He sells grapes to a local cooperative, sells specialty fruits to city merchants who knock at his gate, and sends fresh food regularly to inner-city relatives.

Within his walled compound Ainarov practices some of the most advanced concepts of organic urban agriculture. Grape arbors shade vegetables, and on a patio goats eat alfalfa and crop wastes, while pigeons provide manure enriched from feeding in nearby fields and forests. All solid waste is composted, and all wastewater is used for irrigation. Many products are processed on-site, including wine, dried and canned fruit and vegetables, and pickles and sauerkraut. He harvests most vegetables—potatoes, beans, peppers, tomatoes, mushrooms, cabbages, and onions—at least twice a year. Chickens, pigeons, and turkeys produce meat and eggs. Whereas agriculture in the United States requires eight off-site calories of energy (petroleum and other sources) to produce one calorie of food, Ainarov reverses the ratio and produces eight calories of food for every one calorie of external energy.

During a recent food crisis in Bulgaria, United Nations experts were astonished at the low level of malnutrition. They concluded that urban agriculture is contributing to poverty alleviation, food security, and good health.

Current World Trends

In 1990, 45 percent of the world's people were living in cities; that share is expected to increase to 75 percent by 2040. Eighty to 90 percent of this urban population growth will occur in what are now developing countries. As urbanization and associated economic development grow, so will urban sprawl, consuming some of the world's best farmland; solid waste and wastewater accumulation, with higher disposal costs and health dangers; major strains on infrastructure; and mushrooming social pressures. Urban agriculture can turn most of these huge forces to advantage, creating soil, fertilizer, and water and promoting community participation and cohesion. In an era when farmland is disappearing, urban agriculture can increase the space available for farming.

Today cities everywhere are sprouting farms. In places like Berlin and New York the growth of urban farming is sufficiently vigorous that it has become a hot political topic as neighborhoods defend community gardens from takeover by builders. Fifty thousand Berliners today rent land for gardens, and another fourteen thousand are on waiting lists to do so. In Harare, Zimbabwe, agriculture within the city limits doubled between 1990 and 1994. In greater Moscow in 1970 one family in five was raising food; by 1990 three people in five were devoting 20 to 60 percent of their time to farming. In the United States registered farmers' markets, which rely on locally grown products, increased by 40 percent (from 1,750 to 2,410) in 1994–1996. In Argentina a national community and household garden program grew from 50,000 members in 1990 to 550,000 in 1994. In China 40 percent of urban jobs are categorized as agricultural. In Mozambique's capital, Maputo, the share was 30 percent in 1988. Two-thirds of all families in Dar es Salaam, Tanzania, produced food in 1988, up from one-fifth in 1968. Many cities are now self-sufficient in vegetables—from one of the world's largest, Shanghai, to Mali's small capital, Bamako.

All of these are SCALE One examples, places where single successes have led to replication. A spontaneous, exponential growth is under way. As more and more communities wake up to the potential, an enabling environment is being created worldwide. Many places are systematizing this extension, creating SCALE Cubed types of support structures. Eighty percent of Cuba's people live in cities. When massive infusions of money and food from the Soviet Union ceased in 1992, government leaders opened public lands to gardening; the government provided seeds, training, marketing, and technical inputs; two television programs a week broadcast information and advice to the new farmers. Romania adopted similar policies following the breakup of the Soviet Union, food production in its cities jumped from 6 to 26 percent in six years. In Loudon County, Virginia, the third most rapidly urbanizing county in the United States, farms, farm enterprises, and farm-generated income have increased in every one of four survey periods from 1978 to 1996; and the agricultural sector is still improving, complementing growth in residential, industrial, and commercial development.

Changing Patterns of Food Supply

Urban farming has been around for millennia. The hanging gardens of Babylon, praised by historians for their beauty, were also a source of food. Machu Picchu, high in the Peruvian Andes, was nutritionally self-sufficient. The medieval cities of Yemen produced all their own fruits and vegetables. Mexico City, perhaps the largest city in the world in the fifteenth century, converted swamps into farms and fishponds and produced half or more of its own fish, livestock, fruit, and vegetables.

From Nineveh to medieval Paris, ancient cities tended to expand in ever-widening rings. Food that stored and traveled well was produced in relatively remote areas. Food that spoiled easily or tasted better fresh was grown within or just outside the city precincts. Imperial Rome followed this pattern, importing grain from North Africa and Asia Minor but growing its own fruits and vegetables. In both Rome and the ancient Mayan city of Tikal, in Guatemala, the proximity of production allowed for perishable food to be harvested at night and early in the morning in response to reports about daily demand coming by runner from the central markets.

The industrial age created a different pattern. With more rapid and sophisticated transport networks and work specialization, food production moved farther and farther away from the majority of consumers; foodstuffs were shipped first by rail, then by trucks via nationwide networks of limited-access highways. Today the average item on a supermarket shelf in New York City has traveled fifteen hundred miles. Artichokes picked in fields in California are delivered to stores three thousand miles away in Manhattan, along with fresh fish from the Caribbean. A structural change in the food supply system replaced *proximity* with *access*.

Today still another pattern is emerging, one involving nodal networks, supported by nearly instantaneous computer-driven information. In wealthy Loudon County and in impoverished Port-au-Prince, Haiti, farmers can learn hour by hour what will be in demand in markets tomorrow and make choices about harvesting and shipping accordingly. The structure inevitably favors farmers who are closest to urban markets. Thus in many ways the newest pattern resembles the one prevailing in ancient Rome and Tikal, where runners took up-to-date information to nearby farmers. Once again, urban and agricultural sectors enjoy a symbiotic relationship.

Old and New Technologies

Researchers today are studying sophisticated urban agricultural methods of the past such as the Incas' use of standing water surfaces to fight frost, combined land and water farming in fifteenth-century Mexico, crop specialization in ninth-century European towns, the *marais* system of nineteenth-century Paris, and the dry-climate intensive production of the Navajo and other southwestern Native American tribes. Some of these ancient methods are being adapted to modern uses. Java is applying the old Mexican system; Ghana is using both the Mexican and *marais* systems. Mexico itself has adapted an old Mayan waste-treatment system, using fiberglass containers to coprocess sewage, garbage, and human waste for food production in a residential neighborhood. Farmers in Havana are improving upon the biointensive growing methods of eighteenth-century China, now called *organiponicos* (all compost, no soil).

New technologies are also playing important roles in urban agriculture. The glass greenhouse, invented in 1850, revolutionized agricultural production in the developed world. Since 1980, light, easy-to-assemble, less expensive plastic greenhouses have expanded that revolution worldwide, enabling farmers in rich and poor countries alike to conserve heat and moisture efficiently and to reduce losses from theft, wind, and insects. The development of new plastics has also enabled urban fish farming to become a fast-growing sector of urban agriculture.

Hydroponics, growing food without soil, is the second most rapidly spreading technology. Hydroponic projects range from large, well-financed firms in Rotterdam, to simple, water-filled trays in the barrios of Bogata, to the use of sterile media in St. Petersburg (peat moss) and Hawaii (volcanic ash). Hydroponic produce includes lettuce, tomatoes, herbs, and a score of other crops that sell at premium prices.

New technologies are also advancing treatments of urban waste for fodder and plant nutrients, including the use of worms in vermicomposting and of duckweed (a small, high-protein, floating plant) in sewage treatment. Genetic reengineering is increasing yields, making plants and animals hardier, and improving the taste of many products, from Dutch peppers to Peruvian guinea pigs. Whether mushroom, rabbit, seaweed, or potato, crops are being designed for the particular needs of urban agriculture, as occurred for rural agriculture decades earlier.

Benefits to the Urban Landscape

Savings for Cities

In some poorer cities, more money is spent on waste management than on education. Urban agriculture offers cities a chance to reduce expenditures on waste disposal by using 10 percent or more of waste as fodder for poultry, fish, and livestock, and over two-thirds of all solid and liquid waste for soil enrichment and irrigation. These strategies have a ripple effect, reducing traffic congestion, air pollution, and strains on infrastructure (roads, water-supply systems, sewers) by reducing the number of trucks hauling waste and food on city streets. Urban farming is synergistic with most of these activities: moving food production closer to the dinner plate reduces investments while increasing livability.

Replacing nineteenth-century waste-treatment systems with ecologically more sustainable ones also saves money and benefits the urban environment. Cities in China are adding shredded plastic bags to soil to lighten it. Elsewhere municipalities are recycling solid waste into roads. And some cities are cooperating with local industries to recycle the products of one system into a resource for another; in Texas, for example, a large manufacturing company is transforming waste from making blue jeans into a soil conditioner.

Urban agriculture can also reduce the costs of acquiring, maintaining, and policing rights-of-way for roads, railways, and utility services. Opening these spaces up to farming benefits a city in five ways: farmers pay rent, maintain the soil, diversify and improve the ecology, informally police the land, and feed themselves and their neighbors.

A Broadened Economic Base

Farming favors women, youth, the elderly, and the poor—all groups that are usually discriminated against in the regular workplace. But livestock and produce don't care whether they are being tended by one particular type of person or another; what matters is how consistently and well the farming is practiced. Thus urban agriculture is also frequently a way of closing the equity gap.

Urban agriculture promotes processes and markets while minimizing demand on transport and infrastructure. This replacement factor can be significant. My grandfather lived at the edge of nineteenth-century Amsterdam and worked as a middleman, buying from rural farmers and selling in the city. A food-supply system that brings produce from California or Israel to Chicago has many such middlemen. Their income does not trickle down to the farmer. In contrast, urban farmers often sell their products directly to the consumer. For example, in my hometown the direct sale of a crate of lettuce returns fifteen dollars to the farmer, whereas selling that same crate through middlemen to a distant market brings five dollars. Higher profits for small producers expand economic opportunity for the poor. In addition, by being in daily contact with the grower, chefs and greengrocers are better able to serve their customers.

In Ho Chi Minh City, Vietnam, 70 percent of all family expenditures in 1994 were for food, a rate that is not unusual. In Bombay and Kinshasa the rate is 50 percent. In cities like Zurich, food is only 10 to 15 percent of the economy, but as a result of packaging and transport the demand on the environment is three times greater; so even in wealthy cities, where a lower percentage of income is related to food, the change to urban agriculture brings other savings. The first benefit of urban agriculture is to the small producer, but the radiating impact can be many times larger.

Increased Stability and Civility

Farming promotes a more stable and more civil urban society. In communities with small-scale agriculture, interactions between neighbors intensify, with more face-to-face communication and sharing of concerns. People who deal with each other about food-related matters have a common denominator, one with longer-term implications than the immediate moment. Building a more beautiful and healthier place to live strengthens social cohesion and collective empowerment. In the 1980s studies in Seattle showed that community gardens delivered more social benefits per dollar invested than did libraries or community centers. Building on this rationale and working under tight budgets, cities from California to Canada to Colombia to Cuba are supporting school-based instruction in urban farming. Now it is time for SCALE Squared intentional training to begin. With so many SCALE One demonstrations and SCALE Cubed enabling policies, there is a current vacuum worldwide that assistance from nongovernmental organizations could begin to fill.

Urban agriculture promotes civil society. Home business of any kind promotes other home-based activities, including those that strengthen positive influences in the raising of children. Cities where economic pressures compel both parents to work outside the home, leaving their children unsupervised before or after school (if schooling is available at all), often have greater alienation and higher crime rates. By providing income, urban farming can enable one parent to work at home, and it provides an activity for the entire family for an hour or two a day or on weekends, along with the bonuses of larger income, better food, and social benefits for the person staying at home.

With investment in the productivity of urban land, local residents promote sustainable communities and help reduce social and physical chaos. Farming in open city spaces fills in social as well as physical gaps, enabling people to come together as neighbors rather than as potential adversaries and creating spaces where people can congregate in productive work. Further research may also reveal the potential of urban agriculture to reconnect urban citizens with nature.

Improved Health

From their lower altitude, children often experience the city as a more hostile habitat than adults do. They are more likely to breathe ground-hugging ozone. Their hands are more likely to be covered with unattended trash. And if their families are poor, they may lack access to good food, since in many cities stores are the only source of food. At this interface urban agriculture makes a fundamental contribution to a healthier city. Plants grown in the city change the urban environment, cleaning the air at street level and making food more available to residents.

Fresher food brings better health. The more time that passes between harvest and consumption, the greater the loss of micronutrients, especially vitamins. Week-old spinach has lost half of its vitamin D. The poor in Dar es Salaam get better spinach than the wealthy in London, since 90 percent of the leafy vegetables eaten in Dar are grown within the city. Protein sources tend to be still more costly; not only are they higher up the food chain, but often they also require transport and special storage. Production of small livestock—poultry, fish, rabbits, guinea pigs, and the like—in the neighborhood lowers costs and makes protein sources available to the poor.

Agriculture in cities benefits human health by improving the soil and reducing the volume of solid waste and wastewater. Production of fruit, vegetables, and ornamental plants brings birds, bees, butterflies, and with them a more interesting and pleasant environment for humans. A city with green growing things is also cooler in the summer.

Going to Scale with Urban Agriculture

The largely spontaneous expansion of urban agriculture around the world differs fundamentally from the coordinated agricultural expansion of the Green Revolution. Both were and are central to improving human well-being. But urban agriculture self-assembles, expanding in a natural way. It thrives when given an enabling environment—a three-way partnership of experts with ideas, pro-active city governments, and citizens who embrace the vision. In city after city a new pattern of behavior is unfolding as people start farming and relate to one another to support this effort. And as locally sensitive information accumulates, diversity expands.

In this expansion, urban agriculture displays the three dimensions of SCALE. Small gardens have always been present in cities, but a huge and continuing increase has occurred in the past two decades wherever municipalities have adopted supportive policies. Where policies were not supportive, expansion occurred more slowly. Entrepreneurial individuals and third-sector organizations joined together to lead the way—the best among them serving as demonstration and experimental sites. In this information-based age, news about changes in technology and policy is moving more easily and quickly for adoption and adaptation by communities throughout the world.

Urban agriculture and rural agriculture are complementary activities. Urban agriculture provides clear advantages for certain crops. It involves different types of stakeholders and responds to different demands. It enables towns and cities with tight budgets to gain green space at minimal cost along with people to tend it, perhaps also bringing in taxes or rent, rather than the more expensive approach of increasing green space simply by creating parkland.

Agriculture directly helps the most needy in a city. It creates economic options for many subgroups that otherwise experience food insecurity. It expands and improves the food supply. It creates a nonmonetary livelihood for people with little money and allows scarce financial resources to go to other needs such as medicine, shelter, and clothing. For the wealthy, farming in the cities provides fresher food than was previously available. By diversifying food production, it also fosters export opportunities: locating food production near airports allows regions to take advantage of their climates to produce perishable foods for other economies. Aided by quantum advances in technology and communication, small-scale, community-based urban agriculture represents an especially efficient and productive new arena of development.

CHAPTER 17

Peru

*Communities and Government
Learning to Work Together*

Patricia Paredes and Carl E. Taylor

Those who have tried only top-down or outside-in stimulus often think that promoting community participation is a very slow process, but the CLAS (Comites Locales de Administracion de Salud; Local Committees for Health Administration) movement in Peruvian villages demonstrates that the process can scale up very quickly. The main requirements are a truly enabling environment for community empowerment and patient persistence by officials and experts in establishing that environment to foster trust and partnerships so that the capacity of the people has time to mature. Then growth can virtually explode.

Origins

In 1994, after decades of violence, the Sendero Luminoso, or Shining Path, a Maoist terrorist movement, was driven out of villages in the Peruvian Andes and into the slums of Lima. The Ministry of Health was eager to reestablish social services in the mountains, but in many villages the people refused to let health centers be reopened. Officials were baffled by community demands that local, nonmedical people be involved in running local health facilities. We were part of a team from the Ministry of Health that visited these villages.

In a public meeting one community leader from Quinua, a village near Ayacucho, said, "We showed we could defend ourselves from terrorists. Now we want responsibility for protecting the health of our families and children." The women said that it wasn't the American helicopters or the Peruvian army that defeated the Sendero, but the *ronderos,* or self-defense groups formed by village people, and especially women, who sat armed with guns in stone pillboxes around their villages and shot guerrilla gangs when they came to kidnap teenage boys to join the Sendero.

The villagers said the old health system did not meet their needs: doctors from Lima were interested only in getting back to the city and making money in private practice. People especially complained about payments for drugs. "Money we pay for medicine should replenish our local health post's supplies. Some people are too old and too poor to walk to distant health centers. Work in each community needs to be strengthened. We need *promotores de salud* [health facilitators] to extend outreach for public health and pregnancy monitoring." Such community self-reliance fitted well with the policies being advocated by President Fujimori during that preelection period.

A proposal for community-based health services was drawn up, and in May 1994 President Fujimori signed a decree creating CLAS. Under its provisions each community would have a committee composed of local residents: three members would be selected by the community, three by the Ministry of Health, and the chair would be the senior doctor of the health center. Each community committee would sign a contract with the ministry as a registered nonprofit organization and then receive authority for controlling the health center and hiring personnel beyond those assigned by the government. They could use funds raised by the health center and create programs to meet their own priorities so long as they also facilitated national programs and priorities. Accepting part of the SEED idea, the committee and health center staff were to conduct an annual household survey and set local priorities to create an annual community health plan.

Pilot programs were started under the guidance of a small ministry team working directly under the minister of health. The project started with 4 CLAS committees in the Ayacucho subregion and 9 villages in the Ica subregion. Huge national demand quickly overwhelmed initial planning, and about 250 more CLAS committees were organized in the next six months.

Four years later, in 1998, 548 of the 5,060 government health facilities were CLAS centers, with another 150 waiting to be recognized. By mid-2000 more than 1,200 CLAS centers were providing care for more than one-fifth of Peru's people.[1]

Friction with Regional Health Offices

From the outset the regional health offices had problems with the CLAS concept. Previously the regional offices had sent pharmaceutical supplies to local health centers and received the money that health facilities collected from the sale of drugs. Now CLAS committees could keep the money from the sale of drugs to purchase their own resupply. As they did so, they found they had money to hire additional staff, get equipment, and do regular maintenance. Several CLAS centers even put up new buildings. The regional offices objected strongly because they had lost a major source of financing.

As the communities took control, regional differences emerged. In Tacna the regional director enthusiastically supported CLAS, every health center had a committee, and the regional office directly influenced who was on the committees and what was done. Other regional offices resisted the CLAS concept and delayed transmitting funds to CLAS centers. The CLAS committees in these areas were necessarily especially strong and independent, hiring their own staff and using voluntary workers. On one evaluation visit, we found a large poster on the front door of one regional health office saying: "Health Workers Boycott CLAS." The regional personnel director had been visiting health centers that were discussing forming a CLAS to tell staff to resist the movement or they would lose their jobs. Many of the most effective CLAS centers were in places where regional offices took a neutral stance, helping when asked but letting local committees make decisions as long as people didn't complain.

Formal Evaluations

In 1998 two independent evaluations were done of the CLAS program.[2] The first was by the Research Center of Universidad del Pacifica, and the second was by a consultant for UNICEF. Both used data from a 1997 national survey of quality-of-life indicators from a random sample of 3,843 households in CLAS and non-CLAS areas. CLAS centers accounted for 14 percent of all centers on the coast, 39 percent of those in the mountains, 6 percent of those in Amazonian forests, and 6 percent of those in Lima. Two-thirds of the people served in CLAS centers came from the two lowest economic quintiles; their homes had dirt floors and usually no electricity. Thirty-nine percent of CLAS clients were between zero and five years, 20 percent were between six and thirteen years, and 10 percent were over forty-five. Patients going to non-CLAS government services had a considerably older age distribution.

The response to improvements in quality care was strong, particularly where government collaboration was good. Performance was evaluated as low where relationships were poor. Services were best where community participation was greatest. Significantly greater use of health centers was found in CLAS areas; in non-CLAS areas patients were much more likely to use pharmacies or a hospital.

Most CLAS committee members were women who had worked in public-service programs; 70 percent were housewives, and 90 percent had finished high school. Committee members worked an average of fourteen hours per week. Both studies showed that women had a particularly strong leadership role in CLAS. They were leaders in mobilizing communities, and they continued as volunteers, performing a variety of essential functions. For example, they promoted behavioral changes in their communities that supported preventive activities such as immunization, nutrition, and maternal care. As expected, women and children were the primary users.

In some urban areas CLAS committees raised enough money to expand both facilities and activities, such as building a maternity hospital while also organizing effective community outreach. Ancillary programs included building basketball courts on health-center grounds and sponsoring youth basketball and soccer leagues. Mothers' groups were particularly effective in building relationships with government and nongovernmental programs for women and children.

The UNICEF evaluation confirmed the effectiveness of SEED-SCALE principles: the strengths of CLAS derived from "the involvement of community members in: (1) identification and prioritization of community problems based on a health assessment via household survey; (2) planning solutions in ways unique to community needs and resources and formalization of solutions in the annual work plan; (3) decisionmaking on the use of funds for personnel, supplies, equipment, maintenance; (4) monitoring and evaluation of the local health program; and (5) monitoring of personnel, in terms of attendance and treatment of patients."[3] CLAS committees met regularly; meetings were led by a community member; women participated in meetings and decisionmaking; the needs of the socially and economically disadvantaged were addressed; services provided flexibility in clinic hours, waiting time, and the number and kind of personnel available; there were more home visits and promotional activities in the community. About 90 percent of CLAS health facilities reported such involvement in the community; non-CLAS figures were much lower.

Many government officials continued to object to this level of community involvement. They maintained that untrained people could not manage a facility or do the paperwork, and they had special concerns about financial mismanagement. Both evaluations, however, found that CLAS communities consistently had transparent management and financial accountability, and where people did have difficulties with paperwork and regulations the studies recommended government training to enable them to handle these tasks. The evaluations also showed that local programs were disappointing officials' hopes of reducing health expenditures. This outcome was not surprising, given local committees' use of surplus drug revenues to expand subsidized services.

Information Systems and Community Statistics

Local data are fundamental to impartial, community-based decisionmaking. CLAS and non-CLAS centers were uniformly dissatisfied with the government information system, claiming that too much time was wasted on maintaining records and filling out more than ten report forms every month. Immunization records were especially confusing. Some centers said the most complex task imposed on them was a new management information system that took as much time as the rest of the recordkeeping combined. Layers of financial accounting added further burdens.

In CLAS centers each committee did a household survey. Because local data were gathered in partnership, coverage was typically close to 100 percent, in contrast to household surveys by professional teams, which averaged 60 to 70 percent coverage.[4] The resulting statistics were more accurate and reliable than the usual government figures, which tend to be based on norms established at the central level and have little relation to local reality.

As CLAS centers became aware of the number and needs of the poor, most created a sliding scale of fees for services and medicines. Community members identified the neediest families, and some developed computerized databases of these. Systematic home visiting then targeted these indigent families. Chincha's CLAS centers, for example, worked regularly in the neediest areas and concentrated on home visiting. In Quinua, in the Ayacucho region, CLAS committees translated announcements of vaccination and sanitation campaigns into the local languages to encourage families who otherwise would not have come to the center.

CLAS and the National Program of Health for All

Frequent changes in ministers and officials in Peru's Ministry of Health greatly complicated national policy relating to CLAS. First it was promoted, then ignored, but centers continued to proliferate dramatically because of the enabling framework that had been created at the beginning. When officials learned that CLAS had grown to be the basic service for almost 20 percent of Peru's population, they decided the program could no longer be ignored. As stories spread about the enthusiasm of committees, officials worried that negative comparisons would be made about services in government programs. At policy meetings most officials continued to oppose the community concept, claiming that the loss of control by professionals could jeopardize quality of care. They wanted to bring the CLAS centers under ministry supervision, with only a symbolic role for the committees. At the regional level the issue of who should get the funds from the sale of medicines remained unresolved.[5]

Two additional internal and external evaluations of CLAS, presented at a meeting of regional health directors in 1999, persuaded the skeptics to compromise, and the government decided formally to extend the program in response to growing demand. At four regional conferences in 1999 and 2000,

CLAS committee members were able for the first time to share their experiences and promote new learning and progress. In February 2000 Peru's Ministerio de la Presidencia issued a working paper citing the contributions of the CLAS program: "With stronger community institutions we can now transfer to the people competencies, responsibilities, and resources. Among the impacts of our communities' institutional strengthening is the emergence of the people's capacity to manage programs and projects. The Local Health Care Services Administration Committees (CLAS) are an example of participation in both identifying needs and managing services."[6]

The apparent success of CLAS is still fragile, and its relations with government services remain uncertain. The momentum for expansion depended mostly on the local people's enthusiasm when they were allowed to take control of their services and direct them toward meeting the priorities that the communities felt to be important. The enabling framework that was created to allow this community-based leadership drew directly on the paradigm described in this book. But although CLAS has grown rapidly and well, the project's very success may threaten future flexibility if it induces the national government to co-opt CLAS by incorporating it into a cumbersome and largely unresponsive government structure or by developing CLAS as a parallel system within the Ministry of Health.

Communities are eager to organize and solve their own problems. If appropriate support is provided by government and outside experts, this extension can occur rapidly. Expansion in Peru ran into difficulties for many reasons. There have been repeated changes in the small supporting team in the Ministry of Health and in most of the midlevel health-care centers, and government support has been inconsistent or ambivalent (especially with regard to centralized control of the money paid for medicines).

Lessons from CLAS

In advising on the creation of CLAS, we were not in a position to implement key components of the SEED-SCALE approach. Most unfortunate was the omission of SCALE Squared centers to systematize a process of evolving sensitive and practical responses to local needs. A rapidly expanding program requires support even if it is designed to be locally led and locally adapted.

Many committees still have few places to turn to for help. Funding and implementation of a SCALE Squared system would help bring together concrete and tested answers to expand learning and adaptation in yet more communities.

We also were unable to persuade decisionmakers to integrate health services with other sectors to gain broader community support and create important linkages between health and food security, education, and environmental protection. The CLAS experience demonstrates the essential weakness of a program limited to a single sector. Health professionals in community-based systems must link their services with other development sectors if solutions are to address underlying conditions and promote healthy communities in a healthy environment. These linkages may yet come into being if CLAS is used as a demonstration project in a national policy of decentralization. Discussions are under way about addressing the wider needs of communities, perhaps by joining CLAS with programs such as women's income generation, school gardens, and environmental protection in the fragile Andean and Amazonian ecosystems.

Finally, we were unable to implement a regular system of data collection and feedback in revising annual work plans. The first CLAS centers did a good job of gathering data, but this activity did not spread uniformly along with the CLAS program.

Peru's tremendous cultural, economic, and physical diversity—ranging from industrialized cities along the coast, to ethnic and physical isolation in the high, dry Andes, to the lush low ecosystems of Amazon tropical forests—requires decentralized decisionmaking to address local conditions. No centralized system can meet such various needs. In contrast, a community-based system can self-assemble and adapt to local realities. This flexibility in community-based capacity-building was a major factor in the initial rapid spread of CLAS.

CLAS began with the efforts of women in the Andean highlands to strengthen their own communities. Their vision has gone nationwide in less than a decade. Peru's history of political instability indicates that for long-term development, the nation needs a steady and yet active base of citizen organization. CLAS committees can help engage the people of Peru in creating a more promising future.

CHAPTER 18

Tibet, China

Integrating Conservation with Development

"It all depends on one's point of view" should be an axiom of development. Circumstances that are viewed as progress for some define catastrophe for others. One of the most intriguing examples of contrasting values in development has been (and remains) Tibet, today an autonomous region of China. For centuries, Tibet defined development in terms of the pursuit of spiritual values. Today it is seeking a more sustainable balance with natural resources as well as economic prosperity. We have followed the Tibetan case closely since 1984, working through two nongovernmental organizations and UNICEF.

Until the middle of the twentieth century, the government was controlled by religious leaders. Much of Tibet's agricultural, economic, and human potential was channeled to support thousands of highly developed monasteries, several of them housing more than five thousand monks. Many families traditionally gave one of their children to serve in a monastery. Paralleling the religious structure was a feudal system of local lords. Taxes by monasteries and lords often took one-third of the average farmer's crops in this difficult, barren land.

In 1950 the Chinese army entered Tibet, and in 1959 China took over direct control, asserting that Tibet had agreed more than two centuries earlier to a suzerainty relationship. The new rulers deplored the total absence of schools and health services, an agricultural system that used serfs, and a theocratic system of government. China destroyed what had gone before and imposed a new order in its Tibet Autonomous Region. Thousands of religious monuments were torn down, and compulsory communal experiments resulted in famine and vast social dislocation. The Cultural Revolution of the 1960s and 1970s added to the destruction wreaked by the initial "liberation." Chaos and much suffering followed as the new system crushed the old.

From this collision of values a new order began forming, one that included a new approach to preserving the environment. Today a large demonstration and experimentation SCALE Squared center in the Mount Everest area has become a model for wider development in Tibet, showing the potential for people to address economic, social, and conservation needs simultaneously. In most of the world, conservation programs remove land from development activities and people from the places to be preserved. Development is viewed as incompatible with conservation. In Tibet the conservation effort is redefining the way land is used. Conservation has become a means of ensuring the long-term well-being of people even while protecting large ecosystems.

While the conservation momentum builds, most Tibetans focus on social and economic advancement. Local entrepreneurs race to make money, and outsiders move in by the thousands to do the same. A debate is under way between those who seek to exploit the environment as a way of creating economic options and a rapidly growing array of those who advocate protection.

The harsh environment determines all action in Tibet. The climate is one of the most extreme on the planet; the air has one-third less oxygen than is available at sea level, the average temperature is 30 degrees Fahrenheit (17 degrees Celsius) lower than at the equivalent latitude at sea level; annual precipitation is frequently less than 10 inches (25 cm). In such conditions only the hardiest of trees, bushes, grasses, animals, and people can survive.

Historically, as people have sought livelihoods they have damaged the environment. Our comparisons of populated areas and protected pockets of habitat reveal that several hundred years ago the ecology of Tibet was very different. The vestigial forests still found around ancient monasteries—for example, Samye, south of Lhasa, or Reting, in central Tibet—and in the sacred valleys such as Tsari, in southern Tibet, show that forests once existed on mountain slopes and in valleys that today are barren. Pollen studies show that centuries ago trees grew beside rivers along valley bottoms and on the slightly moist north-facing slopes below 12,000 feet.[1] Comparisons of grass species and variety on inaccessible cliffs show that Tibet's original vegetation was more diverse and luxuriant.

Evidence of home construction dates in villages throughout Tibet suggest that with the blossoming of Tibetan civilization in the seventeenth and eighteenth centuries, the human pressure on the land increased and changed the balance of flora and fauna. Monasteries demanded fuel both for cooking and for warmth. A consolidation of control by the monasteries seems to have brought stability to the scattered human population and the opportunity for their numbers to increase. As a result, trees that once grew by the rivers were cut for the many monasteries and tens of thousands of homes. Flatter lands that usually had better soil and richer grasses were plowed to make fields. Herds of domestic animals became more numerous than the wild, and the grass types that survived this more intense grazing became selected for hardiness.

The pace of human-initiated environmental change accelerated with the arrival of trucks and the construction of roads during the 1960s and 1970s. During the Cultural Revolution and into the early 1980s, entire forests started to disappear with the advent of organized timber and mining operations. The inflow of modern guns, which began as a trickle with muzzle-loaders until the 1950s and swelled with U.S. and Indian government support of Tibetan revolutionaries in the 1960s and 1970s, grew to flood proportions with the arrival of large numbers of Chinese military. All this opened up a large-scale killing of wild animals.

This exploitation of the environment in Tibet resembles trends in all parts of the world. What is different in Tibet is how quickly conservation efforts began. One reason may be greater sensitivity because of the deep tradition of innate spiritual values; another may be that Tibetans are learning from other societies. Another advantage, uncommon to societies in this phase of development, is the existence of a strong governmental structure that has been able to take the long view and engage local communities and utilize expert help. For any or all of these reasons, the environment has benefited in the following ways:

- In 1985 less than one percent of Tibet's area was protected. By 2000 fourteen nature preserves protected 31 percent of the land, with additional preserves being planned that by 2002 will protect over 40 percent.

- In the mid-1980s reforestation started around major urban areas, then along the rivers, extending to more than 150,000 acres in fifteen years. The impact has been substantial: in the Lhasa Valley the local government claims that these efforts have decreased average ground wind speed by one kilometer per hour.
- In 1994 a Tibet-wide ban on the commercial sale of wild animal skins, horns, and body parts was followed by dramatic arrests of poachers and sellers. As of 2001, throughout much of Tibet wild animals were noticeably less fearful of humans, and population counts suggested that animal numbers had doubled. For the exceptions—high-value animals such as musk deer and antelope—protection was increased in 2000.
- A commitment to solar energy began in 1984. Fifteen years later, solar cookers had penetrated to approximately one-quarter of villages, and photovoltaic solar lighting had come to thousands of nomad camps and monastery reading rooms.
- By 1980 electricity had come to virtually all towns and many large villages. Over 90 percent of this electrical generation is from hydroelectric or geothermal sources.
- Since 1980s simple conservation technology (window glass, small greenhouses, outside latrines that create compost, and energy-efficient metal stoves with chimneys) has become common in nearly all wealthy homes across Tibet and is spreading to other homes.

The cumulative impact is that in one of the planet's most isolated and socially disrupted societies, where severe hardships are the norm and human dependence on the environment is starkly clear, conservation has now become accepted as a basis of development. This ever-wider acceptance is based on the realization that beneficial change will not endure if Tibet's natural resources are consumed in the process of achieving that change. It is also supported by the Chinese cultural characteristic of seeing civilization as part of millennial progressions and the willingness of their people to sacrifice for society. Finally, the interconnectedness of development and protection of life is supported by Tibetans' religious respect for all life forms.

The three principles of this book were easily implemented in this context.

In particular, three-way partnerships formed among communities, leaders, and experts. In this partnership a few dedicated officials consistently worked hard over two decades in cooperation with an outstanding American-Chinese expert, Chun-Wuei Su Chien. Throughout this period other experts gathered data, and action followed from plans that allocated new roles for people by matching needs with human and economic resources. Extension of this process to a regional scale followed the three-dimensional SCALE approach. In this extension the Qomolangma (Mount Everest) National Nature Preserve served as the key SCALE Squared center.

Qomolangma (Mount Everest) National Nature Preserve

In October 1989 negotiations had been under way for four years to create a new nature preserve in the heart of the Himalaya. Six months earlier the government of the Tibet Autonomous Region had launched a large conservation experiment across four counties around Qomolangma, the Tibetan name for Mount Everest. Initially called the Qomolangma Nature Preserve, as its successes mounted the Chinese government elevated the park's status to a "national treasure," and it became the Qomolangma National Nature Preserve (QNNP).

The preserve that was created is mostly high plateau, averaging 14,000 feet (4,500 meters) above sea level. Descending from that height are five deep, forested valleys with high rainfall and a great diversity of plants and animals. Eighty-five thousand people live in the area at elevations from 7,000 to 17,000 feet. Two of the four counties encompassed by the preserve are the poorest in all China, with half the people living below the national poverty line and 98 percent illiterate. When the preserve started, the area had one bank; now there are five. There were five schools; now there are thirty-eight. None of the water supplies of the area's 320 villages was protected; today those of 64 are protected.

One day when the preserve was just starting, a meeting was under way with villagers in the eastern part of the new park. "It's fine for you outsiders to talk about integrating conservation and development," said an elderly Tibetan community representative. "We all want to preserve the scrub juniper bushes. But my family needs fuel to cook with and a fire to keep us warm, and cutting the juniper is our only option."

"But if you cut juniper this year, you won't have it next year," replied one of the officials of the new preserve. I sat on the other side of the room watching this standoff. It was not the first. We had been going from village to village, explaining the new preserve and how it would help local people and protect the environment. Why should the people stop killing snow leopards that killed their domestic sheep? Why stop killing wild asses, which invaded their crops? Why stop cutting trees to sell to merchants from the cities who paid them hard cash?

"We must discover new ways to protect nature and to use nature so our children will have better lives when they grow up," continued the official.

Then an old man dressed in simple homespun quietly spoke up, and the others immediately fell silent. "Perhaps we first take care of our needs. But as we start with our needs, we should also ask: 'One hundred years from now, what will be the consequences of the action we take today?'"

Thereafter the challenges of implementing both development and conservation were repeatedly resolved by what became known as "the Qomolangma question." So simple; yet by extending our time horizon it engages the interdependencies of real life, in which every action has consequences. This question links environment and development in a way that people can understand.

In 1989, when the park was established, both the local people's needs and the environmental threats seemed impossibly great. Qomolangma, the Goddess Mother of All Mountains, was in danger: the forests around her base were being ravaged, her slopes were littered with the garbage of those who sought her conquest, and visitors were shooting the wildlife in the surrounding valleys. On our way to one of those early village meetings, we saw a Tibetan gazelle beside the dirt track. The Tibetan driver turned the jeep and went after the animal. At first I thought he was chasing it for fun or even to enable me to photograph it, but then, before we could stop him, he pulled a pistol from under his seat and blazed away at it a couple of times out of the window. For behaviors to change, even in a culture that values life, the way people think about their resources has to change.

In creating the QNNP, the planners knew they could not afford to pay wardens from outside to protect the land; nor would outsider wardens be effective workers in this harsh, isolated place. The local villagers were on-site, and so was the structure of county administration. So, since outsiders could not be brought in, the pragmatic decision was taken to put protection in the hands of local people. They would not be asked to leave so that the land could return to a wild state; instead they would restore the land by learning new ways of using it.

The QNNP planners also realized that because the ecology of each valley was different, the management of each valley must also differ. To ensure site-specific management, teams collected data on the wildlife and plants in each valley, their rates and ways of changing, how people were changing, and the imminent dangers.

The preserve that was created on March 18, 1989, is a new model of nature protection. Three features distinguish the QNNP approach:

- Management uses existing systems; no separate park structure and warden force were created. Utilizing the existing administration of the four counties allowed new initiatives to grow without adding layers of bureaucracy.
- Management follows the biosphere reserve concept, creating a zone-based mosaic of land-use patterns. How land and wildlife are treated depends on where they are. Eight core areas strictly preserve key habitat. In surrounding buffer zones people can use the land as long as natural balances are not disrupted. Towns and villages are zones of intensive human use—called development zones—where more-disruptive activities are permitted so long as they do no harm to the larger environment.
- Nature conservation and development are interdependent. Visitors pay permit fees to visit the park, and the revenues are used to improve people's health, education, housing, fuel supplies, animal fodder, and the like. Park ownership of lodges provides a second stream of income; there is no outside ownership of hotels. Because people are benefiting, they work to implement conservation policies.

The Pendeba project illustrates the process of self-assembly by which ideas were first implemented, then adapted, and, after further refinement, able to go to scale. Surveys in 1988 showed that villagers had three priorities: reliable energy sources, acute health care, and transport services. (Outsiders had expected the priorities would be food security and poverty alleviation.) Of these priorities, primary health care is the fastest and least expensive to provide, so the planners decided to follow up on this first. Subsequent village-based data showed the most urgent needs to be diarrhea, pneumonia, cuts and broken bones, and childbirth assistance.[2]

The project then created a new type of worker. The workers were given a name coined specifically for their new function: *pendeba*, "the worker who benefits the village." Twenty-four villagers were selected to go to Shegar, the central town of the park, for three weeks of training in primary health care. They returned to their villages with a basic drug supply, knowledge of how to use these medicines, and an understanding of preventive medicine. To pay for medical care, the villages established their own payment plans: simple insurance schemes, fees for services, taxing families one or two sheep, or creating village cooperatives.

Pendebas' skills and services grew incrementally. At first they provided little more than first aid, vaccinations, and oral rehydration for diarrhea using a homemade solution of roasted barley flour and salt. With supervision and more training, they were able to meet two-thirds of village health needs. Villagers where the more competent pendebas worked and where a modicum of support was present (a school, cooperative, or government administrator) were designated "teaching villages." Pendeba numbers grew, from 24 in 1994, to 87 in 1997, to 234 in 1999. Ultimately there should be 450 pendebas to serve the park's 320 villages.[3]

One venture pushed by an international funding agency demonstrated sharply how the QNNP's orientation to strengthen local capacity differs from conventional donor-designed development. In 1996 this donor became enthusiastic about the pendeba concept and offered support on the condition that pendebas be paid salaries. The donor reasoned that since these were the poorest villages in China, it was impossible for the project to expand with the people paying their workers. QNNP leaders resisted this modification but worked out a compromise: the donor would set up a parallel project with the goal of promoting income generation, and revenues from these projects would be used to support other development activity. Two years later the number of specially funded workers had not increased beyond the original fourteen. The donor was not in a position to increase the funding, and villagers, who saw the services as gifts, had no incentive to figure out how to pay for this expansion.

Elsewhere villages and pendebas were expanding their services as well as their numbers. Tree nurseries had been started in the QNNP in 1992. By 1998 they were producing thousands of seedlings. Pendebas distributed these and trained families in tree care, in the hope that eventually every household will have a stand of fast-growing willows and poplars whose leaves will provide fodder for animals and whose branches will supply fuel for human use. In 1998 a few villages opened shops to sell solar cookers and metal stoves with chimneys, both of which consume less fuel than open fires on floors. Demand for these items usually exceeds supply. By 1998 some small shops were selling window glass to hold heat inside homes. Villagers sought new ways to do things, made or saved some money in the process, and tried still more innovations.

To relieve pressure on ecologically fragile valleys, a multilevel resettlement program was launched. To support better living standards and thus promote acceptance of the resettlement areas, people and government joined to dig irrigation channels and build access roads. Whole valleys were opened to settlement, and hundreds of families were offered the chance to relocate from fragile or overcrowded lands.

The extent of internal innovation by midlevel administrators is striking. For example, one village could not afford to pay a salary to its pendeba, nor did villagers have the equivalent of twenty U.S. cents per person per year to create the insurance scheme proposed by an outside expert. So the local administrator taxed owners of larger sheep flocks one sheep each, reasoning that they could easily lose one sheep a year to a snow leopard. The sale of wool and offspring from this new flock supported the village pendeba. Another midlevel administrator noticed unused land outside the village, had access to a QNNP tractor, and offered fields to the landless and the use of the tractors to plow them. If the families successfully grew crops for two years, the land would become theirs. Other villages quickly adopted this innovation.

Another midlevel administrator started cooperatives. His villages wanted roads, walls to keep wild asses from invading fields, and more money for the revolving drug fund, which got depleted as pendebas gave away drugs to the most needy. By pooling resources in a cooperative, they increased their leverage. The coops sell machine-made clothes, drugs, candy, plastic jugs, and other items from the outside world. In 1997 there were four cooperatives, two years later there were twenty, and the year after that there were fifty. Many are started by a one-time tax on the barley harvest. In a recent conversation, one pendeba said, "It's not the money we get that's important, but the strength we build from putting our resources together."

Successes such as these have raised expectations from government and outside donors that these simple villagers cannot possibly meet. They are now asked to help with village administration and with complex decisions on health, agriculture, conservation, income generation, and public policy. Villagers do not hesitate to ask pendebas, who have only a few weeks of training primarily in health, to build a retaining wall to stop flooding, to start a village school, to stop wild animals from invading crops, or to engineer a bridge. Western tourists who get sick on their way to Mount Everest increasingly stop for treatment from the person the villagers call "doctor," and sometimes get upset because the treatment they receive is so basic. In some cases pendebas themselves overestimate their competence and take on inappropriate leadership roles or tasks for which they have not been trained. There is a danger that as expectations rise, pendebas may come to be seen as failures because they cannot do everything asked of them.

Yet the QNNP's successes are breathtaking. Wild animal populations appear to have doubled, and deforestation, the most pressing environmental problem when the preserve was established, has been reduced by two-thirds. (Illicit felling is hard to stop completely, because individuals can transport timbers clandestinely by yak over unwatched passes.) Community capacity continues to build as village councils take on more complex projects and mobilize larger internal resources. In 1998 the United Nations selected the Pendeba project as one of its fifty success stories for that year. The American Museum of Natural History in New York City selected this demonstration around the slopes of Mount Everest as a permanent exhibit in its Hall of Biodiversity. Chinese television, international journals, and local and foreign newspapers give coverage to the hard-working pendebas.

From garbage cleanup on Everest, to schools, health clinics, and libraries, even to archaeological excavations of fossilized three-toed horses and dinosaurs, action is being proposed in many forms. Donors from around the world are excited by the success (and by the chance to work near Mount Everest) and offer free money for all sorts of projects. It is almost impossible to turn down free money. The QNNP offers the chance to spend relatively small amounts to leverage big projects: $20,000 will restore a monastery, $2,000 will run a village training program, $200 will start a pendeba revolving drug fund. Today so many offers of aid are coming in that the administrative infrastructure lacks the capacity to oversee the projects. The promise of the QNNP could be smothered by outside love and the magnetism of the highest place on Earth. The only durable response to this global force lies in building up community capacity—a very difficult task when social reconstruction must start building from a feudal state.

In the early months of the QNNP, a cynic quipped, "It will be a sensational conservation achievement if the fox can guard the henhouse." Today villagers are succeeding because they have been enabled by a genuine partnership: the government partner has been both strong and flexible, and the experts have been helpful rather than controlling. Visiting officials point out deficiencies, and, when necessary, the QNNP takes corrective action. With this support, villagers are the ones who implement the activities. There is no one else to do the work in this isolated land. The greatest success of the QNNP is not that the fox is indeed guarding the henhouse, but that a three-way partnership is building a new house, a demonstration that holds promise for a better future for Tibet. The uncertainty is whether this positive community empowerment can build as fast as it must given the outside forces that increasingly impinge on people's lives.

Four Great Rivers Nature Preserve

The Goddess Mother of Mountains is an almost ideal site for a showcase and demonstration: it attracts attention, has great need, and had few previous failed attempts at solutions to reverse, so the QNNP project launched there was able to take advantage of the most advanced world knowledge.

Other areas of Tibet faced far more pressing environmental challenges. The most critical of these was the heavily forested region along Tibet's southern and eastern borders, where a major ecosystem collapse was under way.[4] The upper drainages of the Yangtze, Mekong, Salween, and Brahmaputra Rivers hold one-seventh of China's timber reserves. Beginning in the 1960s and continuing into the 1990s, people were cutting down whole mountainsides of trees in response to economic expansion in China. On days when the frail roads notched into these slopes were not closed by landslides or winter, an average of 200 truckloads of cut timber left for Sichuan and Yunnan to the east, and from the western edge of the area another 100 embarked on a circuitous 4,000-kilometer journey over the Tibetan plateau and Tang Shan Mountains to central China.

The potential consequences of this deforestation were huge. Whole valleys with steep slopes thousands of feet high were being cleared. Continued destabilization would lead to massive soil loss during the rains through topsoil runoff and landslides. Now that flora was disrupted, the megadiversity of the fauna would decline. The biodiversity here is the second greatest in mainland Asia; estimates are 8,000 species of vascular plants, 600 species of birds, and 150 species of mammals. Trauma to this complex ecology would immediately affect the livelihoods of the 800,000 people of this wealthiest region of Tibet, one-quarter of Tibet's population.

Damage was likely to be equally severe downstream. Lower in these four watersheds live 1.2 billion people in eight countries, 20 percent of the world's population. Fluctuating water levels could reduce essential irrigation to the paddies supporting their rice-based diet and would also disrupt river transport, fisheries, and hydroelectric generation. Without a stabilized water flow upstream, flooding, the age-old scourge of massive death in China, would increase, along with siltation. The latter would particularly affect China's largest development project, the Three Gorges Dam on the Yangtze, jeopardizing energy production, planned water supply, and financial investment.

The four valley systems cover an area the size of Italy, spanning two prefectures of Tibet, so conservation solutions would have to cross prefecture lines. Coordination would be difficult, since travel between prefecture centers takes five days when the roads are clear. And nowhere else on Earth is the land so fractured. These four valleys are among the deepest, steepest, and geologically most unstable on the planet. For four months each year monsoon rains effectively cut off communication to the area. Roads are regularly broken in dozens of places by landslides and each year must be rebuilt. The area is also politically sensitive, forming international borders between China, Myanmar, and India. Any proposed conservation action would have to take into account national security issues.

China's national government committed itself to creation of the Four Great Rivers Nature Preserve by writing it into the Ninth Five-Year Plan. The Tibet Science and Technology Department became the implementing agency. In 1995 the government of the Tibet Autonomous Region initiated a master plan to conserve this complex area and expand social services and economic activities. The government adopted the QNNP zonal management approach but added the uncommon step of having people from the area instead of outside experts create the plan. Although experts would be more familiar with nature-preserve design and sustainable-development planning, the QNNP experience had shown that local administrators ignored plans designed by outsiders because the administrators had no incentive to cooperate with them and resented being told what they must do. The first major obstacle to having local administrators lead the planning initiative was that none of them had experience in planning a nature preserve. So a six-year training program was launched for them and for local foresters and scientists so they could learn skills and see examples of community-based conservation and social change at other sites around the world. Simply offering the QNNP as the model and ratcheting it up tenfold would not be enough. As they were being trained, the teams also gathered data for the master plan, conducting valley-by-valley surveys to establish zonal boundaries. For community-based services, the pendeba project provided a model, but three thousand pendebas would have to be trained, and the earlier model needed to be adapted to widely varying services in the different locations.

Forest management was the key to the preserve. Given China's need for timber and the huge revenues being garnered by powerful economic interests, harvesting had to continue. The challenge was to replace clear-cutting with sustained forest management, including forest plantations. Cutting would have to be restricted to gentler slopes to minimize soil loss, preserve biodiversity, and stabilize water flow.

Major flooding of the Yangtze during the summer of 1998 took thousands of lives and threatened millions more.[5] The floods washed out roads and towns and heightened public awareness of environmental threats to the construction of the Three Gorges Dam, downstream from the proposed Four Great Rivers Preserve. These events stimulated political will to stop all timber cutting in the Four Great Rivers region until the master plan was formulated. In November 2000, after five years of planning, gathering data, and widespread community dialogue, the master plan was presented on an informal basis to the government. Intensive final writing followed through early 2001, and the final plan was submitted to the government in May. Also in early 2001 Beijing designated Four Great Rivers a national priority for the western region of China. Seventy million dollars a year over five years was allocated in China's Tenth Five-Year Plan, thereby providing the preserve with access to significant financial resources.

The Four Great Rivers Nature Preserve confronts a central environmental management challenge: how to deal with large political and economic forces outside the project area. Chiefly because of its uncommonly diverse membership, the preserve coordinating team in the Tibet Science and Technology Department has been able to turn unexpected events (such as the flooding of the Yangtze) into program-friendly opportunities, sometimes playing the larger forces off against one another and sometimes using public opinion to influence decisionmaking. Only when local people, officials, and experts are acting together can they resist pressures that arise not from local conditions but from the fact that the developed world tends to discount environmental exploitation when it is far from home.

Other Preserves

During the decade that the QNNP and Four Great Rivers were developing their community-based management approach, in other preserves Tibet tried the traditional approach of policing preserves. For these preserves wardens were hired and assigned to track down poachers and illegal timber cutters.

Of these preserves the largest and most important was the 120,000-square-mile Changtung Nature Preserve, in northern Tibet. Here, across an area the size of Germany, an area of rolling grasslands at altitudes averaging seventeen thousand feet, roamed vast herds of Tibetan gazelle, antelope, wild ass, and other animals. The high altitude and low precipitation create an exceedingly fragile habitat, but the seemingly unending space affords ample room for the herds to search out food. This high plateau is the last refuge of many key central Asian species.

Despite the region's isolation, poaching increased here during the 1980s, threatening one species in particular, the Tibetan antelope. Well-armed, mobile hunters seek this fleet-footed animal whose exceedingly fine *shatoosh*, or belly fur, is woven into shawls bringing five thousand to ten thousand dollars. Each antelope that is shot yields a couple of handfuls of fur. The challenge of dispersing wardens in vehicles across such a huge area to find poachers is punishingly expensive. As experience with a community-based approach comes in the QNNP and Four Great Rivers, work is under way to mobilize the few local nomads still eking out a marginal existence in the region to provide a new protection system.

A very different experiment is simultaneously taking shape in the rapidly growing capital city, Lhasa, where there is still a large, uninhabited wetland. In arid Tibet, this green space was a stunning treasure and ornament. Urban growth had encroached into the marsh, reducing its original size by 60 percent, to 1,500 acres (625 hectares). In 1999 the government set aside this remnant, creating Asia's largest urban park. Grazing animals were prohibited, and the vegetable-growing squatters were expelled. But although this forceful approach got the job done, it did not provide a long-term solution. A probing discussion followed concerning how to involve Lhasa's residents.

A firm boundary was needed that would both protect the wetland from encroachment and make the wetland visually accessible. After consideration of several options, the solution chosen was to construct roads along the outermost limits of the wetland. The roads formed a tangible barrier that also allowed people to look at the area as they traveled past—and to monitor activity there as they did so. This solution affords both visual enjoyment and protection.

Lessons from Tibet

Tibet presents a dramatic example of going to scale with positive change under very difficult circumstances. An affordable, community-based model of conservation allowed preserves to self-assemble: once people saw that the model worked and could be adapted to their own circumstances, the effort expanded rapidly. In the efforts to address people's needs, many factors converged: values in Tibetan culture that respected the environment, a recognition of accelerating environmental destruction, a strong political structure that could foster action and control, a national policy of sustainable development, and, with expert help, a model that offered an effective, affordable response. This is very different from traditional approaches to national parks, although it has an analogue in the parallel approaches used in the Adirondack State Park in the United States. The model and the process can be transferred to still other parts of the world.

Tibet, whose environment has been drastically changed across the centuries, is taking huge strides to reconstruct that environment without displacing people. In a dozen years, from 1989 to 2001, it has increased the share of its land under protected management from one percent to more than 40 percent in sixteen nature preserves. The evolution of sustainable land management there paralleled the writing of this book. The creation of the QNNP, the Four Great Rivers, the Changtung, and urban Lhasa provided excellent prospective field trials of the SEED-SCALE process that refined our understanding of how to help foster consensus among participants who otherwise have little reason to work together.

China's Model Counties

Going to Scale with Health Care

Carl E. Taylor, Robert Parker, and Zeng DongLu

From 1980 to 1995 a maternal and child health initiative in China expanded from 4 million people in 10 counties to more than 160 million people in 400 counties in every province. Together, China's Ministry of Public Health, UNICEF, and the communities used components of the SEED-SCALE process to extend rapidly to national scale a child health initiative that was adapted to local conditions.

In 1949 China's new Communist regime (building upon its wartime experience, which shaped so much of its philosophy, and upon the Ding Xian Experiment, described in Chapter 7) launched health services that dramatically reduced disease and death. By the 1960s, "barefoot doctors" (a name meant to show solidarity with the poor) provided primary health care for most villages in the country. The communal health cooperatives became famous as one of the world's most equitable health-care systems. In about two decades 22 percent of the world's population achieved high general coverage and a quality of care that produced excellent health benefits at a fraction of the cost of services in developed countries.[1]

But the system collapsed during the 1980s, when communes were dissolved and land was returned to families as part of new economic reforms. The work-point system that had provided payment for the barefoot doctors was eliminated along with the health cooperatives that had financed and managed the health system. Inequities and discrimination increased as women, children, and the poor had more and more trouble getting access to adequate care. A singleminded focus on economic growth shifted priorities away from funding services that maintained equitable and community-based care.

In 1980 Madame Lin JiaMei (the head of the Maternal and Child Health Bureau in the Ministry of Public Health and the wife of the president of China) organized a project to address the nation's health-care crisis by seeking local solutions and developing local funding. Using an early version of the scaling-up concepts outlined in this book, the program evolved and expanded through local innovations over one and a half decades to permeate the national health system.

The Initial Ten-County Project

We started with ten "model" counties, one in every region of the country. A team from the central Maternal and Child Health Bureau and one of us conducted weeklong workshops to plan priority maternal and child health services in each county. Attending the workshops were sixty to one hundred community and county representatives, health officials from Beijing and the province, and faculty from the departments of maternal and child health, pediatrics, and obstetrics at regional medical and public-health schools.

After these meetings, detailed household surveys were organized in each county to determine local needs. Six priorities emerged: pneumonia, diarrhea, perinatal deaths associated with pregnancy and delivery, faltering growth as a result of protein-energy malnutrition, micronutrient deficiency, and immunizable diseases. Each county worked out one- and five-year plans to change how services were organized, provided, and funded. For each of the six priorities, Chinese and international experiences were integrated to focus on activities that upgraded barefoot doctors could implement.

Experts and officials learned early the importance of greatly simplifying community-level solutions. For example, in one workshop a group of professors of obstetrics and former women barefoot doctors who were being retrained as maternal and child health village doctors for this project were seeking to define indicators for prenatal care to identify high-risk mothers. The professors so dominated the early discussions that the village doctors were moved to another room. A short time later the coordinating committee dropped by and found the village doctors in a vehement argument: some were punching with their fists while the others were waving their arms in large circles. The first group was insisting that the correct way of measuring pelvic size to predict obstruction at the time of delivery was to push a clenched fist into the area between the pelvic bones where the baby would come out. The others wanted to use a simple tape to measure the circumference of the pregnant woman's body at the upper pelvis. With the choice narrowed to these alternatives, the professors were brought back in. They agreed that both indicators could be used together more quickly and more easily than the sophisticated methods they had been recommending.

The main cause of death in all villages was neonatal and infant pneumonia, responsible for between one-quarter and one-third of deaths in various parts of the country. Academic centers conducted field trials in six counties and found the high pneumonia mortality in infants could be brought down by adapting the World Health Organization's case-management approach, first reported from Narangwal (Chapter 10). Case management based on diagnosis by direct counting of rapid respirations and prompt treatment with antibiotics worked well. Community-based village doctors explained the process to parents and obtained good results when babies got sick. However, it proved very difficult to change the ancient and common practice of tight swaddling, which prevented babies from doing the deep breathing and crying needed to open up their lungs; by restricting respiratory function, the practice contributed to the development of pneumonia.[2] To address this problem we needed more than a technical intervention. We made some headway in changing this deeply ingrained practice by offering mothers a practical and convenient substitute: zippered sleeping sacks that simplified changing diapers.

Diarrhea was the second most common problem. Morbidity levels under age one were equivalent to the very high rates in Bangladesh, but deaths from dehydration were only one sixth of the Bangladesh rates. An ethnographic study revealed that health workers and mothers would willingly modify the traditional method of oral rehydration, using diluted rice porridge or liquid herbal medicines. Care improved by mixing a small amount of salt in diluted rice porridge.[3] Longer-term prevention of diarrhea through sanitation was accepted less rapidly. It has also been difficult to prevent health workers from treating diarrhea with inappropriate antibiotics. China's extreme overuse of drugs reflects a societal overconfidence in technology, and the commercial promotion of pharmaceuticals has led to serious iatrogenic (doctor-caused) diseases; for example, toxic complications from overuse of antibiotics are now the number-one cause of deafness among children in Shanghai.

Third, growth retardation among infants in southern China was found to be associated with the widespread use of rice porridge—mainly starch and a large amount of water—as the main weaning food. Research in Guangzhou indicated that it would take eighteen bowls of rice porridge a day to meet the energy requirements of an eight-month-old child, and forty bowls to provide minimal protein requirements. But adding calories in the form of oils and a protein source (fish powder, egg, peanuts, or soybean) could convert rice porridge into excellent weaning food. Cost-effective methods were developed to expand immunization among poor communities, to reduce perinatal mortality, and to introduce iodized salt to prevent mental retardation and cretinism in mountain areas.

Each county evolved its own financing system. A 1985 study to improve local financing found that a marked difference in immunization rates was directly related to the economic status of counties. The Ministry of Public Health advised counties to have families pay village doctors 10 fen (about three U.S. cents at that time) for each immunization. However, poor counties set the rate at 5 fen to make immunizations affordable, yet these counties still had poor coverage. In rich counties families were paying 40 fen, and coverage was almost complete. Then one county tried a different approach, one that addressed the concerns of parents rather than government interest in recovering costs, and the innovation spread quickly and spontaneously to most of the other counties. Each family with a new baby signed a contract with the health system, and for 10 yuan (about three U.S. dollars at that time) the baby received all immunizations. The contract specified that if the baby developed any of the six immunizable diseases, all medical care would be free and the health system would pay the family an indemnity of 100 yuan or more, depending on the disease. The indemnity provision convinced families that this was a good deal and that immunizations could be trusted.

Scaling Up

Over thirteen years the project moved from 10 pilot counties with a high per-capita cost to implementation in 400 counties with much lower per-capita costs. Scaling up occurred in the following stages.

Stage 1: In 1982 ten counties were covered, with an average annual allocation per county of $250,000 in outside funds. Much of this funding supported local research. A focus on the major health problems of children significantly reduced disease and death.

Stage 2: In 1984 twenty more counties were added, with an average annual allocation per county of $200,000 in outside funds. The impact in these counties was equivalent to that in the original ten.

Stage 3: In 1986 sixty-five more counties were added, with an average annual allocation per county of $100,000. Both the impact and support from officials and experts were smaller, and implementation was considerably slower and less effective.

Stage 4: In 1988, 300 of the poorest counties were added, with an average annual allocation per county of $70,000. The emphasis shifted to systematic training of staff in how to use the interventions, drawing on the experience in the first two sets of counties. (This move taught us the importance of establishing the SCALE learning process instead of merely hoping that learning would occur spontaneously.) We also focused on stronger management and evolved a useful tool: at a special conference in Xian contracts were signed between the counties and government, clearly stating the expectations for all partners. We soon incorporated this contractual concept into every county's annual work plan. These efforts produced improvements in mortality and quality of care, and project innovations began spreading to nonproject counties.

Stage 5: In 1993 five more counties were added, where action focused on integrating family planning with maternal and child health services.

Stage 6: To help additional poor counties and those with high mortality, a World Bank loan to the Ministry of Health in 1995 supported extension of maternal and child health services in selected poor provinces, with an emphasis on training and management.

National Policy Framework and External Funding

Rapid extension occurred thanks to a clear, consistent, top-down policy. At the start of China's economic reforms in 1980, the director of planning in the Ministry of Public Health told us: "The new policy is that in Beijing we decide what will be done, but local units will decide how they will do it." (This is a good definition of the difference between strategy and tactics.) Throughout the project, county officials were encouraged to adapt and to give considerable autonomy to community-based programs.

As decentralization proceeded, local units gained confidence and took more initiative in implementation and local problemsolving. At first local decisionmakers used UNICEF funds chiefly to purchase sophisticated equipment from outside the country. As the project matured, county governments began using donor funds to purchase locally produced equipment and supplies while allocating their own funds to improve staffing at township and village levels. A continuing major problem is that so far, efforts at simplification have not discouraged the potentially dangerous overuse of drugs, which is a major source of income for village doctors.

Mobilizing Province, Prefecture, and County Support for Change

In the first ten counties, social mobilization depended mostly on the interaction of national and international maternal and child health experts with local officials and community representatives. County personnel joined with community staff to run services in experimental townships and to develop local adaptations. Community representatives suggested many of the best adaptations. Once a new, comprehensive approach had been developed, the experimental townships served as training sites for workers from other townships (SCALE Squared extension).

In the second and third stages of expansion, national MCH officials again worked directly with county and township leaders. Direct replication worked well in the first twenty counties, but in the next sixty-five the contributions of national and provincial staff were greatly diluted. Little effort was devoted to training. The experience made clear the needs for more-cost-effective training methods and for better management of innovations.

Planning for the project's extension to 300 counties led to development of a new strategy for mobilizing and managing sustained expansion. Dr. Wang Fenglan, director of the Maternal and Child Health Department, had observed the success of community-level negotiations ten years earlier, when commune land had been returned to individual households and contracts between families and local authorities had redefined their respective obligations. In 1989 the Maternal and Child Health Department convened a major meeting in the city of Xian attended by county governors and health officials from the 300 counties and by provincial government and health officials. The leaders who attended were politicians, and the political focus in China was on making money. This meeting proved to be an exceptional opportunity to show the relationship between good health and a prospering economy. When they understood the relationship, then it was possible to set up a contract system in which the leaders made commitments.

In these intensive negotiations among county, provincial, and national levels of government, the concept of contracts emerged as a particularly useful tool to keep the partnership in balance. Discussions went late into the night as leaders from some of the poorest counties and provinces struggled with decisions about how much money they could commit to solving their own health problems. Eventually most counties, prefectures, and provinces committed at least three yuan for every one committed by national and international sources. The most promising outcomes were the participants' recognition of the long-term implications of the contractual commitments and their decision to include maternal and child health for the first time in many county and provincial five-year health plans.

Mobilization of government leadership did not stop with the Xian meeting. In 1992 the Maternal and Child Health Department organized an inter-regional program in which county leaders traveled to other counties to assess each other's progress in meeting the Xian commitments. Selected county and provincial government leaders participated with health professionals in management training and in study tours, where they observed successful county efforts with maternal and child health problems such as supervision of village doctors and promoting oral rehydration therapy. In 1994 the Maternal and Child Health Department expanded social mobilization efforts by encouraging prefecture leaders to establish and supervise training activities in still more counties.

Key Components in Going to SCALE

Action learning. Training for community health workers has become increasingly experience-based and participatory as they practice technical skills and learn new ways of communicating knowledge to local people. At the 300-county stage, the project invested heavily in building capacity at all levels by introducing new techniques for encouraging participation (such as intervention modules and role-playing) for better management of the extension of training. A village midwife from rural Xinjiang Province, when asked about the new training methods, told evaluators: "Before, the teacher never knew who was sleeping or who was learning or who was writing in the notebooks. All the teaching, all the notes were just for the exam. This time we didn't have notes, but we could understand. This new method is good for us. The role-playing—we laugh a lot, but we learn, too. We get drawn into it in spite of ourselves. You can't help yourself, you just get drawn in."

The Maternal and Child Health Department evaluated the training continuously. When grassroots workers needed more practice in specific skills, their next training sessions included supervised practice of those skills. Training also focused on communication and counseling. Project research revealed that many women and children lacked access to maternal and child health services and needed to learn self-care. Health workers learned how to counsel clients about their own responsibility to improve health practices, such as home management of diarrhea and knowing when a sick child or high-risk pregnancy should be brought to a hospital.

Priority interventions. On the basis of surveys, practical experience, and national research on carefully selected interventions, each region focused on cost-effective solutions for its priority health problems. Six "packages" of interventions for priority problems were developed nationally with the option to include additional local concerns. Standard modules and manuals were prepared for village and township health staff.

In 1993 five new counties focused on improving the quality of reproductive health services by integrating family planning and maternal and child health activities. The project tested low-cost interventions for childhood nutrition, maternal mortality, childhood accidents, and injury from cold. Follow-up projects supported by the Ford Foundation and the United Nations Fund for Population Activities continued to promote integration of services as China moves away from rigid implementation of its one-child policy.

Exponential extension. By 1995 the Model Counties project was reaching 160 million people distributed in every province, including half of the poorest counties in China. It had become large enough to generate a movement toward use of its simplified interventions, training approaches, printed materials, and supervision methods in every county of China. Many provinces deliberately selected at least one county per prefecture as a training center (SCALE Squared) so that project innovations and capacity building could reach the largest possible number of health staff. The capacity of all provincial training and health education staff was substantially upgraded, and the national government announced its intention of extending participatory training methods to at least one-third of nonproject counties in every province.

Institutionalizing Innovations

Reconfiguring roles into a three-way partnership. The key to sustainability and continuing development in the provision of routine maternal and child health services was to combine bottom-up and top-down approaches, thus institutionalizing the new practices and values. For provincial and local leaders and health staff to take ownership, they had to learn new roles. A cascade strategy extended training: national and regional experts trained provincial trainers, who trained county-level trainers, who then trained the grassroots workers. Some slippage in quality was more than offset by the participation of a critical mass of trainers at each level. The first training materials were developed with guidance from international specialists. In 1993 Chinese master trainers independently created the third set of training materials and a complete set of manuals that included audiovisual aids. They then organized training-of-trainers workshops for the whole country and used their new skills to plan and implement other health projects.

Data-driven decisionmaking. Evaluation activities helped foster a culture of learning from experience. Outside evaluation was used to validate local self-evaluation. For the first 10 counties, six of China's best medical universities did the field research to test interventions and adapt them to Chinese conditions. They also guided implementation in the counties. For the 300-county expansion, Shanghai Medical University had an external evaluation team monitor new implementations by gathering precise quantitative data about the training and its results. They also conducted surveys on knowledge, attitudes, and practice and quality-of-care studies to track improvements, identify gaps, and help in reprogramming project activities. An evaluation survey in 1994 found statistically significant improvements in infant, child, and maternal mortality over the findings of the 1989 baseline survey.

Financing and role reallocation. Alternative approaches to financing health care were needed, especially for the curative services that people were usually willing to pay for. The earlier barefoot doctors had stopped working when their communal funding through work points was terminated. Officials knew that China was too diverse to permit implementation of a single model of self-financing. Some counties pursued strong control by county authorities; others decentralized decisions to townships and villages. In most counties curative care permitted fee-for-service private practice by village doctors and referral hospitals. Some affluent and well-organized counties retained health cooperatives with mixed patterns of local insurance. Some counties used money from county business enterprises to fund essential services for education and health. Preventive services also had mixed sources of financing. In some poorer counties, in exchange for the privilege of having a private practice, village doctors were expected to provide preventive services for their needy neighbors with little reimbursement, while in other counties they were paid well. The diversity of field trials spawned vast experimentation. As counties exchanged information on their methods and results, the most effective were commonly adopted.

Emerging Problems in the Poorest Parts of China

Large regional differences in economic status have recently created major problems in poor areas and for poor people in all areas. As China's Ministry of Health continues to experiment with various financing arrangements, including different kinds of cooperatives, dedicated taxes, a variety of insurance schemes, and projects to link improved health and economic development, the problems of rural health financing, the nationwide trend toward privatization, and growing inequities in services are creating a rapid decline in coverage and in quality of care for the poor.[4] On a visit in 2000 to poor villages in a northwestern province, we found that quality of care is worsening in the poorer half of the country. Where economic conditions are rapidly improving, the programs described in this chapter seem to be having a continuing positive impact. In the poorest counties, however, local health units tend to overuse medicines and injectables to augment their low salaries. Another growing problem is the reuse of inadequately sterilized equipment, a practice that increases the potential transmission of viruses such as hepatitis B and C and HIV/AIDS. This problem illustrates the importance of ongoing national surveillance. Without outside supervision, community-run health programs may not identify such dangers or mobilize a response. This is especially true if commercial interests are concurrently promoting practices (such as the excessive use of drugs) that may be exacerbating the problem.

Lessons from the Model Counties Project

Health systems around the world can learn much from what a large, poor, and densely populated country accomplished in its thirteen-year transition from a communal structure to family decisionmaking. Working in balanced partnerships, communities, officials, and experts used bottom-up, top-down, and outside-in methods for scaling up. At the beginning of the effort, officials moved as a group to each of the early experimental counties for intense dialogue with local people. This approach stimulated surprise and then enthusiasm as people gained a sense of control through shared participation and shared commitments in the form of contracts.

The Maternal and Child Health Department's heavy investment in educating and mobilizing government leaders at all levels paid off in the leaders' continuing support for maternal and child care. This priority in turn motivated field staff. As academic experts shared control with local people, they began to see the difference in usefulness between solutions based in scientific theory alone and solutions that were both practical and economically feasible. Village people learned much by being able to ask on-site experts practical questions, but they also realized that they had much wisdom to share with the experts.

Although China's efforts to improve the health of women and children equitably still face major challenges, the Model Counties project shows the potential of the SCALE approach to support rapid and effective implementation through sustained modifications in programs.

PART V

SEED-SCALE Handbooks

Typically books advocating social change only describe the process. The next three chapters are designed as handbooks for those who are actually implementing community-based programs. Here we consolidate the lessons drawn from fieldwork worldwide and explain how to implement the SEED-SCALE approach. Although we believe that SEED-SCALE offers a standard process for finding solutions in widely different situations—fitting the ecology, economics, and culture of each locale—we are also well aware that for those attempting to effect social change the core guideline must always be: "Be prepared for surprises."

SEED-SCALE Principles
and Criteria

The Three Operative Principles

Our field experience indicates that three activities are so important that they become principles for successful social action:

Forming a three-way partnership of community members, officials, and experts

Basing action on locally specific data

Using a community work plan to change collective behavior

If one of the partners seeks to control the others, if one or more partners believe they know beforehand what the data will say and therefore skip data collection, or if any partner refuses to change behavior, development will fail to move toward just and lasting change. Together, these three create the foundation on which community action can grow.

The three principles operate synergistically. Our review of development efforts over the last few decades shows that when only one or two of the principles were used, even spectacular initial successes eventually lost momentum and effectiveness. When all three are functioning simultaneously, the impact is greater than when only one or two are operating.

Principle One: Forming a Three-Way Partnership

Two types of partnerships are needed for sustainable development. One is external, involving collaboration among community, officials, and experts. This is the basic three-way partnership. The other is internal, involving collaboration within a community to frame and act on priorities. We discuss the second type of partnership (calling it collaboration) in the latter half of this chapter as one of the criteria by which successful action can be measured. Collaboration within the community will often grow when the external three-way partnership is in place.

Many involved in development planning continue to debate the issue of who should be in control, a debate sometimes called the question of leadership. On one side are top-down activists, who say: "Development by the people is too slow. Someone with authority is needed to get things going and hold factions together." On the other side are advocates of grassroots, community-led development, who say: "A community develops only from itself. People's control should determine all activities, or there will be no sustainable action."

The debate is artificial; both approaches are needed in a constantly shifting balance. Top and bottom must work in partnership, putting an end to wasteful arguments about who is in charge. Yet even a genuine two-way partnership will not accomplish change, not only because communities and officials tend to remain stuck in their separate perspectives, but also because neither of these partners is likely to know the most current ideas and research findings or to have the special skills needed to put them into practice. All successful development leadership that we have studied closely has included a third viewpoint, that of experts (EmpowerMentors) who brought to the process an understanding of local causal relationships and knowledge of a wider range of options. An outside-in perspective is as essential as the bottom-up and top-down.

Communities. Communities, not officials or experts, are the foundation of sustainable action. A *community,* as we use the term, is any group that has something in common and the potential for acting together. Communities are whole groups, not one or several factions that try to speak for the whole. Communities are hard to get functioning early in the change process—often certain factions stay outside at first—but in time larger participation can grow. Community mobilization builds most reliably from successes. Here we explore their central role in the partnership.

Communities, whether through ambition or through romanticism, often overestimate their capacity, believing that they can do more than in fact they know how to do. Overconfidence in community capacity is especially common when several community members perceive themselves to be experts on a subject and want to press their neighbors forward. Such people can do much to empower their community, but they need partners to create an enabling environment for their commitment and to provide skills and ideas that they lack. It is useful to have knowledgeable people on hand (who may even be experts in other community applications), but it is confusing when local citizens also try to be the experts (as we found ourselves, in the episode described in Chapter 5). Experts are better off staying in their role as community members and serving as links to experts.

China's Great Leap Forward in the 1950s was perhaps the most massive demonstration ever that people cannot develop on their own. An erroneous belief that community capacity was present led national leaders to persuade local people to industrialize on their own. The result was a famine that caused over 30 million deaths and set back development for hundreds of millions of people for a decade.

Similarly, local charismatic leaders, though providing inspirational starts, seldom produce more than short-term success. They may be effective in bringing factions together and in speeding up effort, but they tend to lack the creativity and breadth of vision needed to nurture a community's goals and to sustain momentum. They need to be part of a community team, stepping back as others develop competence. Charismatic leadership may over time build dependency on the leader, not interdependence in the community. However, this is not always so; Abraham Lincoln used his charisma to build the capacities of his partners and to launch policies that transformed the capacity of American communities.

Officials. Officials are most often politicians or administrators who represent the government; they are the decisionmakers overseeing budgets, policy, laws, administrative regulations, and in some cases the issuing of professional credentials. Often they are service personnel in health, education, agriculture, and local administration—people who are paid to help. Or they may be outside government but with formal affiliations in business, nongovernmental organizations, religious agencies, and civic groups. This is the group that creates the environment for making change occur. Officials are not the same as leaders who represent the community. They may live in the community, but their authority comes from outside, and it is this authority that allows them to shape an enabling environment.

Because officials are usually interested in protecting their positions, they often pose great obstacles to real, systematic change. Seeing themselves as the sponsors and conduits of all development services, they may feel threatened by new initiatives that are not under their control. Officials will therefore usually see a balanced partnership with either community or experts as unnecessary—they will see themselves as being in the senior position. Even if they accept the need for partnership, they may try to imbalance the partnership and assume control through directives, detailed control of services, or money. This orientation of officials makes it hard for them to accept the community as other than employees; as a result, *officials are usually the main obstacles to forming an effective three-way partnership.*

Increasingly now others are claiming the mantle of officialdom. Business, religious, and NGO leaders try to acquire official legitimacy and displace government officials by alleging that the official structure has proven itself incapable in a particular way. But attempts to isolate officials ultimately weaken initiatives. Each partner must fulfill his or her role. Where there is weakness, the role or the partner needs to be strengthened, not side-stepped. Where capacity is weak, we have found SEED-SCALE an effective way to break into doable steps the tasks that each partner needs to do.

Experts. Experts come in many types, and with a wide range of costs and qualifications. Their knowledge may be scientific, social, fiscal, managerial, or derived from one of any number of technical fields or disciplines. The primary contribution of experts is to provide knowledge and skills. These commodities can then empower the process of change.

One type of expert, the donor, stands apart. Donors almost deserve separate categorization as a fourth partner. But they should most emphatically *not* be permanent partners, for then their donations will breed dependency instead of development. Donors very often blend opinions and technical skills with financial incentives in order to gain cooperation. The resources they contribute can be catalysts for development; this is both the role that is desired and the role that can get out of hand. Donors very often are susceptible to falling into the three expert traps described below.

Experts in their many types usually enjoy sponsorship by academic, governmental, or private institutions, large businesses, international agencies, or professional associations. They fill several essential roles that neither a community nor officials bring to the partnership:

Knowledge of development processes (what has worked and in what circumstances)

Technical skills to simplify and help sustain options and interventions brought in from outside for local adaptation

The capacity to broker relationships between community and officials to enhance cooperation

Experts bring much that is good, but they may also bring problems: ideas that are inappropriate, outside priorities that override local priorities, an emphasis on professional prestige that distorts local vision, pet hypotheses or experiences that are not transferable, definitions of development or theories that do not fit local realities, and, most commonly, a tendency to prescribe ambitious blueprints for social action. Sometimes experts are engaged because they are available rather than because they have the skills needed. Inappropriate advice by experts is often the reason development efforts fail. Robert Chambers (himself an expert) after decades of field observations has identified three traps that experts must avoid:[1]

Professionalism: they become more concerned about their own roles, embedded beliefs, and personal advancement than about local needs.

Distance: they often work from offices outside the community, rely on secondary data, and are socially apart and professionally arrogant.

Power: their identity as experts leads them to try to control local processes and to exaggerate their own role rather than educating and empowering community members and leaders.

The idea of partnership is not new; nearly all community-assistance documents produced by the World Bank, the U.S. Agency for International Development, and other bilateral and multilateral agencies now include mandates for partnership. But in practice these projects are structured in ways that make partnerships unequal, and most of the power remains with those providing money.

Outsiders (such as the media, skeptics, and academics) can help to assure a balance by asking the right questions to stimulate community action: Who attends meetings? Who speaks at those meetings? Who makes the decisions? Is a three-way partnership operating, or has one or two of the partners taken over? Have weaker partners taken refuge in local cultural traditions and passive resistance? If so, the claims of partnership are false.

Business is a central player in development. Because of the important role business plays, it is often assigned the role of a separate, autonomous actor. But business is not a separate partner. In each of our projects the role of business was different, and that role changed over time. In various cases, business people acted from community perspectives or brought in outside expertise or influenced and joined government decisionmaking. Business can be a vital energizing force because it is almost uniquely able to participate in and cut across all three partnership roles. On the other hand, business can also be supremely disabling if it chooses a short-term perspective for immediate profit and ignores the larger, longer-term vision essential for sustained development.

In our field projects, when we discuss the role of business we say that while communities provide bottom-up input, officials work from the top down, and experts come from the outside in, business, because of its changing roles, operates by "going around." This going-around role also applies to other powerful social groups that in varying communities play different leadership roles: religion, education, media, sports, and, certainly most important of all, women. Each of these is a different part of the community and must be dealt with as a collective.

Principle Two: Basing Action on Locally Specific Data

People are by nature reluctant to face risk, and the more failures the partners in a project have had, the less willing they will be to attempt innovation. Communities that have been exploited more often than helped will shun new initiatives, and in most cases their leaders are reluctant anyway to upset the status quo lest they lose their power base. Experts may be reluctant to try new ways because their reputations are based on successes, not on learning from failures. Officials often view change as a threat to their jobs and established authority.

The surest way to convert risk into probability of success is to base action on locally specific, constantly updated data. When local people can gather accurate information about their perceived problems, natural resources, culture, geography, and financial parameters, the local groundedness of their action makes success more likely, and their shared ownership of that knowledge galvanizes them to work together.[2]

Localized data are the functional opposite of opinions. Most commonly, decisions are made on the basis of the opinion of the person with the most power. Power, however, does not necessarily confer accurate knowledge. But protecting decisions from abuses of power by collecting a wide range of opinions—perhaps even soliciting everyone's opinion, as is the growing practice in participatory decisionmaking—can lead to equally incorrect decisions. Opinions can be passionate and convincing, yet also totally wrong. Moreover, where there are two, three, or more opinions, the result may not be a decision but an argument—or a breakdown in collaboration. But when action is driven by data and based on a clear assessment of priorities, decisionmaking can transcend differences and point toward the most efficient path to change. Data-driven action scratches where the community itches.

Community data-gathering is often not impartial. If one party controls the data, the process may be used only to confirm the party's opinions. Officials can use government data to reinforce their power and influence communities' decisions. Experts are prone to take data out of the community and use it for their own professional advancement, making it sophisticated rather than simplifying it to help local people make decisions. Community members often have data that are mostly a litany of horror stories. Everyone, whether an outsider or an insider, will see what she or he wants to see in the data. Participatory decisionmaking requires a commonly accepted set of data, and to get a database that all accept, it helps to have everyone involved in collecting the data. Working together to collect data is a new activity, but one that is very important for communities.

Existing data can provide a starting point. Traditionally data came from government or academic statistics, but often such information relates only to certain sectors or is out-of-date. Experts may have data, but almost always those are based on onetime surveys. Communities also have data, but they are often descriptive (such as tax, demographic, or production statistics) and do not help to prioritize community needs. Nevertheless it is important to bring these into the overall database, and the need for additional data-gathering may prove minimal.

A further problem is that in the past fifty years increasingly rigorous procedures for data collection have evolved, and now primarily serve increasingly sophisticated research purposes that have their own justification. These efforts to make research more and more precise and objective tend to narrow the focus of measurement to test specific hypotheses, but in doing so they reduce its usefulness to ordinary people in their decisionmaking. Local people, officials, and even experts from other fields now find data collection and interpretation confusing. Practical decisionmaking demands a return to simplified data systems.

During the past two decades several techniques have evolved as alternatives to rigorous, research-oriented data-collection procedures. Newer methods called variously Participatory Rural Appraisals (PRAs), Rapid Assessment Procedures (RAPs), and Planning, Learning, and Action (PLA) achieve compromises between precision and simplicity, speed and local participation.[3] Our approach, called SEED (Self-Evaluation for Effective Decisionmaking) and discussed in Chapter 21, combines the strengths of these methods but avoids their tendency to use opinions and instead focuses on finding objective facts. But any method used, even if it cannot build from facts, should incorporate the following features:

- Community members should perform at least part of the data collection themselves, using simplified methods they understand. Only then will they trust the findings and act on them—and typically the cost will be less.
- Data collection should be ongoing in order to monitor progress and to provide clear evidence over time of what is working.
- The community's perspective of its own reality should holistically balance economics, social needs, natural resources, and aspirations—and not be controlled by one sector.

Principle Three: Using a Community Work Plan to Change Behavior

Communities need help in modifying behaviors; otherwise they would have mastered their problems long ago. But help must be appropriately balanced. Officials and experts will inevitably overestimate how much the community needs them. In this context of shifting perceptions, control should remain with the community, and officials and experts should move to supportive roles.

Allocating roles appropriate to both the community's needs and people's capacities can be difficult if partners see role reallocation as a threat to their status or livelihood. Not surprisingly, leaders are almost always the persons who find it hardest to adjust to changes in their roles. After all, they may be asked to surrender control of legal, financial, personnel, or other decision-making powers and perquisites that reinforce their status. Some of these requests they may simply not be able to grant in the way being asked, but to meet the participatory objective they should seek to find a way.

In the general uncertainty about how to modify behavior, leaders will continue to try to tell others what to do. Experts will think that only they understand the problems and the solutions, and community members may think that all they need is enough money to spend as they see fit. Yet the *expectations for each partner must change as development goes forward.* To guide this adaptation each year following the analysis of data, it is useful to conduct an activity we call functional analysis. Regularizing behavior change in this way not only reduces the risk that one party will grab a dominant role; it also encourages people to achieve a balance between what is best for them and what is best for their community. The next chapter explains in detail how to do this functional analysis.

The needs and roles of communities differ in each of the three dimensions of SCALE. In SCALE One communities need techniques and models to learn from and adapt. When a community is functioning as a SCALE Squared center it needs assistance in monitoring progress and in sustaining dialogue to determine what to attempt next and how best to implement it. When development goes to scale, communities need SCALE Cubed enabling frameworks. All these roles require changing behavior to meet community needs.

Officials have to adapt their roles to changing needs. At the beginning of

SCALE One, some aspects of a traditional, paternalistic role may be appropriate tools for energizing the community. At this point officials are coordinators, providing training through workshops, programs in informal education, data collection and analysis, and possibly offering seed funding to jump-start data-driven priorities. But they need to avoid the easy slide from building capacity to producing dependency. For communities that become SCALE Squared centers, officials work more as teachers, advocating the process, assiduously avoiding trying to make the centers into glamorous but unreplicable showcases. Always officials need to come on-site, get involved, build confidence in simple, adaptable methods, and support appropriate standards that can be extended. During SCALE Cubed extension, officials become cheerleaders and promoters, encouraging other communities to join the process, to adopt and adapt. As successes bring praise to them, SCALE Cubed officials share recognition with the wider network of community members, departments, nongovernmental organizations, businesses, and civic and religious leaders, avoiding the temptation to claim credit for work that everyone knows they did not really do. During this process they concentrate on nurturing an ever more enabling environment.

Experts tend to know what change is possible, and their catalytic role is to integrate local wisdom, scientific knowledge, and experience from elsewhere. With SCALE One communities their roles are to stimulate and train as they bring in new ideas, new data, and new skills. Because they are usually outsiders, they have less to lose and so can take more risks, perhaps challenge local power blocs, and accept blame. Their contributions become most relevant when they do fieldwork on-site, deepening their understanding through local involvement. In the SCALE Squared stage, experts assume a more academic role, teaching, doing research, monitoring, and trying to blend objectivity with immediacy. Experts can help SCALE Squared centers learn how to share their lessons in ways flexible enough to be useful in daily life. During SCALE Cubed extension, experts not only teach but also help organize networks and guide policy reform in bridging actions that nurture a learning revolution. Communication experts can guide a local movement using the SCALE Squared centers to increase the number of SCALE One communities trying to change.

Six Criteria by Which to Monitor Progress

The three principles above seem to be universal, leading to successful implementation wherever development is attempted. But the six criteria that test progress—equity, sustainability, interdependence, holism, collaboration, and iteration—are site-specific. Each community must define what each criterion means in the local context of culture, economics, and environment.

Criterion One: Equity

Inequity seems to be the prevailing human condition, and ongoing global economic restructuring is widening the gap between rich and poor. Robert Chambers, using data from David Korten, has nicely distinguished the worldwide patterns and pervasive character of disparities. (See Table 20.1.)

For half a century, socialism promised to dramatically reduce or eliminate inequity, but in most countries socialism proved corruptible. Capitalism has offered itself as a people-centered alternative, but as the table indicates, there is no compelling reason to believe that capitalism by itself nurtures equity. Under capitalism, those with advantages too frequently seem to take advantage. As corporations continue to restructure human relations through market forces and the political process, they have gained immunity from governmental controls, and global disparities are increasing dramatically.

Perfect equity is surely unattainable. But the pursuit of equity is more than a moral imperative; it is also practical, since it mobilizes a momentum that benefits all. The SEED-SCALE paradigm offers a practical way to achieve equity because it creates communitywide dialogue about whole-community priorities. It will not produce a dramatic revolution, but it can systematically build capacity among the underclass, focus the middle class, and broaden the vision of the overclass.

People know when they are getting poorer, when they are working longer and with less security. People have memories of the past, and today telecommunications enable them to see beyond the walls of privilege. Inequity leads first to fear, then to guards around houses, then to civic instability.

Equity co-opts unrest. In a newly unified Germany, Otto von Bismarck heard murmuring from an aging population and funded pensions and health

TABLE 20.1. Profile of the Equity Gap

Global position:	Overclass	Middle class	Underclass
Category of consumption	Overconsumers (1.1 billion)	Moderates (3.3 billion)	Marginals (1.1 billion)
Income per capita	Over U.S. $7,500	U.S. $700–7,500	Less than $700
Diet	Meat, packaged foods, soft drinks	Grain, clean water	Unbalanced, insufficient grain, unsafe drinking water
Calories consumed	Too many	About right	Too few
Transport	Private cars	Bicycles, public transport	Foot
Materials	Throwaways	Durables	Local biomass
Shelter	Spacious, climatized	Modest	Rudimentary
Clothing	Image conscious	Functional	Secondhand or scraps
Health	Diseases of affluence	Healthy behavior	Infections and malnutrition

Source: Adapted from Robert Chambers, using data from David Korten, in *Whose Reality Counts? Putting the First Last* (London: Intermediate Technology, 1997), p. 8.

services for the elderly. During the Great Depression in the United States, Franklin Roosevelt launched a welfare economy. In the final days of apartheid in South Africa, Prime Minister F. W. de Klerk started expanding opportunities for blacks. In all these instances, promoting equity did not mean taking prosperity from the overclass, but giving impetus to those with less so that their advancement would narrow the gap. Equity is more than a moral argument; it provides a practical glue to hold together collective action. A community with a commitment to equity moves as a whole.

Equity will not come as a by-product of economic growth, leader-community partnerships, tax reform, environmentally friendly action, or even holistic services. Achieving equity requires an intentional focus on narrowing the gap between those with power, property, or privilege and those without. Improving life for the disadvantaged also improves conditions for the wealthy. But communities cannot achieve such a focus acting on their own. Rigidities and discrimination are solidly established in all communities; local exploiters can be more efficient than those who are distant. Achieving equity (like achieving sustainability, discussed below) requires top-down and outside-in pressure and a special role for socially conscious experts, often acting through nongovernmental organizations, who operate as watchdogs over the process of community change.

Outside agents will be most effective when they use objective assessments such as SEED to guide social direction. Because the pursuit of equity builds incrementally, it is helpful to have data that mark progress in an objective way and keep discussions impersonal. A practical method of systematic data-gathering is surveillance for equity.[4] Surveillance is a standard epidemiological method to measure progress in control of specific diseases. It involves monitoring not only changes in priority problems and how these are differentially affecting the community, but also quick-response capacity in services and the community—that is, it monitors both the community's status and its ability to take action when the status starts to change. Since problems tend to concentrate in needy families, surveillance for equity greatly reduces duplication of effort, in contrast to the use of separate systems to track changing needs in categorical sectors such as agriculture, income distribution, health status, and the like. Because equity covers a range of social conditions, monitoring it provides a reliable indication of general social advancement.

Equity and sustainability are probably the two most important indicators to monitor in order to keep development on course.

Criterion Two: Sustainability

A community develops by consuming resources. *Sustainable development,* as we use the term, is a use of resources that assures continued availability. Achieving this goal requires cultural, environmental, and economic adjustments.

Cultural sustainability is crucial. As global change threatens traditional values and social structures, unforeseen rifts threaten community cohesion and even survival. The three principles of the site-sensitive SEED-SCALE process—forming three-way partnerships, basing action on local data, and modifying behaviors—help communities mend cultural fracture lines. Traditions can evolve; new festivals can be created; cohesion can be redefined. Cultural sustainability is not holding to old-fashioned ways, but blending innovations in such a manner that old ways remain beautiful along with the new. It is the remodeling of a house to introduce new conveniences while retaining its heritage and beauty.

Restoring cultural strength comes to seem necessary mostly after it has been diminished or threatened, and introducing practical programs at that point is extremely difficult. It is always difficult to gain support for preventing change that has not yet occurred. Fortunately, the practices that support cultural sustainability, as many case studies in this volume show, emerge when action follows the three principles and six criteria. In particular, regular data collection allows communities to track and anticipate its results.

Environmental sustainability has been a centerpiece of international development discourse ever since the 1989 United Nations Brundtland Commission report made the case for a global reorientation of development action and the 1992 Earth Summit in Rio tried to create an agenda for action.[5] The vision was clear, but the way to get there was not. Some countries, such as China, Costa Rica, and Norway, are building coordinated national programs, but they tend to be limited to protecting natural resources instead of redefining and redirecting development. A new strategy must move toward sustaining resources and reducing pollution by bringing people and nature together in large, integrated frameworks. Development needs to be seen as the whole, balanced process of social change rather than just economic acceleration. Development activities need to be connected to the level on which they are making their impact. Case studies of Kerala, the Adirondacks, Tibet, Curitiba, and urban agriculture offer practical demonstrations of such a strategy.

If the development that all people seek is to be sustained, the consequences of development must be linked to the larger frameworks driving it. A good example is the global matrix of timber. Timber harvesting now exceeds forest regeneration in many parts of the world. Deforestation is at the root of many environmental crises—not only the progressive loss of biodiversity but also soil erosion and loss of water quantity and quality. Some countries such as Japan and Norway have raised the price of their own timber, making domestic timber cutting more expensive. Other countries such as China and the United States are attempting to plant more trees than they harvest so as to have a net positive rate of forest regrowth. However, these activities do not take into account the fact that national timber reserves are a collective global resource, like the air we breathe. A few countries have adopted "certified sustainable lumber" programs in which trees are grown through sustainable practices and sold at higher prices.

Although new national policies are essential, taking action to reconfigure the web of factors affecting timber prices can be done on very modest levels. Paul Smith's College, in northern New York State, is the only forestry institution in the world that both teaches and uses sustainable forestry practices. On the college's twenty thousand acres, trees are grown and harvested so that overall forest quality improves each year; practices are monitored by an external commission that then certifies the timber as sustainably harvested. The added costs are offset by the higher prices paid for the certified "green" lumber.

Increasing global concern for the environment is also increasing economic opportunities. As our understanding of the dynamics of sustainability grows, so, surely, will the options being explored, including the use of wood and recycled wood, the manufacture of plywood and furniture from fast-growing bamboo, and the use of reprocessed synthetics and metals.

Although none of these programs alone will eliminate the critical planetary threat of deforestation, each is contributing one part to a solution. As occurred in the Child Survival Revolution, momentum seems to be building to produce a package of conceptual breakthroughs. To achieve environmental sustainability we will need to adapt this package to each niche worldwide. Parallel packages of solutions will be needed for the other great environmental challenges, such as global warming and sustainable use of limited resources, through finding actions that are effective locally.

Economic sustainability is a third increasing priority, to compensate for distorted practices that have encouraged communities and countries to borrow more money than they can repay. Not only do large loans place unfair repayment burdens on future generations; they also produce accumulated indebtedness, becoming an ever-larger share of current budgets. When communities are encumbered by such loans, their decisionmaking focus shifts from social development to the imperative of repayment.

A second concern is that outside money can destroy self-reliance, that core of integrity necessary for development. Communities are more likely to use money responsibly when at least part of the investment comes from their funds that they must repay or risk losing other resources. When people see money as free, when large (or small) amounts can be claimed without local accountability, their goals change from development to getting more money. The arrival of outside money (especially international development loans) in short-term cycles and with rigid conditions kills self-reliance, creates dependency, and eliminates people's sense of ownership.

A third threat to economic sustainability is the tendency to measure development in terms of the amount of money spent. That changes the focus from community priorities to the donor's magnanimity. World Bank officers are judged almost solely in terms of how much money they move, private foundations in terms of the size of their endowments, and politicians in terms of their ability to access public funding or grants. Such a shorthand characterization of a project makes it easy to lose sight of whether or not the project works. To measure progress in terms of the amount of money spent is to measure in terms of inputs rather than outcomes or, even more usefully, process. Almost every project requires infusions of money, but the definition of need must come from community priorities, not from the number of dollars available.

Criterion Three: Interdependence

The antithesis of development is dependency. Development, when sustainable and equitable, creates healthy interdependencies. Linkages within and between communities are strengthened, as well as linkages between development sectors such as health and education. Interdependence creates webs of opportunities, expanding access to resources, people, economic reserves, technology, skills, and knowledge.

Many communities worldwide are giving up local control over their resources in the belief that they are gaining security as part of a larger, globalized, interdependent system. In reality, when these communities give up control they move backward, becoming dependent on external market forces. When dependency increases—even though people may be making money and receiving more development services—community empowerment shrinks. There is an alternative to simply surrendering control or the equally unhelpful position of isolationism; this alternative is interdependency.

A community achieves self-reliant interdependence by retaining control of its destiny even as it builds relationships with outside groups. Resources from outside—new paradigms, technology, and specialized skills—are essential components of development. Interdependence involves recognizing that one group may have things that others need and promoting access to those things. In forming the expanded relationships that make these exchanges possible, however, communities must ask if these relationships are also making them more vulnerable. The answer is seldom a simple yes or no, since economic and cultural forces pull both ways, in tension and compression. Pressure in one place radiates response throughout the system, and the various parts of the system accommodate the pressure by redistributing it. The process is a manifestation of tensegrity. Such interdependence is impossible when the forces involved are controlled by mega-organizations, whose decisionmakers are not responsible to anyone outside their group.

A useful indicator of interdependence is whether relationships and transactions separate people from their community or engage them in it. A second indicator is whether decisionmaking about the community has moved increasingly outside local control. It is hard to predict whether certain actions will promote interdependency rather than dependency, but assessment in hindsight will make the direction clear. The annual SEED process of creating the community work plan regularizes this hindsight identification and allows corrections that would otherwise be difficult.

Physician-patient relationships afford a useful analogy to the difference between dependency and interdependency. In one pattern, the physician is the expert in control; he pokes, presses, tests, and decides what is best for the patient. The patient is expected to demonstrate "compliance" by following "doctor's orders." In the other pattern, the patient retains control and the physician provides services—diagnosing, listing treatment options, and recommending changes in behavior. Patients are expected to gain understanding as they make decisions and use both advice and medicines appropriately.

Criterion Four: Holism

Despite a great deal of talk about integrated services, an ecosystem perspective, and systems approaches, most community-based action remains sectoral, with discrete projects in agriculture, health, education, roads, and so on. Moreover, the focus of these sectoral projects has increasingly narrowed—from health to AIDS, from income generation to microcredit for women, from agriculture to plant genetics, from nature conservation in all its majesty to campaigns for extremely rare individual species. Specificity is usually a consequence of outsiders' becoming convinced of the urgency of a particular problem or of the issue's potential to exert leverage on large problems. Although the actual issues may in fact be acute, this narrowed focus loses sight of the dynamics producing the crisis.

Holism comes from the three-way partnership. Usually it is outsiders who plan and implement programs, seeking to hold communities accountable to objectives set by outside donors. They go about their work not thinking about its implications beyond their role. Promotion systems in the institutions and organizations that employ them reward specialists who achieve results, not generalists who provide perspective. Cross-sectoral linkages (agriculture, health, housing, transport, finance, politics, and fisheries) are seldom attempted or even understood. Each separate program is controlled by experts who speak different professional languages, and their budgets are organized for competition between units and working teams.

Although specific interventions—finding new seed types, eliminating locusts, preventing soil from eroding, conserving water—are both necessary and useful, they do not produce systemwide change. A holistic response to a crisis in food supply or the potential for famine will combine education, financing, improved technology, increased efficiency in moving food from areas of surplus to areas of need, and surveillance against hoarding. This societal synthesis of solutions rather than sectoral fixes is more likely when the community has a greater voice in decisionmaking.

Holistic action has been tried. The World Bank, for example, lent an impressive $19 billion between 1973 and 1986 for 498 projects designed to integrate all aspects of development. But few of these projects took hold, and the World Bank itself, in a candid self-analysis, acknowledged that the failures stemmed from excessive outside planning, inadequate respect for local circumstances, top-down implementation, and excessive outside funding.[6] In short, holistic projects were not implemented holistically.

The case studies in this book demonstrate that holistic development is possible if it is done right. Communities look at the world from an integrated perspective, not a sectoral one. From the community perspective there are no sectors, only problems to be solved. Pragmatic citizens will turn to whatever sector is available. Action needs to parallel this real-world, community-based view. Relationships established in childhood and sustained through marriages and other activities that all remember are the operational basis for the loan at the bank that supports a trucking decision, helps create more efficient access to markets, allows farmers to move produce, enables the carpenter to get more work, and assures the bank of receiving its monthly payment on a house loan. At the community level, people see these linkages as soon as they hear that a bank loan was given to so-and-so. The links get strengthened each day over lunch and in encounters on the street. When communities talk about the linkages between problems, they are likely to work toward actions that address the root issues critical to releasing community energy.

Conflicting goals will always emerge. In these situations, bargaining, rather than incentives or pressure, is likely to achieve a solution acceptable to all. Recently we were involved in an area where people from several villages were cutting down trees. Our priority was to support a new national park that was being formed to preserve those trees, and we knew that this objective was not something the local people would spontaneously choose over making money from cutting those trees. We struck a bargain: if they stopped felling, we would pay for electrical lines to extend power upvalley. The bargain required accountability: if the tree cutting resumed, the power running through those lines would be turned off. Because a partnership existed, each side held a measure of control. Such bargaining, supported by written contracts to make the balance of responsibilities clear, is one of the more transparent and least manipulative tools of development.

Criterion Five: Collaboration

Earlier we stressed the centrality of partnership among community, officials, and experts. Such partnerships create a supportive context, which in turn fosters collaboration within the community. The more a community gathers around a common vision, the greater the chance that vision will be achieved. Collaboration mobilizes all the community's human resources.

Collaboration comes naturally when communities are faced with outside threats: a flood, a war, fear of the loss of jobs, danger to a natural resource, loss of local land ownership. However, when the outside danger disappears, the common vision usually fades and collaboration ends. The most lasting collaboration comes from a positive goal, not from a threat.

A major obstacle to collaboration is the inevitable competition among communities and subcommunities, which unfortunately often maintain their specific identities by deliberately not cooperating. Another obstacle is people's memories of promises made by community members and then broken. People are chary of rhetoric urging collaboration, especially from political leaders just before elections. They know that those who talk most of power sharing may really be trying to shift the balance of power for their own benefit.

Collaboration does not grow on its own. Advocates of grassroots action, both within and outside the community, sometimes forget that grass requires rain and sunlight from above and other nutrients from outside. Officials and experts are needed to nurture collaboration through strategies that break down factions and promote openness. Once it is clear what the various factions are seeking, action can focus on engaging local leaders. A leader is anyone who has decisionmaking power: business leaders, who have access to substantial and flexible resources; religious leaders, who can catalyze community commitment and legitimate changes in values and social norms; entertainment leaders, who can mobilize a community in a matter of hours; and leaders of the unacknowledged yet very powerful groups, such as women, ethnic minorities, and the poor. Nondesignated or informal leaders also play an important role in bringing factions together. Their leadership comes from earlier performance, character, education, or outside travel. One way to identify these natural leaders is to ask community members whom they turn to for advice, who knows what is likely to succeed. Another technique is to "follow the eyes" in a meeting when a difficult question comes up: whom do people look to for cues as to how they should react?

To build collaboration, seek out the easy partnerships and strongest points of common loyalty. Crossing factional lines is often easiest for women, using their common concern for children. To nurture families through the uncertainties of life, women have learned to cooperate. Women may also be more attuned to relationships than men. However, women cannot be counted on as the only sources of initiative. Because they are commonly the keepers of tradition and values (and especially when they've been denied schooling), they are often less willing to take risks, less well educated, and less knowledgeable about changes in the outside world.

Gaining collaboration is easier when there is an objective base on which to build. Agreeing on data depersonalizes issues that may have defined earlier community antagonisms. When a community coalesces around data, a new collective vision can emerge. From this each individual and group can find a new position and opportunity to contribute. The valuing of individuality differs from culture to culture, but all societies recognize the centrality of community cohesion and working together.

Criterion Six: Iteration

Development requires iterative action. Seldom does a project turn out right on the first try or according to the first design. The development expert David Korten speaks of the need to "embrace error."[7] Progress comes through learning from mistakes and making corrections so that on the next try the activity works better, and on the trial after that, with more corrections, improvements continue. Such refining of partial successes can add momentum as participation grows within the community.

Often people hope for a magic "fix": if a factory will locate in their town, people will have jobs, and everything will improve. A similar false perception is that technology or science will create a breakthrough. But well-being never arrives in a tidy package. Breakthroughs come from careful and persistent iteration, step by step, usually with mistakes along the way. A relevant analogy is the process of writing a book. First there is a rough draft, then changes in organization and wording produce another draft, and the message improves with each successive attempt. In general, the more drafts there are, the better the final result.

Efforts at social change are subject to the same reality: they grow from failures as well as from successes, and the former will be more common than the latter. Progress is an unending process of learning from mistakes so that the next try improves. Iteration is what enables us to work our way to solutions that were inconceivable even a few years ago. We cannot fathom the whole issue at once. Our well-being grows through repeated trials and cumulative successes. Advancement depends not so much on specific inputs such as money, program design, or accountability—the factors commonly considered central by planners—as on how well the community learns from mistakes and then takes corrective action. Better futures are forged by learning from experience and then changing actions accordingly.

Community-Based Action
through SEED

Betsy Taylor, Daniel Taylor-Ide, and Carl E. Taylor

When the intent is to make informed decisions, clearly it is better to get multiple inputs rather than single and to ground those inputs in hard data rather than opinion. Obtaining multiple inputs and making them factually based are at the foundation of SEED (Self-Evaluation for Effective Decision-making). SEED allows communities, experts, and officials to come together around the facts of each locality's situation. SEED has a third feature as well: it takes this informed talk and leads to doable action.

SEED is a system so simple that any community can use it. It is a system that starts simply but can grow sophisticated as users develop capacity and see the need for added precision. The participatory decisionmaking allows community members, officials, and experts to contribute from their positions of respective strength rather than from positions of power. As multiple inputs and data support ever more refined actions and foster equality among decisionmakers, confidence builds among the partnership and extends to the actions being planned.

Four very different strands of research were brought together to create SEED. The philosophical beginning lies in the community perspective that arose from the pioneering efforts of Paolo Freire (see Chapter 4). Out of his work has evolved an approach for involving people in decisionmaking about their futures, called Participatory Rural Appraisal (PRA). From the 1970s to the 1990s PRAs gave local people a practical way to come together, share their perceptions about their circumstances, and move toward collaborative action.[1] Modifications of PRA continue under different labels such as Planning, Learning, and Action (PLA) and UNICEF's Assessment, Analysis, and Action (Triple A) for community nutrition.

At the same time that research was seeking to involve people, experts in virtually every discipline (forestry, education, environmental protection, agriculture, credit programs, and health) were seeking to simplify their assessment techniques to find simple tools that would show what was really occurring in communities.[2] Constraints on donor budgets were a contributing factor in this process—earlier complex research was not being funded, yet donors still wanted to have data-based decisions. Academic disciplines, most especially anthropology, were trying to be community sensitive, making their insights more accessible and more rapidly available. Among their other contributions in terms of speed and simplicity, this research strand worked on the idea of using key indicators whereby a single factor (such as the presence of a certain bird) brought together many variables.

Simultaneously computer technology was reorienting the whole foundation of society. Some of the electronic tools opened up major opportunities, working in parallel with the major simplifications occurring in research design. The manipulation of statistics was simplified so that procedures that had required hours of calculation were completed with the click of a mouse. Geographic Information Systems became accessible, making it possible to put physical systems in a community together with landscape and then on top of social services. Formerly obscure mathematical computations of multivariate modeling now became both understandable and a lot more holistic.

Operations research was the fourth component that came together in SEED. Beginning in World War II and then continuing in business planning, operations research developed the concept of representative sampling used in industrial production to monitor production. Such sampling promotes data-based surveillance and also supports the use of key indicators to assess larger production quality. In operations research the discipline of functional analysis was particularly useful—looking at factors in terms of what performance is desired rather than looking in terms of inputs or products. Having earlier used functional analysis very beneficially in planning national health systems,[3] we now realized that the process could be simplified down to the community level.

Objective Decisionmaking

The first important feature of SEED is that it is factually based, in contrast to traditional community-based decisionmaking, which is opinion based, and which usually capitulates to the opinion of whoever is most powerful in the decisionmaking process. Finding a method to bring together the diversity of perspectives is inevitably difficult, because the viewpoints differ sharply.

Community perceptions are usually embodied in stories, and the more unusual or entertaining they are, the more likely they are to become part of community lore. Tales often recall earlier failures, especially the come-uppance of dreamers. In connection with development issues, the stories often express resentment about manipulation by outsiders. Stories often reach back generations to portray a strong past against a modern era of victimization, cultivating wariness of innovation. Today, as mass media increasingly glorify village chatterboxes as global storytellers, the need for objectivity is greater than ever before, since community members have no way of knowing whether the distant stories are true or false.

Official perceptions support stability regardless of political system. Officials are suspicious of people who are not from their cadre or unable to talk their jargon. Their subculture, too, tends to rely on anecdotes, recounting the missteps of individuals who deviated from official norms. In-group priorities tend to focus on precedent, bureaucratic dominance, traditions, statistics, and holding others accountable. Their concerns and perceptions of accomplishments may differ strikingly from community perspectives. They are especially concerned with balancing judgments about benefits received by each subgroup and are usually defensive and protective for their own group.

Experts see themselves as pursuing impartiality, even though most seem to trust nobody's numbers but their own. Experts can be found to give advice on just about any purpose—at least this is a view common among community members and officials. For their contributions to be useful, experts must be used in roles for which they have had real training and experience, instead of being allowed to rely on secondhand opinions based on theory. Too often, development experts are expected to provide guidance in unfamiliar areas in which they may have more biases than local citizens.

SEED brings these sets of perceptions together. It bases community action not on directives from officials or community leaders or on ideas imported from yesterday's news, but on joint decisionmaking with agreement on community reality and the facts.

SEED has the potential to bring together factions through community-wide participation in data-gathering. When data are owned by all partners—people, officials, and experts, as well as multiple factions—they are more likely to guide real action. SEED reverses prevailing patterns of research, in which leadership and control come from outside the community. Nor does it make any effort to take over the community. Where possible, it employs traditional, well-established methods of bringing factions together, such as town meetings, panchayats, and community caucuses.

SEED does not replace full-scale research about a community; as an annual part of action programs, it merely seeks data accurate enough to enable the community work plan to self-correct. The first half of SEED, Self-Evaluation, starts with an annual assessment conducted by the community to learn about its own conditions. It is followed by collective analysis of the data in order to create objective, shared agreement on priority problems. Self-evaluation is Step 4 of the annual cycle of community action, and it has two parts, each with three tasks. The first part consists of preliminary organization: defining the community and its boundaries of concern, simplifying the options to be studied, and selecting key indicators. The second part consists of conducting the assessment: selecting and training the assessment team, gathering and analyzing the data, and setting communitywide priorities. In the Effective Decisionmaking half of SEED, which is Step 5 of the annual cycle of work, the people create a work plan to solve their priority problems. There are three tasks here: causal analysis, functional analysis, and role reallocation. Thus there are nine tasks in the overall process.

Organize the Assessment

Task One: Define the Community

Our operational definition of a community is any group with something in common and the potential for cooperative action. The traditional view of a community is based on geography, but the actual boundaries of a community do not always match existing administrative or political units. For good relations in promoting development, the definition of community boundaries may need to be adjusted so that irreconcilable factions are not forced to work together.

Preparing a map together is one of the clearest ways to define a community and at the same time to include all groups and generate enthusiasm for participating in the SEED assessment. The eventual map should be as accurate as possible and in a format that can be preserved. It should show clearly where community boundaries are and what subgroups are included. New electronic tools such as remote satellite sensing and Geographic Information Systems (GIS) make mapping easier than ever before. Once the map is created, a means of copying and editing it should be worked out so that it can be used repeatedly to provide the basis for survey and surveillance work, for maintaining equity and inclusiveness, for keeping track of families, and for allocating responsibility for service coverage.

It helps to start by organizing one or more participatory games, community meals, or celebrations to create cohesion. These fun activities should lead directly to collaborative discussion—not just to self-promoting speeches by leaders, however well-intentioned. One way to involve people is to ask them to break up into small discussion groups; another is to use more formal PRAs or facilitator-led focus groups to talk about the community's future needs. Less formal approaches include Paolo Freire's thoughtful listening for "the places that itch."

One technique we find effective is to ask neighborhood groups to build physical models of what they would like their community to look like in the future. (We did this with Lego blocks with the Apache; see Chapter 15.) This exercise encourages shy people to participate, opens up talk about options, diffuses ownership of the process, and focuses thinking on the future rather

TABLE 21.1. Areas of Community Life for which Key Indicators Can Be Developed

Population
    Population numbers and age, sex distribution
    Birth and death rates, and family migration
    Food availability
    Health status
    Education status
    Housing status

Culture
    Historical self-perception
    Expectation for the future
    Common culture (music, folk stories, rituals, etc.)
    Views of equity, justice, etc.

Environment
    Transportation resources
    Soil characteristics
    Water quality and quantity
    Domestic animals
    Wild plants
    Wild animals
    Energy potential and sources

Livelihood
    Types of livelihood and occupations
    Income distribution
    Work opportunities
    Traditional activities
    Government and outside assistance
    Administrative and political structures
    Technologies being used
    Farm and animal husbandry practices
    Forest uses (timber and medicinal plants)
    Consumption patterns
    Energy use

External Factors
    New cultural influences
    Formal services (health, education, agriculture, fisheries, etc.)
    Administrative infrastructure
    Financial institutions
    Food security supports
    Outside business and industry
    Institutions to promote change
    Tourism

than on the past. It directs talk to steps required for community change. Then each neighborhood group can describe its vision to the larger group. We have had particular success with materials such as Lego blocks, children's building blocks, paper, magic markers and pencils, and even prepared wooden models of houses, schools, police posts, and health facilities, which help make the presentations real.

Task Two: Simplify the Options

Once participatory activities have brought people together, talk should move quickly to defining a shared vision and objectives for action. Creating a comprehensive database will take some years, but in the first years community action will also be maturing as people learn to work together. In the first year, data collection may be limited to systematic gathering of basic information such as the number and distribution of households and their main problems. Any formal assessment must begin with asking people what they want to know, testing key indicators, creating the expectation of continuing data-based decisionmaking, and later refining the process.

Trying to include everyone's casual mention of interests is a common temptation. But a community cannot work simultaneously on health, agriculture, income generation, and forestry, and it cannot include everyone's desires in the first several SEED assessments. The first assessments should focus on high-priority interests on which there is wide agreement. The assessment must be kept simple. Only a few key indicators are needed in each priority area. Table 21.1 presents an inclusive list of possible areas that grew out of our work in the Himalaya—far more areas for investigation than a community can reasonably attempt. From this range of options only a few are selected, and for each of these several key indicators are chosen.

Task Three: Select Key Indicators

Once the community agrees on its priorities, experts can help select some key indicators to reflect the status of each area. Most formal surveys done by professionals directly measure multiple variables and then perform complex cross-analysis to determine which are the most important. Such techniques are beyond the abilities of a typical community. The use of key indicators introduces a different approach. Instead of measuring inputs and outputs for all variables directly, key indicators assess understanding and relationships already synthesized by these variables.[4]

Selecting key indicators allows researchers to skip many direct measurements and cross-tabulations. For example, measuring midarm circumference on all children under age three in a poor community reveals the influence of multiple factors on nutritional status. Children with inadequate caloric intake have very thin muscle and fat in their upper arms regardless of genetic or cultural differences, and this measurement is fairly stable up to age three because muscle builds up as body fat decreases. Midarm circumference is not only an indicator of each child's earlier food nutrition, but when aggregated for a group it reflects community food security. Differences among children in various socioeconomic groups reflect variability in food distribution and hence are an excellent way to measure equity within a community.

The findings from key indicators may not meet academic research standards for precision, but they are much more useful in guiding action, less costly, and much quicker. As practitioners gain experience in selecting and using them, precision will increase, and perhaps also their research utility. In the meantime, for community-based research, key indicators reveal relationships that multiple, separately assessed variables by themselves are unable to show.

Several websites provide a wide variety of useful approaches for choosing the optimal indicators for communities. Five such sites are:

- www.sustainablemeasures.com: Sustainable Measures is a private consulting firm dedicated to promoting sustainable communities primarily through the development, understanding, and use of effective indicators and systems for measuring progress.
- www.rprogress.org: Refining Progress offers community indicators that measure progress on sustainability issues, engage community members in dialogues about the future, and seek to change community outcomes. Currently more than 200 communities throughout the United States participate.
- www.iisd.org/measure/compindex.asp: The International Institute for Sustainable Development provides a website on the Compendium of Sustainable Development Indicator Initiatives. This is a re-

view of indicators being carried out at the international, provincial, and state levels.

- www.loka.org: The Loka Institute is a nonprofit research and advocacy organization with social, political, and environmental interests. Loka works to make science and technology more responsive to social and environmental concerns, and it seeks to expand opportunities for community-based groups.
- www.ciet.org: The work of Community Information and Epidemiological Technologies illustrates parallel use of the process of community-based indicators to monitor and redirect community work.

The following examples illustrate the simplicity and usefulness of key indicators. In all cases, data-gathering requires little training.

Indicators of Community Health. Our field trials have shown that three variables allow a community to diagnose its own health with remarkable precision:

- Mortality, particularly for children under age five in developing countries, where mortality is usually highest. Data on deaths should be segregated by age group for the five main causes of death. Interviewers can gather this information from families by using "verbal autopsies" based on a history of symptoms or by using local terminology for broad diagnostic categories, such as diarrhea. These deaths are then spot-checked against medical records.
- Nutritional status of all children under age three, most simply determined by measuring midarm circumference or, alternatively, by growth monitoring of weight for age and height for age.
- Specific morbidity, focusing on a few locally defined priority health needs such as malaria, diabetes, hypertension, anemia, symptoms related to alcohol consumption, violence, and HIV/AIDS.

The Flying Indicators of Ecosystem Status. In a pristine forest, the balance of flora and fauna is complex. Examining all the ecological factors takes a great deal of time and requires extensive training. However, observing representative species of small flying creatures provides a simple and sensitive indication of ecosystem integrity or disruption. Birds may be used, or butterflies, or other insects. Appropriately selected, each of these creatures ties together much information about the biome. Considerable skill is needed to identify the right indicator. For example, in Himalayan forests an indicator of pristine conditions is the presence of pheasants, often more easily heard by their distinctive calls than seen. As habitat is degraded, other local birds such as warblers become more common. When people have destroyed local forests, the indicator birds are sparrows and crows. Similarly, the colors of prevailing butterflies may serve as key indicators: typically white or yellow in settled areas, brown in transitional areas, and colored in forests. Such indicators are so distinctive that even schoolchildren can be taught how to identify them reliably.

Indicators of Land Use. Recent advances in satellite capability offer communities an exciting new tool for local land-use monitoring. High-resolution photographs can be obtained through many sources, and the prices continue to fall. Using such photographs, communities can precisely chart local land use every year or every ten years, objectively monitoring changes in agriculture, forests, residences, roads, wetlands, and many other variables. They can use spectrographic images taken by satellites to monitor vegetation complexes, tracking the specific mix of flora in a given area. Using satellite images as the base maps on GIS allows very precise accuracy. But working from these remote images is not enough; because satellite images flatten three-dimensional space, people need to go into the field and use sample plots to check the data; otherwise results can be misinterpreted. Equally important, the data will be trusted more if people have gone out and seen for themselves that measuring instruments are reading reality correctly.

Indicators of Domestic Water Quality. Health departments have designed portable kits that reliably measure water turbidity and bacterial content. Often these kits are available from government departments, and with simple training community members can gather reliable data on local water quality. Many kits include a small container for culturing coliform bacteria. Other simple indicators are number of larvae and water insects in streams, which decline selectively with pollution. Schoolchildren can make a project of wading in streams, counting the insects on the surface and rolling over rocks to count larvae.

Economic Indicators. A community's economic status is customarily monitored by such variables as inflation, local unemployment, cost of living, and property ownership. An alternative indicator is a shopping basket for a sample of households to determine on a per-capita or per-household basis what was purchased—what came from outside, what was community-grown or family-grown, and what items were bartered. Seasonal and cyclic figures can be compared with those for prior years. Another indicator is the source of family income: is it being earned outside the community and sent in or being earned from within the community? Interviewers can often more easily ask about sources than about amounts. A third indicator is a simple inventory of products in community stores; people are often reluctant to reveal their buying habits, but purchases can be determined indirectly by monitoring the variety, pricing, and sales information from local merchants.

Indicators of Soil Quality. Few factors affecting the welfare of agricultural communities are as important as soil. As population numbers and the desire for export crops rise, soil is often overexploited. Soils vary greatly, and monitoring soil quality by standard techniques can be complicated. But annual counting of earthworms in a standard cubic volume in a planned pattern of sites offers a precise indicator of many vital variables. Specially impregnated paper strips can track the runoff in streams of key nitrate nutrients. A third technique is to examine soil with a hand lens to determine the proportions of organic matter, sand and tiny stones, and clay.

Indicators of Forest Status. Trees have many social uses, providing income, material for local building, fodder for animals, and fuel. Cutting often exceeds forest growth rates. Communities can measure rates of timber growth with several simple tools. Whereas measuring timber volume with standard prisms is expensive, an equally useful measure of volume requires only a thin standard-diameter stick and a piece of string. Or, to assess the height of a tree, use a piece of cardboard cut at a 45-degree angle; step back, keeping the bottom level, until you can sight along the 45-degree angle to the treetop; the distance stepped back from the tree is the tree's height.

The accuracy and usefulness of SEED indicators depend upon the experts who guide their choice and use. Selection of valid indicators that accurately measure local variables is best done by scientists knowledgeable in the subject areas. To find the range of locally appropriate key indicators will require a mix of ecologists, public-health experts, agriculturalists, foresters, and economists. Training community surveyors to do the three tasks that follow requires a second type of expert, one sensitive to local realities in community empowerment, who can mobilize volunteers to gather and analyze data. Special adjustments may be necessary when social divisions are deep. After assessment information is available, a third type of expert is needed to help define workable options in the development of interventions. The most important challenge for any expert is to simplify technical knowledge usefully for local application.

Conduct the Assessment

Task Four: Select and Train the Assessment Team

Although communities will need professional expertise in designing their surveys, professionals are not the best people to do the actual assessment, because local participation in data-gathering will promote later plan implementation. When we first implemented SEED in Nepal, the local coordinating committee compared two groups in their ability to gather data: local people from several villages and professional data collectors from the capital city. When the results came in it was clear that SEED's simplicity eliminated the need for the sophisticated skills of professionals: an unexpected benefit of SEED was that community members got nearly 100 percent coverage of households, whereas professional teams were often satisfied with 70 percent. In subsequent trials of SEED it has been our impression that the neediest families are often left out by professionals because they are the most difficult to track down—and so the omission of the 30 percent probably significantly skews findings. Local data-gatherers were able to enter and leave homes easily, make household members comfortable, and locate the most knowledgeable family member.

If data collectors are hired, they should be local people. However, hiring has three disadvantages. First, it sends the wrong message—that development agencies can be expected to provide jobs rather than empowering communities. Second, employing local surveyors is more expensive than attracting volunteers. Third, short-term employees may not be available for surveys in later years, and it is better to build capacity in the community.

A second approach is to use government or NGO workers already present, such as community health workers, agriculture extension agents, and economic-development workers. These people may have the skills to perform special tasks in the assessment and may need only minimal additional training. Including such workers in the assessment has the further advantage of integrating them early into a larger, longer-term planning framework, which may help them to think about issues outside their sectoral discipline. Using these professionals also has problems. They are few in number and probably cannot be spared from other essential tasks; for example, no one should stop treating sick children to conduct an assessment. Moreover, they may resent being expected to do work not in their job description, especially when fieldwork outside their office is involved. Or, if given special duties, these people may enjoy participating. A frequent problem is that they often rotate away, go on leave, or abide by strict work hours. Perhaps the biggest barrier is that they are often not from the community and may have little familiarity with local people even though they may have worked there for some time. Finally, if employed workers take over, and if community members do not have a major role, the SEED process may be perceived as a job for service workers rather than a community-owned initiative.

Third, in communities with strong civic organizations, volunteers may already have the capacity to take major responsibility for the SEED process. Local organizations—mothers' clubs, sports teams, town councils, civic societies, or religious organizations—all want to advance community welfare and may see taking this kind of leadership as enhancing their credibility. They may have financial resources or physical space to contribute. If it is not appropriate for them to lead the process, they can still be a good source of volunteers. However, no one group should take exclusive control, for then action is no longer a whole-community effort, and SEED will lose credibility as a base for community mobilization.

A fourth group who may be effective in data collection and analysis is local secondary school students. In some situations, students have participated in an annual cycle of assessments built into their curriculum. Students may not be able to conduct a SEED assessment on their own, but working as part of a community team provides both them and their communities with some outstanding benefits:

- The process builds knowledge and concern about development among the community's future citizens.
- Because schools are somewhat standardized from community to community in a region (unlike development workers, professional surveyors, and voluntary organizations), replication of the assessment is often easy.
- Schools are usually integrated into a community. Because their facilities host sporting events, fairs, and meetings, they are seen as more open to all segments of the community and may be less identified with those who are politically or ethnically important.
- Because they have access to many homes, students can cover a high percentage of households quickly. This is especially true in traditional communities, where most students have extensive family ties.
- Student interviewers require no payment.
- The information that students gather enriches the school curriculum. Math classes can use the data to teach analytic skills. Laboratory work in science can incorporate medical and ecological tests. Writing courses might include compositions based on household interviews. Social studies discussions provide a forum for reflecting on SEED findings that reaches back into families for traditional wisdom.
- Learning practical skills in subjects such as conservation, agricultural innovation, health, economic analysis, community organization, and political action can help students find meaningful careers.
- Learning about their community makes school more interesting to students. This increased interest may reduce dropout rates and increase participation in other activities.
- Students may be among the more knowledgeable individuals in the community in literacy, conservation, health, agriculture, and numeracy and therefore more capable of handling assessment tasks.

The four options for staffing a SEED assessment are not mutually exclusive. Teams are often most productive when they involve multiple groups.

People will be most effective in research work that fits with their everyday roles and knowledge. For instance, if women are the ones who spend most time gathering timber or other forest products, they might be most effective in gathering data on forest sustainability. However, if men are hunters who spend much time in the forest, this might be a natural area of research for them. In societies in which women stay close to home and men are more mobile, women might be the most effective in household assessments, while men can gather data on infrastructure issues such as trade.

Our field experience has shown that a combination of mothers' clubs and students is often an especially effective team for data-gathering. In addition, we have found that students get enthusiastic about environmental data collection. (This occurred with the Apache youth; see Chapter 15.) Outside professionals, on the other hand, are useful in developing assessment design, validating indicators, training volunteers, and helping analyze data.

Training the assessment team involves explaining clearly what the indicators assess and how to measure each indicator in ways that make sense to surveyors and to community members being surveyed. Where interviews are involved, training must also make surveyors comfortable with intruding on family privacy. One way to build comfort for both the workers doing the assessment and the community is to have trainee workers role-play the assessment process; another technique is to open the training up so that citizens can watch the process. After their training the workers should go out and gather data in pilot trials that are later repeated as part of the actual assessment. Including the local coordinating committee in the training will help them prepare the community for the later interviewer visits.

Task Five: Gather and Analyze the Data

In the first assessment, all participants will have anxieties, and mistakes should be expected. Support from the local coordinating committee and visits from experts can help build confidence. Community meetings are essential for two-way communication about what is going on. Too much should not be expected, especially the first year. *It is essential that the entire process be completed so that final data come in, even if the quality or quantity is low.* The next year, results will be better because the process will be more familiar.

Once data have been gathered, the local coordinating committee should arrange for all partners to share in deciding how the data will be compiled and analyzed. All factions should be represented in decisions about which community members, working with expert help, should handle the data. Compilation cannot be done in public, since recording data accurately requires precision and care. But sharing expectations of how this collective community resource will be used is helpful in taking the next step. Analysis should include those doing the compilation, community leaders, and representatives from most community factions. Transparency is essential. In analyzing the data it might be helpful to compare data from other sources to see the larger context. Results that differ from expectations should not be made known before the community dialogue, since all perspectives should be involved when the data are discussed.

Task Six: Set Communitywide Priorities

Once the data are compiled, as many community members as possible should participate in the dialogue to plan actions. Up to this point the local coordinating committee may have done most of the work, and various factions may have chosen not to participate. During the community dialogue, however, leaving out any group will handicap collective action in fundamental ways.

Officials and experts should attend when the coordinating committee presents the data to the community. Charts are helpful if they are kept simple. Seeing one's community reflected in objective measurements is like seeing one's own photograph for the first time: the experience brings both a special fascination and new self-understanding. The data must be discussed in ways that give community members time to adjust to what the data tell them. Many may reject some or all of the findings; if that happens, the leaders of the meeting should postpone action on a particular data cluster but not on data-gathering in general. Errors in data collection are likely, and these should be noted with care to avoid giving the impression that the whole assessment process is invalid.

The idea of promoting dialogue is simple, but the practice is difficult. In open meetings with data available, community members immediately become involved in talking about the relative value of various options and how they relate to the main priorities. The data must serve as the touchstone, prompting people to think about interconnected factors. Presentation of the findings and analysis of the implications will almost always meet with challenges about validity and accusations that preferences were shown. A meeting intended to promote objective analysis can easily degenerate into fractious debate. Groups may threaten to walk out and may even do so.

Experience has taught us some practical steps to reduce the chance of chaos in the first year or so of implementing SEED. First, make sure that people agree that the assessment idea is worth trying; get this from the broadest base in the community, not just from the local coordinating committee. Then ask them to agree that although the first year's data may not be absolutely complete and accurate, they do generally reflect the community's reality. Before presenting the data, walk them through the processes that have been and will be used; don't just spring conclusions on them. The one prevailing rule is that the discussions must be based on data not on opinions. If the data collected do not reflect reality as perceived by the community, then decisions should be deferred while people go back to collect new data, solving any methodological problems identified and including the people who have raised objections. Usually people will let one year's data stand if they know that next year their concerns will be addressed. If large groups of people are participating, they can be divided into smaller groups. It is essential to have many more community members than officials or experts, and also a balanced representation, including people from groups usually left out, such as women, youth, minorities, and the poor.

After the data are presented, use of a simplified nominal group method often prevents domination by people who talk a lot. The initial task of suggesting priority issues circulates around the group, with each person mentioning a problem of particular concern. Items are listed on a blackboard or flip chart without any discussion at this stage. The roundabout is repeated until the group can add no more ideas. Although the suggestions will seem repetitive, it is essential to express and record all ideas. Then the items are condensed in active dialogue into a smaller number by combining wording. A vote follows, with each participant writing down the three items from the list he or she considers most important. The votes are tallied, and almost always the participants feel that they can live with the consensus and work on the highest priorities at least until next year. The aim in this step is to set priorities for action—not to define what the action is.

Create a Work Plan

Task Seven: Causal Analysis

Separating Tasks Six and Seven is important: agreeing on priorities makes it much easier to move forward with analysis. Once priorities are set, causal analysis enables people to discover effective entry points for change. Since SEED recurs annually, it is not essential that all problems be remedied in one year, only that changes begin. To keep the focus on genuinely inclusive collective planning, and to prevent causal analysis from degenerating into finger-pointing and recrimination, a neutral authority from outside the community may be necessary. It should be someone who can keep the agenda focused and not show favoritism to any faction. Such a person may be an official or expert, a businessperson, a religious leader, or even an international friend.

As people seek a common ground for action, it often becomes clear that several priority problems have the same underlying causes, such as poverty, discrimination, inadequate water supply, or poor training. Where circumstances permit, the discussion leader should encourage the community to seek root causes and to focus on activities that will bring multiple benefits. Focusing on the data should help preserve impartiality. Where circumstances do not allow the community to talk openly about the most troubling deep-rooted causes, addressing those causes may have to be postponed for a year or two. If the group analysis polarizes communities, accentuates class separation, or attacks one side for having caused the problem, there will be no community momentum.

Analysis then leads naturally to intensive inspection of possible solutions. Suggestions will emerge spontaneously. It is vital that outsiders not assume a dominant role, since doing so will divert attention from the underlying realities the community is groping to understand. Experts usually focus on what seems to them a theoretically correct method. In meetings outsiders almost always fail to understand much of what is said, even if they are fluent in the local language, because they do not know the community context. A legacy of subtle references and common history is buried in every statement or argument. Old factional disputes may emerge that make people uncomfortable. People will grasp at simplistic fixes and opportunities to make money. Without taking control, outsiders need to keep the focus on deeper causal analysis.

One way of channeling debate and depriving comments of personal sting is to encourage participants to turn in written comments on each possible solution to an experienced secretary who can condense them on a flip chart, blackboard, or computer. Such methods build confidence that proposed actions may be considered in the next year if not at this time.

Task Eight: Functional Analysis

Once people have agreed on what solutions to try—for example, saving babies dying from diarrhea, expanding the food supply, bringing electrical power into homes, increasing jobs for young people so they don't move away—they must decide *how* to do it and *who* will do it. At this point most groups start talking about money. Money may well be a necessary issue to address, but first there must be agreement on the functions to be performed and who will do what.

Questions need answering: What will most effectively correct the priority problems? What skill levels are needed? How many people will be needed from inside and outside the community? How can activities be simplified and brought close to homes? Would a method that is 70 percent effective be better than another that is 95 percent effective if costs for implementing the first method are much lower and implementation is possible in the home? Can problems be simplified enough for people with little expertise to do them? Can the more complicated cases be referred?

Functional analysis requires that activities be classified according to the technical and human resources required to achieve objectives. For example, if diarrheal death is a priority problem, teaching the community the use of oral-rehydration therapy with supplies already in the home can cure about 90 percent of the cases. But to prevent diarrhea itself, different action objectives are needed, such as providing clean water to homes, perhaps creating a pure community water-supply system, helping families get safe water storage, and improving handwashing and hygiene.

A functional analysis of why young people are moving away might find that no more land is available for farming. If the causal analysis has suggested the need to promote nonfarm employment, then a subanalysis might identify what expansion is possible and what resources are available in the community. The analysis might explore more-intensive cultivation on smaller units of land, changing to higher-profitability crops, starting secondary processing of local yield, developing more-efficient technologies, and the like. For each option additional resources, training, and tasks must be allocated.

Task Nine: Role Reallocation

The third principle of development is behavior change. People need to adapt their behavior to suit new circumstances. This last step of creating the work plan gives people jobs, bringing together resources, training, and the tasks to complete the functions. This role allocation is usually difficult, because people like to hold to existing frameworks of responsibility; but all partners need to start each development year knowing what the expectations are for their own new roles.

As roles are reassigned and resources allocated, it helps to work out details publicly. In traditional communities whose leaders have long told people what each should do, it takes time to adjust to new ways and expectations. People may continue to do as they are told for traditional activities, but development, by definition, means changing to new ways. Public assignment of roles allows people to participate in deciding who is getting what job.

In some cases, professionals in health care, information technology, and environmental action may find themselves displaced by inexpensive simplified technology that ordinary people can use (such as oral rehydration). Threatened with "losing market share," the professionals may become major obstacles to community progress. It then becomes necessary to help them see that they will be able to focus instead on tasks that require greater expertise.

A long and wordy plan will probably never get used. A simple matrix chart lets people see at a glance where they fit. The chart may specify the levels at which roles are to be performed—household, community, region, with subcategories as needed—and the functions or jobs with major tasks as subcategories and due dates for each. At the intersections of these matrixes, boxes can specify the jobs, people responsible, and dates of completion or other verifiable targets. Notes can be added, detailing key resources and substeps; or separate tables can display specific training or other resources required.

By completing these nine tasks, SEED presents clear statements of the community's priorities, the causes (both proximate and underlying) of each problem, the actions to be taken to solve the problems, what changes people need to make in their behavior to accomplish the objectives, what resources are needed, and how they will be provided. Because every step is public except the actual compilation of the data, expectations are clear; people can see how they will get the services they agreed to and who is accountable. Experts and professionals are usually also pleased, not only because they like to see order, but also because role reallocation may relieve them of many boring routines. Thus the process generates commitment among all the partners.

Another major benefit is that confidence increases as simple tasks are accomplished through decentralized routines. A more filled-in vision of what the future could become grows among the partners as the causal analysis moves systematically to long-range, underlying solutions based on behavior changes. Functional-analysis matrixes can help resolve long-standing conceptual conflicts in debates, particularly ones with a history of polarizations between established hierarchies and points of view.

The recurring cycles in the SEED process encourage communities to focus on long-term objectives such as equity and sustainability. Linking data-gathering to informed decisionmaking creates an orderly framework for moving communities systematically toward previously elusive goals. The recurring cycles also encourage growth in capacity despite limited human resources. People who learn to handle their own information flow move from dependency to a sense of control over their future. In more affluent communities, SEED offers a way of allocating resources more efficiently. In both poor and rich contexts, SEED enables communities to scratch where they itch in ways they can afford.

How to Go to SCALE

From studies in many parts of the world we have observed that the most vexing problem in changing communities is learning how to take small successes to scale. Many good pilot projects point the way, but how can these grow up and out into a new way of life for communities? There are far fewer examples of successful scaling up than there are examples of promising starts.

Among the four approaches to large-scale expansion outlined in Chapter 3, the biological seems most promising for community-based action. Its main advantage is that it creates solutions that more frequently evolve to fit local needs. Other approaches often go to scale more quickly or in a more controlled fashion, but the pattern that then emerges seldom fits local conditions. For example, whereas in rapid construction of housing it may be most cost-effective, though not aesthetic, to have a standard tract house multiplied hundreds of times across a growing city, in changing community behaviors or efficiently using resources in an ever more competitive world, a standardized solution creates a less adapted fit. Each community is different—and each community optimally thrives when its solutions so fit its differences that it turns these into advantages. Local specificity is an axiom of successful communities.

We have defined commonalities in how the scaling-up process works. There is a loose parallel to a plant growing: a seed must be chosen that fits the soil, seasons, and situation. This is the node of success, the real demonstration, the example that can grow, what we term SCALE One. But for that growth to multiply, there needs to be an active farmer who works with the seed, adapting conditions, transplanting, and constantly learning how to be a better farmer, a process of action learning and experimentation we term SCALE Squared. But large-scale growth will not occur unless the right climate and conditions exist for that plant, the enabling environment of policies, financing, and education that is put in place by outside forces, what we term SCALE Cubed.

We aggregate these clusters of commonalities into three dimensions. Large field trials in places such as Peru, Tibet, and China (Chapters 17, 18, and 19) have allowed us to work with the interlocking aspects of these dimensions. We have found that breaking down the complex task of going to scale into these three dimensions enables each partner to see what he or she needs to do, and when. Awareness of these three dimensions helps the planning and direction of expansion. When they come together correctly, replication can occur exponentially along with site-specific adaptation, features that characterize biological species when they fit their ecological niches.

We use the acronym SCALE (Systems for Communities to Adapt Learning and Expand) to designate the overall process. However, we also apply the acronym to each of the three dimensions of going to scale:

- SCALE One (Successful Change As Learning Experiences): In a community the understanding grows that a better life is possible and builds systematically into local successes and empowerment.
- SCALE Squared (Self-help Center for Action Learning and Experimentation): Clusters of communities build the capacity to help other communities. Demonstration communities are selected to experiment with and perfect simplified methods of solving problems in their region. Then they help surrounding communities adapt and learn how to develop.
- SCALE Cubed (Systems for Collaboration, Adaptive Learning, and Extension): For rapid extension in a region or nation an embracing, enabling context is created by policies, financing, training, and rising expectations. This environment nurtures and directs change in all communities. The SEED systems of collaboration, adaptive learning, and extension stimulate the empowerment as people continually refine their solutions.

Using one acronym to designate four aspects of a process may seem confusing at first. But in teaching the SCALE process to communities, experts, and governments we have found that this interlinked nomenclature reflects the process of going to scale. Each acronym defines a different and complementary dimension of the extension process. The SCALE acronym highlights the fact that for extension to occur, three sets of tasks must be under way.

When we first observed the SCALE pattern in historical demonstrations of development (such as Ding Xian, Kerala, and the Adirondacks), we assumed that there was a standard sequence in implementing the three SCALE dimensions—that they progressed from SCALE One through SCALE Cubed.[1] However, in our work since 1995 in field trials using the SCALE framework to guide action, we have seen that any one of the three dimensions can lead the expansion. The key is not sequencing, but assigning appropriate tasks to each of the three partners. Each dimension provides very different entry points, but work can start in any one dimension or in multiple dimensions. If the felt needs of people predominate, SCALE One can start first; if there is commitment from donors, nongovernmental organizations, or academic bodies, then SCALE Squared can start first; if a government determines to create an enabling environment, SCALE Cubed can lead the process. But if change at the community level is to go to scale, all three dimensions must ultimately be included.

Unless it is a demonstration model in a SCALE Squared center, it does not matter to a community what is unfolding in the larger context. Individual communities seeking to develop want to know what they should do next and how to access the help they need. The work of communities almost always remains within SCALE One; a given community is continually rebuilding upon its own successes. Or it may look to a SCALE Squared center (or to some partial substitute) to learn tested techniques. SCALE Cubed puts into play all the larger systems that can support internal changes. Sequencing stages are of interest only to planners. Therefore, we have chosen to describe the going-to-scale process from the perspective of communities.

SCALE One: Successful Change As Learning Experiences

For development to take hold, communities must believe that their future can be better than their past. For that change to occur, human behaviors must change. Government or an outside donor cannot provide the energy that makes such change possible; it must come from within the community.

Self-confidence and self-discipline in uniting the community's vision and energy are more important than technical project design or the availability of resources; these outside factors do not generate internal capacity and can easily increase dependency.

Once a community experiences success, energy builds along with expectations. Each success extends the horizon to possible new successes. Progress in one sector, such as health or creating new jobs, nurtures initiatives in others, such as worker productivity or trying new crops in the fields, and this in turn can increase confidence to try changes in other areas such as housing or childcare options for working parents. All these can circle back in a reinforcing loop to prevention of health problems, creation of jobs, or the like.

Successful change is an iterative learning experience in which one change builds upon the one before. Each community must start this process from where it happens to be. The challenge is to identify priority issues that are locally important and doable. Because constructive community energy grows mostly from success (and only occasionally from pressure or crisis), often the best starting point is whatever project is already mobilizing the greatest energy. The starting point need not be an indigenous success, nor is it critical who started it (it could be a nongovernmental organization, university, government agency, or the community itself). The paramount criterion is that the community see the success as its own.

Outsiders often push for action to begin with the neediest people in a community, but beginning with the neediest may reduce the chances of sustainability. Development is momentum, and momentum is unlikely to begin when the first step is too steeply uphill. Projects should target the neediest sectors, but only once there is confidence in the community on which to build. In general, the groups that can least afford failure should not be expected to take the lead position in the first project, when uncertainty is greatest and competency lowest. On the other hand, there are exceptions to this rule. Repeatedly we have seen that those who are most exposed or in some crisis may be the most open to trying new ways. (See Chapter 6.) Those in greatest need may have the greatest enthusiasm for working hard, taking risks, trusting old enemies; they may be most aware that they need to initiate new behaviors.

To identify the right starting point and partners, the local coordinating committee should consider not only whether the activities inspire community confidence, but also whether they promote coalition building and whether the groups involved show potential for growing and widening their visions. With enough community participation, finding the starting point is usually not difficult; people know success in their community when they see it. And when improvement is visible to everyone, the community is more willing to spend time, resources, and money on extending that success.

Empowered by success, communities will start not only to build in confidence but also to attract attention. Outside attention will usually also be accompanied by public recognition and offers of money. There is a great deal of money available to support projects that seem to be making a difference. The management of that money is crucial. Outside resources are usually crucial to success, but they are most effective when they are focused on building community capacity—through training, demonstrations that can be adapted, removal of barriers, and construction of infrastructure. They should not be used to fund routine activities. Targeting money on community capacity and not on operations becomes more difficult as success continues to build. Experts will try to take over. People who were important in creating the success will seek to consolidate positions of power. Money can be justified (and used) in creative ways, but paying direct salaries or providing subsidies usually builds dependency, not capacity.

Success can breed failure as easily as it can breed momentum. Some internationally funded projects spend as much as 50 percent of their budgets bringing in consultants to plan or evaluate. A much better investment is to have community members and also regional policymakers visit other projects and learning centers. Consultants come and go, and usually their comments are based on experiences distant from the local challenge. Taking local people who will stick with the work to learn new ideas promises a more certain return. It opens doors to new areas of knowledge and provides role models to help communities adapt what they see working in other places. Seeing change under conditions similar to their own has many benefits. People come back to the community and explain what they have seen. Seeing success in neighboring communities often reduces fears that change will threaten important traditions, power bases, identities, and practices. Similarly, taking regional policymakers on such trips provides valuable educational exposure and the potential to create an enabling environment for local efforts.

Seed grants can stimulate innovation and willingness to take risks, but they should not come as handouts. Rather, they should be capacity-building capital to strengthen local conviction and skills. Money given in the wrong way pulls communities from local control to outsider control. Officials concentrate not on supporting community energy, but on checking fiscal expenditures. In other words, money from the outside tends to turn attention outside the community. Often pilot projects are too expensive to continue. Or donor money can shift priorities. When promises of money, jobs, or travel are made, they should be made publicly, with clearly stated expectations of what the recipient will do with them. These offers should be part of the community work plan, not freestanding projects that may supersede community decisions.

Seed grants from SCALE Cubed enabling funds should support community action with explicit, transparent, reciprocal accountability. The best way to avoid blurring the relation between seed grants from government and political support is always to put funds into the hands of the local coordinating committee, which balances local priorities and which the community holds accountable. This strategy puts local priorities first and the donor's priorities second and makes clear that development is not benevolent patronage.

Some successful SCALE One communities will become part of SCALE Squared centers. Whether a community remains at SCALE One or evolves into a SCALE Squared center depends on its aspirations and on the incentives provided by government or donors. When the transition is made, an agreement needs to state clearly benefits and responsibilities that are truly reciprocal. There are costs involved in training others and letting people come for action learning. Experimental trials will have a high failure rate. These tasks are in the larger collective interest and justify subsidies. Therefore, in return for agreeing to become a learning and experimentation center, the prospective SCALE Squared center should be assured of covering its costs, continuing to improve its services, and, perhaps most meaningfully, having its status acknowledged among peer communities. SCALE One communities that do not become SCALE Squared centers do not need such financial

COMMUNITIES BUILDING FROM SUCCESS

Fig. 22.1. SCALE One: Successful Change as Learning Experiences

underwriting, but they will thrive from recognition and the multiple support systems of SCALE Cubed. Care is needed in differentiating support given to SCALE One communities and SCALE Squared centers; both are clusters of communities in the society, but they have different roles in sustaining the larger momentum.

SCALE Squared: Self-help Center for Action Learning and Experimentation

Few good interventions can be transferred directly from one setting to another without some adaptation. People adopt ideas and methods most readily when they see them being applied successfully in conditions similar to their own by people who are like them. Formal systems for development training are nothing new. For centuries the guilds of Europe passed along skills through apprentice education in artisan trades, city planning, medical care, and finance. The Green Revolution's demonstration farms persuaded farmers to change practices by showing them how new seeds and methods worked in comparative test plots. Transportation and communications have become global through similar strategies: one company opens a new route, acquires new technology, adds capacity, and other entrepreneurs copy and adapt the demonstrations of success.

Projects such as Jamkhed in India, the QNNP in Tibet, Curitiba in Brazil, and China's Model Counties are recent examples of large-impact SCALE Squared centers, but now many more are needed in each region. They experimented with and evolved new approaches and are now training others to use their methods. Control remained with communities, but in each of these examples the extension function required active participation by officials and experts.

SCALE Squared action learning and experimentation centers bring in external resources—ideas, training, money, organization, even directives—and become showcases for innovation. As points of growth in a larger region they inevitably attract the attention of outsiders. These centers are where donors will want to (and can most helpfully) invest start-up money. But after centers are functioning well, it is important for government to assume the major funding role, as these places have now become centers to promote the public interest.

A SCALE Squared center is a community-based laboratory and a school without walls. It needs teachers who can help explain its lessons. It needs experts resident in the community who can conduct field experiments that improve processes and ideas. Comparative trials should use scientific methods to test the effectiveness of alternate approaches. One lesson builds upon another; findings from one demonstration open up understanding of new problems as capacity and knowledge expand.

Arranging visits to a SCALE Squared center may cause competition in SCALE One communities, especially if the distance to travel is long and outside assistance is needed to meet expenses. Who gets to go? To prevent visits from becoming perquisites for the privileged, a series of visits may be desirable, allowing the powerful to go first, followed by those who are the real workers. Representatives from as many groups as possible should be included to maximize dissemination of the lessons.

When people come to the SCALE Squared center they should see activities in progress. Our experience suggests that instruction should be structured

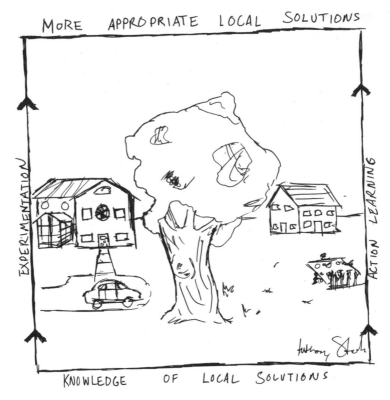

Fig. 22.2. SCALE Squared: Self-help Center for Action Learning and Experimentation

around formal learning objectives so that visitors do not ramble around and take home a hodgepodge of ideas. Lessons are most convincing when people see principles and procedures being employed by people whom they can relate to—people using them routinely under conditions similar to their own.

Whenever possible, the training curriculum of SCALE Squared centers should make the following points through real activities:

- Change is possible.
- Partnerships within the community must be collaborative and sustained.
- The community, officials, and experts should build incrementally together from community data and mutual priorities.
- What the community undertakes should be carefully selected from among many options. Selection should not maximize money

or status for individuals but be chosen for how well it fits local needs and conditions.

With success, there is often a tendency to let one partner take over, or to continue with the obvious decisions instead of gathering annual data and reviewing causal analyses to optimize progress. Development projects that were initially successful regularly run into trouble when they stop customizing action to new challenges and participants. A key reason why social development in Kerala has evolved steadily over more than a century is that Keralans continue to adapt as they adopt. The same explanation accounts for the progress in the Adirondacks, which began its park life as a half-baked compromise and through feedback on its problems and evolution of services turned this large, fragmented area into a world-class, multiple-factored-and-balanced demonstration. Lack of evolution partly explains why the great promise of the Ding Xian Experiment scaled up only partially in the Philippines.

Change typically starts in one part of a community—perhaps an unexpected part—and spreads. Surveillance is very important to identify such successes as well as problems. New information technologies also help identify what makes particular activities successful and relevant to wider community action. Projects may tend to lose focus if surveillance is not continually more sensitive each year.

The momentum of change brings news of ideas to be tried, but only a few of the promising pathways actually lead to more equitable and sustainable futures for a community. Natural resources in particular must be used carefully to avoid reducing future opportunities as a result of pollution, toxicity, and environmental damage.

Training needs to focus on respecting differences. When communities learn to value the skills of other members, there can be a fundamental shift in the way they work together. The SEED process is particularly effective at promoting collaboration as people learn positive lessons about community potentials, share in creating priorities, and work to reallocate roles.

SCALE Squared centers must address divisive issues openly in order to evolve answers to remedy them. The most explosive issues often relate to money: How much comes in? What use of money has made a difference? Can community action reduce the cost of services? Does outside money produce quick results, or are changes only superficial? Does it deflect attention from long-term benefits and behavior change, or take key people away from communities? Does it place more attention on administrative power than on community empowerment? Formal, open, and public discussion of money may help keep utilization transparent and honest. It may help teach visitors how they can use their own money wisely.

SCALE Squared centers should resist the temptation to be made into showcases. Communities understandably want status; outsiders want to take credit for helping a good project, and activists in the community want affirmation. But making SCALE Squared centers spectacular also makes them obviously not replicable for neighboring communities, either as role models or as training grounds for specific lessons.

As SCALE Squared centers become established in a region, it is useful to form a network for sharing among them. New centers may be recognized because of good performance, and they will need support. Centers that grow less effective need to be juxtaposed with the more successful, or they may opt out of the role. Modern technologies can help extend the reach of traditional experiential learning. Moreover, international networks of SCALE Squared centers can share experiences. There will be lessons to learn in teaching, experimental methods, and perhaps in specific solutions.

SCALE Cubed: Systems for Collaboration, Adaptive Learning, and Extension

The SCALE Cubed dimension supports exponential transformation and is most effectively initiated by officials. It involves the creation of a larger societal framework to nurture the extension of social change.

Within a larger systems framework, extension accelerates as communities are energized by the enabling environment. When official restrictions are removed, people change behavior and social norms in an expanding mass movement. When supportive incentives are put in place, people learn new packages of appropriate skills, gain access to new ideas, experience financial and administrative support—and extension occurs at truly exponential rates. Extension is a very different proposition in a supportive SCALE Cubed environment. Trying to escalate change only from a SCALE Squared center can feel

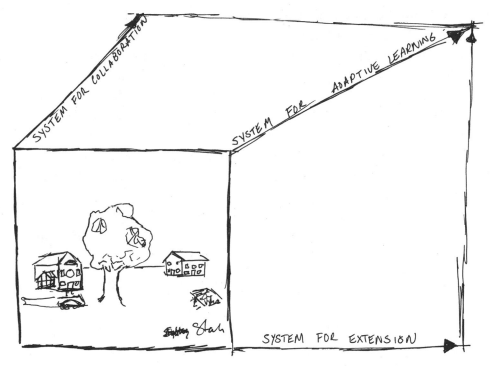

Fig. 22.3. SCALE Cubed: Systems for Collaboration, Adaptive Learning, and Extension

like a steep uphill climb. But when government is out front trying to nurture the rapid spread of change, community energy follows quickly. Expectations soar, people rise to sacrifice (and others move in to take advantage), but the momentum is palpable. The quickest way to sidetrack this energy is to have people see leaders using the momentum for their personal benefit.

As change moves across the three dimensions of SCALE, action becomes more complex. SCALE One has the single focus of building from success. SCALE Squared has the dual tasks of experimentation and training. SCALE Cubed uses three systems to promote collaboration, adaptive learning, and extension.

System for Sustainable Collaboration

The most important but most difficult activity in SCALE Cubed is promoting attitudinal and behavior change in officials and experts, shifting it away from control and toward the collaboration that fosters behavior change in communities. To stress the imperative for behavior change, we have sometimes used another version of the SCALE Cubed acronym—Stimulating Change in Attitudes of Leaders and Experts. This change inevitably meets with great resistance, since officials and experts are not humble students. To remind them of their place in the process, it is useful to make sure that their learning occurs in the field, as communities will have gained enough confidence and capacity that they will not accept lectures about what they should do.

In SCALE Cubed, officials and experts need to relinquish control systematically to allow capacity within communities to grow. Whereas in SCALE Squared the role of officials and experts is to instruct, in SCALE Cubed their role is to empower, not by getting out of the way but by positively affirming communities' capacity to achieve change. Four key tasks ensure that this shift occurs:

- Change policies, regulations, and administrative infrastructure. Financing and information systems in particular will need to be reconfigured. Ownership structures of common resources such as land, water, and trade may need to be changed. Transport, communications, and marketing sectors may need incentives to expand services. And, most important, training must be greatly extended.
- Provide seed grants in the form of either small, outside awards of money or material donations to leverage community self-financing and the mobilization of internal resources. Control over these grants must rest with local partnerships through SEED-based decisionmaking. Prescriptions by donors—so much to health services, so much to road construction, so much to projects proposed by outsiders rather than to the internally determined priorities of communities—will defeat development. A useful rule of thumb is one-quarter of a project's operating budget, including initial investments, may consist of external funds. In our experience, when the share of external funding is larger, allegiances shift to outside the community. Flexibility may be needed, however, in calculating noncash contributions from the community to respond to disasters and in compensating for discrimination against particular groups.

- Share information about what other communities are doing. Networks of SCALE Squared centers can most effectively arrange this information transfer. In a larger region there can be awards for groups that have done something special, and publicity in the form of stories about how specific problems were solved. Special recognition should be given to people who have taken the risk of making innovations successful. All cultures have appropriate ways of sharing such experiences.
- Hold special events—fairs, sports competitions, concerts, workshops, festivals—for the larger region to promote a sense of celebration, build awareness of varied experiences, support larger social change, and provide stability to the development process (a feature especially important for most officials and politicians).

System for Adaptive Learning

Meetings and workshops—all-inclusive regular meetings to decide upon action, and workshops for practical teaching—can provide the structure for helping communities learn how to adapt. Officials and experts can provide ongoing facilitation and technical assistance to help people mature in their capacity to work together, to adapt ideas, and to find more comprehensive solutions, but throughout this process officials and experts must share control to build capacity in communities.

In these meetings the SEED framework keeps discussions focused on facts and helps prevent factionalism. SEED becomes most effective when findings are regularized and real information from communities continues to flow through the system, creating an ever-larger regional or national network of information-based decisionmaking—instead of the archaic official systems now used, which can be easily corrupted. Through Self-Evaluation, objective data-gathering enables communities to assess their changing circumstances and set priorities. Through Effective Decisionmaking, an open-ended analysis of causality followed by subjective functional analysis helps communities reallocate roles and resources through collective agreement on joint action.

Such meetings serve as forums for establishing the annual cycle that leads to a new annual work plan. They also encourage informal, unstructured learning, as individuals who have gone to a SCALE Squared center share their experiences with community members who have not gone, and as individuals tell of their experiences since the last meeting or the last experiment. These spontaneous transfers carry great credibility.

System for Extension

As development goes to scale, the tasks of experts and officials become simpler. (It is often surprising even to them when they think back to why they had so much difficulty letting go of the desire to control.) The major SEED indicators will have been worked out (but will always need to be revised and made more precise). The major development options will have been created. Patterns will have been established for community meetings, and organized options will exist at the SCALE Squared center to which others come for training. For extension to occur for mass implementation of ideas and doable solutions, there is tremendous need for training—cascade training of large numbers of leaders and people.

Direct service providers in the various sectors—health, education, agriculture—are usually the government officials with whom communities have most continuing contact. Continually retraining these workers and reorienting their values are essential, for they are almost always the people at the forefront of action and can be counted on to influence the attitudes of officials and experts. These service providers can become on-site teachers supporting the change process and local experts in the participatory process. The more they feel part of the process, the more they will share their knowledge with others.

SCALE One, SCALE Squared, and SCALE Cubed must ultimately come together as three dimensions of the same process. But how they come together depends greatly on how the three partners cooperate. In the following sections we summarize the roles and actions appropriate to communities, government officials, and experts (NGOs, academic groups, donor agencies, and others).

How Communities Can Promote SEED-SCALE

What launches collective action in one community may not be appropriate for another community. The primary requirement is to find the best starting point in each from which to build community confidence and self-reliance. For example, improving children's health, though a noble goal, may not be as successful in creating a common ground for action as creating a winning sports team. In one community in the Philippines, a guitar-and-banjo team that became popular on television fostered community identity and focused people's attention on the possibility of change. In Tibet communities began by working to create a nature preserve. Curitiba had success with better bus transportation. Very often some money is available from a donor to start a specific activity—but more often the donor's priority is different from the community's. It may be that no one need predominates, that it is more important simply to coordinate existing services.

Two keys to successful community action are to start with a project that involves as many people as possible and to choose a project that shows results quickly. Whether or not a particular decision meets the greatest need identified by experts, whether or not all the partners are ready to cooperate, confidence and capacity will grow once action starts. If the local coordinating committee keeps its meetings and membership open, it can co-opt critics by giving them opportunity to implement their own suggestions.

To launch action and momentum that will self-correct and grow year by year, it is essential to complete the cycle of seven annual steps. Starting simply may help the community to achieve its goals.

Step 1. Create (and then recreate annually) a local coordinating committee and carefully build its capacity. An individual leader tends to get caught up in factions or fluctuating demands. A coordinating committee brings groups together and distributes responsibilities and accountability among those who will act. The group does not need to be highly organized, and at first a dozen people can efficiently do a great deal. The more they represent the diversity of the community, the better.

Step 2. Identify past successes and publicize them to raise awareness of what works, and has worked, in the community. Development grows from successes, and what people do best is the most likely basis for success in the future. On its own a community may not recognize what its successes really are. Experts can help a community identify its successes and how these may be redirected to build potential capacity and do better. A month or two

Fig. 22.4. Step 1: Create and Recreate Annually a Local Coordinating Committee

Fig. 22.5. Step 2: Identify Past Successes

of focused effort in building specific kinds of capacity may prove to be a wise investment.

Step 3. Study successes elsewhere. Divide those who will actually do the work (not just the powerful) into groups and have them visit other communities that seem to be "ahead" of your community. Find options that work for other people, and then adapt the good ideas to your situation. This step can run simultaneously with Step 2.

Step 4. Self-Evaluation. Create a community-specific database by collecting objective facts that are relevant to recognized needs. Don't make the first data-collection process difficult or time-consuming. Select key indicators and gather data on these instead of details on a multitude of separate variables, and use information that may have been collected by others. Gather information on resources for addressing specific problems, include people with special skills, and determine who the best candidates are for forging agreement on how to meet needs.

Step 5. Effective Decisionmaking. Announce a problemsolving meeting and encourage wide participation. Start working from specific data to reduce factionalism and unify divergent subjective opinions. Discuss causes of problems and explore alternatives. As people agree on priorities, draw up a work plan that assigns jobs and functions to all. Make it clear that this is part of an annual cycle, so priorities not addressed this year can be taken up in the next cycle. Try to reach this step each year in less than six months from the time you began Step 1.

Step 6. Take action on at least one achievable agreed-on priority. Seek issues that have the greatest emotional appeal in the community. Involve as many people in the community as possible. Start activities and delegate tasks, giving work to anyone who will work. Involve the people in greatest need, women, and youth. Shape momentum so all can contribute. Each participant and each achievement builds more progress.

Step 7. Involve people in monitoring activities to make midcourse corrections. Monitoring must follow the way work is actually performed and help show how functions can be reallocated. Don't hesitate to admit errors and to

Fig. 22.6. Step 3: Study Successes Elsewhere

Fig. 22.7. Step 4: Self-Evaluation with Key Indicators

Fig. 22.8. Step 5: Effective Decisionmaking—
Setting Priorities and Functional Analysis

Fig. 22.9. Step 6: Take Action on at Least One Achievable Agreed-upon Priority

Fig. 22.10. Step 7: Monitor Activities to Make Midcourse Corrections

adjust actions accordingly. The issue is not to get action right at the beginning but to try options, adapt them, and keep improving. As progress and capacity build, prepare to relaunch all seven steps next year, taking on a new priority in what will become an annual cycle of improvement.

How Governments Can Promote SEED-SCALE

Our experience suggests that governments are less efficient at operating local or regional projects (such as SCALE Squared centers) than at creating enabling environments by launching innovative policies and creating new organizational structures that encourage community-based action (as Lincoln did despite his preoccupation with the American Civil War). The following checklists summarize governments' roles in creating this enabling environment.

Changing Internal Attitudes

- Make financing flexible to support community action, for example by allowing budgeted funds to be reassigned from one sector to another in a new community work plan.
- Retrain government officials in empowering communities, mobilizing experts, and speeding up and simplifying action, so that they learn how to facilitate without taking control of the process.
- Promote community access to government records to obtain locally relevant data.
- Provide direct services through government agencies in ways that support community activities.
- Encourage openness by using balanced policies, incentives, reminders, and even reprimands so that officials and experts support community ownership of programs.
- Support SEED by (a) using and aggregating data from community work plans as a basis for government action and support, (b) instructing government personnel to provide technical help for the SEED process, and (c) promoting publicity that recognizes the annual achievements of communities and distributes information to encourage wider trials of innovations.
- Promote early action on ongoing crises (such as epidemics of diarrhea or HIV/AIDS, loss of groundwater reserves, and widespread changes in soil quality) by funding experiments to make breakthroughs and by adapting successes from other places.
- Arrange regular visits and workshops for government field staff and communities to SCALE Squared centers to learn new ideas and receive training.

Providing Support to Communities

- Facilitate communication and regional meetings among SCALE One communities to learn what others are doing, and promote regional events such as fairs, competitions, concerts, and workshops to create a larger sense of an expanding regional or national movement for change.

- Organize and fund a seed-grant program to leverage internal community resources by providing catalytic capital; outside funds should typically not exceed one-third of total project costs.
- Provide technical support to communities in the annual seven-step process. This task could usually be contracted out to nongovernmental or academic groups or to SCALE Squared centers.
- Organize a SCALE Squared support office with the tasks of (a) supporting communities in visits and workshops at SCALE Squared centers, (b) supporting these centers to do more effective research and training, and (c) creating a network of sharing among the centers.

How Experts Can Promote SEED-SCALE

Nongovernmental organizations, academic centers, donor agencies, and leaders in business, entertainment, religion, and sports can promote synergistic relationships with communities by contributing research expertise, technical innovation, flexible thinking, fast action, access to information, and (perhaps the most talked about) money. These sources of expertise have access to and control over a wide range of information and services, and their independent status may make them politically less accountable to both government and community. Their purposes may be narrower, and their objectives usually relate to global (as opposed to local) priorities. Because there is a tendency for NGOs, academic groups, and donors to try to speak for or act on behalf of a government or community in order to push their own objectives, it is important that both government and community monitor their activities. SEED-SCALE keeps this monitoring from being a hostile or controlling activity by specifying experts' assigned roles and responsibilities in the annual work plan.

NGOs, academic centers, or donors can work at two distinct levels: directly with the community or in planning and research. Many groups do both.

Direct Action with Communities

At the community level the wide variety of tasks that experts perform can be grouped according to the annual cycle of seven steps.

- In Step 1—in creating the coordinating committee—an expert group can help bring factions together, facilitate dialogue, train community members, or assume temporary leadership of the committee to help local leaders develop their own capacity. One coordinating role may be to establish linkages among professional associations, businesses, civic groups, religious communities, and part-time residents.
- In Step 2—identifying past successes—experts can point out achievements that may not have been recognized as successes by putting local experience in a larger perspective of needs and failures. One special parallel task here is to bring together new resources from within communities (such as business, religious, or entertainment sectors) that can make unique contributions to social change.
- In Step 3—studying successes elsewhere—experts naturally have access to wider experience and know relevant places and successful programs that can be visited. They can organize and lead study trips to such places and can provide technical skills that assist in adapting these outside experiences to local conditions.
- In Step 4—Self-Evaluation—experts have a specially vital role in gathering data, providing assistance in setting priorities, identifying solutions that are within community capacity, selecting the appropriate key indicators, and training workers in assessment skills.
- In Step 5—Effective Decisionmaking—experts will be central in helping to move from objective data to dialogue for community-based decisions. The tasks here involve first helping the community analyze the results of the assessment, then working that information through a causal and functional analysis, and facilitating maximal collaborative discussion to create the annual work plan.
- In Step 6—taking action—experts can provide a constant source of technical help as surprises come up. Without flexible and swift help, action is likely to halt as a result of early frustrations.
- In Step 7—monitoring activities to provide midcourse corrections—experts are particularly well placed to observe social change in the community objectively. While communities are good at anecdotal monitoring, they typically lack objectivity. Most particularly, com-

munities will not automatically look at the two central criteria of equity and sustainability. In these areas, experts can fill an outside-watchdog role to make sure that change is beneficial to all and does not slip into resource exploitation.

Planning and Research

In the planning and research function NGOs, academic centers, and donors can also fill some of their most important roles. Some groups will seek to fill several roles at the same time, but all too frequently the single role that an organization is asked to fill is that of financial donor. A donor that accepts only this role will have missed the opportunity to make clear its potential for greater service. If money becomes the focus, given the many demands on any donor for money, the amount the donor is able to give will be smaller than the community feels it needs, and the donor will increase the sense of restriction by adding a number of proscriptions on how the gift is to be used. The more sustainable functions, and the ones that nurture equity, are listed below.

- Open awareness to world knowledge and experience; identify particularly relevant successes, places, or techniques and share knowledge of these with officials and community members.
- Conduct basic research to make the sort of conceptual breakthroughs achieved at Narangwal (described in Chapter 10).
- Conduct applied field research, setting up experiments under real-life conditions to adapt ideas to local situations, such as occurred in the demonstration farms of the Green Revolution.
- Develop more-effective, more-accurate assessment tools (particularly SEED key indicators) that communities can use to make their actions more sensitive to local conditions.
- Teach communities as well as officials and experts useful skills, ideas, and, most important, attitudes and values that build capacity and reduce dependency.
- Develop research and training materials, training workshops, and information resources for citizens and officials to draw on.
- Organize involvement by international or national business forces,

religious groups, entertainment leaders, and the mass media in its many forms.

- Publish local successes; this activity can range from systematizing yearly SEED data, to aggregating it with other data, to bringing wider media attention to local progress and successes.
- Bring in new, nonmonetary resources from outside.
- Serve as an objective monitor of equity and sustainability.

Conclusion

Patterns for Action

As we walk through our lives, pursuing existing opportunities or trying to create new ones, visible just off the path are one tragedy—the widening gap between rich and poor—and, farther down the trail, a potential tragedy—the legacy we leave to our children as we persist in disrupting Earth's systems. Both are threats to our well-being today. They make clear that in our preoccupation with maximizing benefits in each step of our lives, we've been thoughtless and selfish in choosing our direction.

More than a century ago, experiments began (under President Abraham Lincoln, in Kerala, and in the Adirondacks) that carved out a community-enabling path for social change. After World War II many countries began large-scale systematic efforts to replicate planned development, both internally and internationally. We believed that what had brought our newly developed countries abundance and well-being could be transplanted to societies such as India. More recently we have realized that well-being comes from a process, not from a specific answer. It is the overall journey that determines the direction and length of our steps, not the other way around.

A century ago we viewed many of life's relationships as inherently adversarial, particularly our relationship to the natural world. Nature's threats were different then; the dangers today are no longer tigers and wolves. But the fact that we no longer fear wild animals when we step out into the world each day doesn't mean that our lives are not still defined by the forces of nature. The processes that will check us now are larger and seem more distant. Nature's systems will adjust—and make us adjust. The problem can be framed in terms of a story. It is almost inconceivable that the following tale of our closeness to nature could occur in the life of a person today. Such stories sound like fables from the founding of Rome.

But the following story is true. In the winter of 1916, in the jungles of northern India, the Taylor family was camped in a large mango grove by Dhanpura village, in the foothills of the Himalaya. Carl was an infant. Here is what happened as it was told so often by our ayah, the nurse who cared for many of us Taylor children:

I was asleep, my head leaning against the foot of Memsahib's camp cot. The bed shook, and I opened my eyes to look up at a large she-wolf above me, standing on the bed. The kerosene lamp was dimmed, but I saw the wolf reach down and pick up Carl, who was then four months old. I screamed—and you know that I can scream well. My hand found Memsahib's *topee* [pith helmet], and I slammed it into the side of the wolf. She dropped Carl Baba and turned to snarl at me. Again she reached to pick up Carl. We were alone in camp; everyone else was in the village at a meeting, I kept screaming, and Sahib's two hunting dogs charged in, barking. The wolf jumped over me and escaped out of the back of the tent.

In the excitement after everyone returned, the villagers said the wolf would come back, that she was looking for a replacement for a lost cub. Memsahib wanted everyone to pack and move camp, since the night before, when Sahib was away at a meeting, she had been suddenly awakened by a large, doglike animal on the foot of her bed and had kicked it off. Sahib said that Indian stories about wolves taking babies to raise were sheer superstition. He would guard the tent with his gun. But each of the next two nights the wolf came back, trying to get in through the opening at the back of the tent, which was now tied shut. Sahib did get one fine look and saw it was a wolf. So on the third day, we broke camp . . .

As the architects engaged in redesigning the planet's systems we have had fair warning. There is today ample evidence that Mother Nature is looking for something she has lost and has come onto the foot of our bed. And although we may succeed for some years yet in kicking the danger off, ample evidence exists that nature will keep returning to remind us of that loss.

Today's technological weapons will not remove the threat. Whole systems are being disrupted—not just natural systems but societal systems as well; violence rises around us, as does a force more pernicious: fear of, rather than partnership with, our neighbor. We may have mastered how to keep stock markets from crashing and famines from erupting, but we have not learned how to put nature or society into a box and shape what will come out. Nature is not a computer for which we write software. We are part of the software, perhaps even a virus.

The ability of humans to work together in communities—and, now increasingly, through networks as citizens of the planet—places us in a fundamentally different role within the systems of life. Although we are part of the larger software, we also write some of its algorithms. Increasingly we are able to see how life's complex equations work and how to shape our actions to direct the formulas. As our experiments give us more understanding, we are beginning to have the potential to write not just destructive code, but an operating system for a better way of living.

The challenge seems overwhelming: planetary social and natural systems are shifting, and we are like people being asked to change a tire as the car rolls along the road, or to rebuild a boat while it's sailing. We may look back with nostalgia to when change was slower, but we cannot go back. The choices before us are two: either we work out a process to address our problems or we let ourselves be buffeted and driven into the future by forces we do not control. In either case uncertainty and risk lie ahead.

Moreover, past experience shows that whatever we do is likely to create another, larger set of problems. The changing world we live in operates under a mostly forgotten postulate of the nineteenth century called Jevon's Paradox: breakthroughs designed to advance civilization usually also do the reverse.[1] A century ago it was noted that increased coal-burning efficiency made steam engines more useful; that progress led to more steam engines, which led to more demand for coal, and more cinders, soot, smoke. Thus each step of progress brought more environmental destruction instead of less. Jevon's Paradox explains why increased fuel efficiency in cars causes people to drive more miles and ultimately to consume more fuel. It explains why more-efficient chainsaws and sawmills lead to more timber cutting, and why more-efficient petroleum technologies lead to more exploration and exploitation of offshore, Arctic, and other sites. It is why technological progress in medical care is associated with iatrogenic disease and why the control of one infection leads to the emergence of other infections.

How to break through? We should not be romantic about the power of community transformation, believing that age-old patterns of greed will now vanish because we see the looming implications of our way of living. Most of us live in a state of blinkered complacency, not in one of perpetual idealistic commitment. Only for brief moments in human history has generosity transcended selfishness. We need to assemble a system of living based on more than self-interest. It does not matter whether our homes are in China, Chile, or Chicago, middle-class or traditional poor, urban or rural. Most families are so absorbed in their established patterns of daily tasks that they cannot focus on the larger world—and even at those moments when they are willing to, it is unclear what they can do.

In this book we have presented examples of how ordinary people have gone about meeting great challenges, taking small, specific steps that do not entail excessive risk. Each small success addresses community concerns and builds forward momentum, reaching wider in nonthreatening ways to address larger, more distant problems. As confidence and capacity build, so do sophistication and trust.

The communities described in the case studies undertook actions day by day, at a pace that people could handle. Change for them was not disruptive, because they had a voice in deciding which needs were most urgent and a direct role in taking action. Often they were frustrated that change was not occurring fast enough, but the momentum of change carried them along, and ultimately the achievements were transforming.

In most societies the most effective agents of change tend to be women. Women, though keepers of tradition, are also reliable activists, particularly when they see that action will serve their children. Time and again women are more willing to mobilize, more willing to change old social norms, and quicker to scale up to new groups of organization if they see that a process provides hope for making their children's future better. But to support them as they put together truly beneficial frameworks, women need clear demonstrations, not just words.

A recent experience illustrates these dynamics. In the fall of 1999 we were conducting research in central Nepal on how that society had changed during the fifty years since Carl had first visited the country. Lumpek village sits on top of a ridge reached by a five-thousand-foot climb, a perch from which a fantastic panorama embraces the snowcapped Himalaya and luxuriant, undulating, green valleys below. A focus-group discussion was under way with fifteen women who were health volunteers in their communities, women who had taken time from preparing for the semiannual distribution of vitamin A to children to talk to us.

They were outspoken in describing their difficulties. One said, "When I get home tonight, I'll find the buffaloes hungry, the cows hungry, the pigs hungry, the children crying, and my husband unhappy because the food isn't cooked."

We replied, "Then why do you do all this work helping the village? Why not just stay home and do your tasks?"

Another shouted back, "Our neighbors won't let us quit! They say their children's health depends on us. But though we do the work, they don't help. They force us to keep working, and then criticize us because they think we're making money from the rotating drug fund. The village development committee and health post don't help either; all they give is orders, and we do the work!"

The Lumpek villagers were halfway. Some of the women had organized, but their community had not. This group of women recognized the shared imperative for change, but still the other villagers were not joining in to create a truly collective force that would define the future they all wanted and knew was possible. To mobilize the community it was necessary for all women, not just these few, to divide up the work, preferably in data-based annual work plans that all of them helped to shape. To do this, they needed enabling support, not just officials or experts telling them what to do.

How can transforming change occur in our ordinary communities? To some readers of this book the cases presented will seem to describe extraordinary people and places. Yet every community sees its own situation as both normal and special, given its circumstance and time.

Wherever we live, our everyday lives are increasingly shaped by larger forces—corporate actions, newly emerging cultural values, distant financial decisions, environmental change. The challenge is how to respond to these pressures. The uncertainty is not whether a response will be possible, but whether we are going to decide to direct the response so that it benefits both us and those who follow. SEED-SCALE is an incremental approach that gently redirects these forces, looking to the implications of our actions. It changes the system by changing the foundation on which decisions are made, by introducing a different, community-friendly basis of paperwork. It grows from the annual community work plan and seeks to make government direc- tives and budget allocations support it. The plan is grounded in local reality, and it sets out objectives that are priorities people are willing to work for, assigning duties to each partner. This new piece of paper can be the founda- tion that agencies and communities build from.

A wise Iranian friend, Torab Mehra, described the process for making change in his country's rigid bureaucracy:

> The first need is to set your own top priorities, have a clear idea where you want to go. No one else in the bureaucracy has such a vision, people move back and forth in Brownian Movement like molecular particles. So start your process of change. Quickly, you will find that the person above you in the hierarchy will not see the possible benefit of change and will block your idea. If you are right and are willing to take a risk, you can go around him if you have the right connections. But be care- ful, because he will try to get even. In the meantime, work on two smaller things you want to change with people who will cooperate for personal reasons. This will build momentum and your credibility. There are always people willing to try ideas that sound good and will improve their status. After a while the first person who blocked your first priority will move his attention to other activities or change to another position. Then you can go ahead with your idea. Since others don't have a clear vision for change, you can use and mold the system from the inside even though at first it seems hopelessly rigid.

The change produced is iterative and therefore need not be threatening. Each of us must learn to find our own doable tasks. Each of us, even if an official or an expert, is basically a simple person, and what we cope with is our daily duties. Sometimes one of us will stand out slightly from the crowd, but only for a moment. By and large, each of us does the best we can to balance complex demands. The government and institutions we are part of are pretty much like us; they like us to do their simple tasks and keep in place systems that reduce risk for themselves. In this prosaic context SEED-SCALE can slip in a new piece of paperwork at the foundation of the process and become the basis for action that redirects societal change to be site- and need-specific.

SEED-SCALE appeals to both conservatives and liberals. On the one side it promotes self-determination at the community level and cautious extension of exposure, and on the other side it promotes looking beyond individual self-interest to see larger responsibilities and looming implications. The annual work plans change the orientation of community processes, creating a fact-based foundation of aggregate community priorities that can flow into and influence official policy even as they define local actions. The process becomes most successful when it results in another acronym of SCALE: Stimulating Changes in Attitudes of Leaders and Experts. In new partnerships work plans provide concrete steps to guide the people who have authority and money. By giving officials a framework of community priorities and action, work plans help officials to shape local, regional, and national direction.

The genius of the SEED-SCALE work plan is that it is simple. Although the movement of large forces is complex and unclear, and although the bureaucracies that manage our systems are confusing and self-serving, the work plan focuses away from this complexity. This simple focus is what makes it possible for everyone—citizens, experts, and officials—to succeed. Until now it has been hard, amid all the complexity, to sift out what to do. With so many possible directions, our actions have resembled the behavior described in an ancient Chinese fable: "We are like a big fish that has been pulled from the water and is flopping wildly to find its way back in. In such a condition the fish never asks where the next flip or flop will bring it. It senses only that its present position is intolerable and that something else must be tried."[2] The fish had two problems: it was out of its element, and it did not know which was the right direction to take. As communities, we, too, need to find our element; the process of creating the work plan determines where the stream is that is right for each of us. The tasks specified in the work plan tell us what to do once we find that stream and have chosen the way, speed, and direction to go.

It is tempting to attribute our inability to find the river or, once we arc in the river, our inability to swim, to not having resources adequate to the magnitude of the tasks. But most problems have had enough money, people, and ideas thrown at them to show that more resources are not the solution; nor are the resources we need more experts, more buildings, or more any-thing. Like a fish trying to get under way, we cannot fairly be accused of failure if we are valiantly trying. People are working hard. To resolve our random flopping we need both greater clarity about direction and a more supportive, enabling environment in which to make our way.

To find consistent direction each group needs clarity and a vision of core objectives. This book presents a vision with two major objectives: justice (which gives hope to current generations) and sustainability (which gives hope for future generations). In moving toward such grand objectives, suc-cess comes only if we remain humble, expecting more mistakes than suc-cesses, being always open to learning from our mistakes, making a correction, and then expecting that the new path will lead into more errors. The process that carries us forward is not one that maps the whole future, but one that gives us better next steps.

The global conservation imperative needs to be part of all our efforts to improve human well-being. In this book we have repeatedly used the Green Revolution as a worldwide project that showed how programs can grow to global scale and how concerted action can avert a catastrophe that seemed inevitable, such as the famines that Malthus and others predicted. The Green Revolution is also an ideal example to show how something good must continue to get better, self-correcting and learning from its problems. The successes of the 1960s that produced four times more food for the world are today also considered environmental, economic, and social failures be-cause this revolution is not self-correcting and continuing to learn from its mistakes.

We return to India's Punjab, an area where we've watched the Green Revolution. When it began in 1960, the Punjab (where as a father-and-son team we searched rolling savannas for black buck, as described in Chapter 2) was only partially farmed and produced 1.7 million tons of wheat and 2.2 million tons of rice. After four decades of the Green Revolution, the same region now produces 5.1 million tons of wheat and 6.8 million tons of rice—

8 million tons of new food annually.[3] Hundreds of millions of people have been fed because of the new agricultural practices in what is known now as the breadbasket of India.

But negative consequences have already appeared. While they were averting famine for current generations, the planners of the Green Revolution were not adequately aware of implications for future generations. In the words of David Seckler of the International Irrigation Management Institute, "At some point, this house of cards will collapse, and when it does, India's grain harvest could fall by as much as twenty-five percent. In a country where the supply and demand for food is already precariously balanced . . ."[4]

Old seed varieties adapted to Punjab soil and water were exchanged for new grains that flourished with intensive applications of water and fertilizer. The planners assumed an abundance of water in the Punjab (the name means "Five Rivers") and introduced the water intensive practice of transplanting young rice in hot May. This nearly doubled the amount of water needed compared with what would have been required had the transplanting been a month later, at the start of the monsoon. The intense irrigation caused mineral salts to rise from the lower soil and poison crops. Irrigation also caused nitrogen to filter down and contaminate the water below. Carbon, zinc, and iron were eroded from the soil. As soil lost natural fertility, the need grew for artificial fertilizers. In the early years, only ten thousand tons of fertilizer were needed for the whole Punjab, but by the end of the third decade, one hundred times that (one million tons per year) was required. In response to that hundredfold increase, grain output increased fivefold.[5]

The old canals could not provide enough water, so tube wells were drilled. Eventually there was a tube well for every four hectares of land around Ludhiana, where we had lived. To keep them pumping (and the politicians in office), the state gave farmers free electricity. Farmers pumped with abandon. How could they put on their fields too much of something so wonderful as water? Four decades later, the water table is four meters lower and falling still further. By contrast, in northern and southern Punjab some soils are now so waterlogged that they have lost virtually all agricultural potential, and the area of such soil degradation increases.[6]

The Green Revolution is an excellent example of how well-intentioned development goes awry when it violates the three principles—three-way partnerships, data-based decisions, and work plans that change behaviors. Expansion was directed by officials and experts, much like factory managers running a manufacturing process to increase output and efficiency; the community of proud, strong-minded Punjabi farmers believed their techniques would continue what seemed at first to be a miracle. Overly confident in the new, outsider experts ignored historical experience from the British times, experience that was also in the memories of many local farmers, about how earlier irrigation had produced similar waterlogging and salinization.

The data that were gathered focused on aggregate indicators of outputs and inputs. Green Revolution data tended to ignore information that included the larger context of changes in the environment. For example, the new land required by the Green Revolution came from turning savannas and jungles into fields. Plans to put this land under the plow did not factor in what would be lost in natural spaces, wildlife, and a larger ecology. Choices did not balance the food gain against what was removed from the larger web of life. The outsiders who planned the program are gone. The extra food will be eaten. What remain are less biodiversity, lower water tables, and toxic soils—and, hopefully, communities, experts, and officials who will now have learned some very important lessons.

By 1968 the director of India's Agricultural Research Institute, M. S. Swaminathan, had enough information to foresee today's reality: "Intensive cultivation of land without conservation of soil fertility and soil structure will lead, ultimately, to the springing up of deserts. Irrigation without arrangements for drainage will result in soils getting alkaline or saline. Indiscriminate use of pesticides can cause adverse changes in biological balance and lead to cancer and toxic residues in the grains and other edible parts. Unscientific tapping of water will lead to exhaustion of this wonderful resource."[7]

The leaders of the Green Revolution were as well-intentioned and informed as leaders of a high priority project are likely to be. They had a surfeit of financial and research resources. Their lack of attention to the wider context reveals the limits of traditional top-down, outside-managed action even when done in the best way. A larger ecological perspective is needed for such projects, one that includes better checks and balances to readjust momentum and to keep on course. Without such a process, the Green Revolution in India became a two-grain revolution from which we can learn a great deal.

Our local crises are microcosms of global ones. International conservation conferences struggle to find rationales and funding to protect 10 percent of the land on Earth. But this vision is inadequate. A sustainable future will not be put in place by preserving only 10 percent of the planet while activities under way in the other 90 percent warm the atmosphere, reduce the amount of fresh water, erode the soil, and toxify what we breathe. The affluent development model that is causing this damage is given prime time (and virtually all time) as it anchors our economy while seeking continual growth. It is a model, however, of glutted well-being that is available to not much more than 10 percent of people on Earth—the new nobility. As this model grinds on, destroying so much and benefiting so few, current prescriptions for protecting the environment focus on the periphery: the most exotic biodiversity, locking up the last wild places, and investing huge resources in saving a few endangered species. Although conservation advocates advance grand designs to check the momentum of destruction and loss, they then have to compromise so significantly in implementing these agreements that the action is never equal to the need. The conservation momentum worldwide has missed the core of the problem: we need to advance a model that incrementally redirects the way we live.

We face a planetary problem. While saving our wild remnants, we must reassemble, piece by piece, appropriate planetary solutions that address people's core behaviors, particularly those of the affluent. The needs for restitution and reconstruction are urgent, and growing more so every day. We can no longer just pay tithes to nature. We must do better than address the problems of 10 percent of the planet and 10 percent of its people. We have both examples and an understanding from which to build. Now we must take these beginnings and keep evolving them to make them more beautiful and more satisfying.

All partners must join in this effort. In some instances government agencies will lead. In others, nongovernmental organizations, market forces, corporations, or spontaneous movements will initiate change. But communities should never be left out, because they are both the core of the problem and the core agents in the solution. Creating that participation with communities is not a matter of becoming more cunning in community manipulation. In many places citizens have awakened, and their aspirations and actions are ready to take off. But this community energy cannot be left to burn on its own like an untended fire; a simple structure is needed that focuses energy on specific tasks. SEED-SCALE has the potential to systematically focus human actions. The design must take into account global environmental needs to bring forward local solutions that build to achieve large-scale responses.

No single solution is a panacea, and no process will ever assure full protection against human selfishness, stupidity, and shortsighted greed. Daily we risk the evolution of ever more virulent diseases, accelerating global climate change, economic meltdowns, genetic engineering with unknown implications, and an information glut that gives ever-widening access but narrowing wisdom. In seeking a process we must put in place systems that catch our mistakes and allow us iterative trials to build better answers.

For just and lasting change we need structure, but we also need flexibility. The development challenge has been stated succinctly by Amartya Sen: the underlying solution is to enlarge our freedoms.[8] Each community must select the expanded freedoms that are most urgent for it at a given time: better health, greater knowledge, leisure, food security, religious fulfillment, economic well-being, quietude. What expands freedom for one community may not be a priority for others. We may very likely need a lot more of some of these freedoms than we need more money.

Our Muslim neighbors have a useful concept: *sabat,* which means "what we have is only lent to us; we must pass it along." The abundance and well-being that we possess today have come to us from prior generations. To expand our freedoms, we must make small sacrifices for the greater good, both now and to come. To understand how to pass along our human inheritance, we can refer to another old Middle Eastern desert concept: hospitality. We need to welcome our adversary into our tent. To leave any person outside is not only contrary to our responsibility as fellow creatures; it is also bad judgment, as the unknown and unseen will always be more dangerous. Even though we may disagree one with another, we need to learn to live together. Diversity gives strength to our society—and being considered different and special is also how we would like to be treated.

As humans, we have expectations that consistently outstrip performance. We will never achieve the complete satisfaction we seek. Fulfillment recedes ahead as our achievements accumulate. Moreover, most specific achievements do not provide the satisfaction expected. When we lay hands on a part, the objective has moved on. We seek completion, and we find that more remains to be accomplished. Each question answered reveals three others that are more demanding. We know development when we experience it; but we have trouble repeating it. Our needs are immediate, yet there is something timeless about the process of improving the world. As we pursue our separate visions, we are members of a cavalcade of earlier generations also seeking. We exist in a moment that is better than the moment before, but the process of change must and will go on. We cannot stop time or human initiative to experiment. What gives ultimate meaning is fundamentally a spiritual paradox: we can never achieve an ideal life, and yet we can always take another step closer. Satisfaction comes in moving, not in arriving.

To rephrase Aristotle's observation: development is not the life end we are seeking but merely the process that allows us to seek something else. The pace of our progress has so entrapped our attentions that we have come to believe that progressive development is the chief end of humankind. It is not just theology that asks: What is that something else?

The initiatives presented in this book show it is possible to grow in our collective lives toward ends that are more just and lasting. The course of this journey need not and cannot be charted. All that is required is a beginning, and thereafter a process for continuing what is fulfilling to every community. The ancient Chinese proverb "Any long journey starts with a single step" is a helpful reminder that the challenge for each of us is indeed the next step, not the longer journey. We hesitate to take that simple step usually not because of danger or difficulty but from fear of change. But change will come anyway. We need mutual support to select the specific steps for our community. The value of SEED is that communities can cooperate with officials and experts to create an objective database to determine immediate direction. The value of SCALE is that it systematizes steps in an effective order so action can extend across a large region, yet remain specific to local circumstances. Like a long journey, the process unfolds in repeated iterations and along an enabling and evolving path.

It is unrealistic to predict a schedule for SCALE extension; too many variables influence the process. But with a consistent focus it is possible to telescope the pace of the steps. If they occurred in the usual unplanned sequence, a process that would have taken five or six decades can now be compressed into perhaps two decades. But two decades is still longer than the time spans politicians promise or the five-year funding cycles by which donors commonly plan. In the beginning, setting the direction of change requires particular patience. Behavior change takes time. People may turn to partnerships early, they may readily start to use data, but to learn new ways sustainably takes repetition. On the other hand, as the case studies show, once the process starts, with one step, and then another, it can spread faster than anyone planned for.

It is hard to start. It is easier to talk and to investigate options. Communities do not need more beginnings; they need a framework to enable them reliably to continue. Albert Einstein's enduring observation that "the world will not evolve past its current state of crisis by using the same thinking that created that crisis" points toward the imperative that the framework for progress must be a new understanding of old problems. Most people in the world today have better health, more secure shelter, and the hope that things will get better. However, more than one-fifth of us live with rising hunger, vulnerability to violence, and exposure to tragedy from disaster and resource depletion. But there is hope for progress among these neighbors, too—if we reach out. They cannot do it on their own.

As humans, if we are humble, we can take real, next steps and sequence them into a continuing journey. In taking these steps we must remember that development is not a product, but a process; it is not a solution, but a way by which each community can create an evolving and unique pattern to achieve a more just and lasting future.

NOTES

Prologue

1. John C. Taylor, Sr., *India: Dr. John Taylor Remembers* (Atlanta: World Presbyterian Missions, 1973), pp. 34, 85.
2. Letter from M. Feiber, quoted in ibid., p. 4.
3. Carl E. Taylor, "Care for Childhood Psychological Trauma in Wartime May Contribute to Peace," *International Review of Psychiatry,* 10 (1998): 175–78.
4. Jesse Oak Taylor-Ide, "In Search of the Clouded Leopard," *National Geographic,* September 2000.

Introduction

1. United Nations Development Program (hereafter UNDP), *Human Development Report, 1999* (New York: Oxford University Press and United Nations Publications, 1999).
2. Daniel C. Taylor-Ide and Carl E. Taylor, *Community Based Sustainable Development: A Proposal for Going to Scale with Self-Reliant Social Development,* UNICEF Children, Environment, and Sustainable Development Series, no. 1 (New York, 1995); Carl E. Taylor et al., *Partnerships for Social Development: A Casebook* (Franklin, W.Va.: Future Generations and Johns Hopkins University, Department of International Health, 1995).

1. Getting Started

1. See Tom Athanasiou, *Divided Planet: The Ecology of Rich and Poor* (Athens: University of Georgia Press, 1998).
2. David C. Korten, *When Corporations Rule the World* (West Hartford: Kumarian and Barrett-Koehler, 1995), p. 18.
3. See Harry C. Boyte and Nancy N. Kari, *Building America: The Democratic Promise of Public Work* (Philadelphia: Temple University Press, 1996).

4. See Lester C. Thurow, *The Future of Capitalism: How Today's Economic Forces Shape the World* (New York: William Morrow, 1996), pp. 245–6.

5. See Boyte and Kari, *Building America.*

6. The discussion of Lincoln's administration is drawn from Carl Sandberg, *Abraham Lincoln: The War Years,* vols. 1 and 3 (New York: Harcourt Brace, 1939); J. N. Kane, *Facts about the Presidents,* 6th ed. (New York: H. W. Wilson, 1993); and L.W. Levy and L. Fisher, *Encyclopedia of the American Presidency,* vol. 3 (New York: Simon & Schuster, 1994).

7. D. H. Bates, *Lincoln in the Telegraph Office* (New York: Century, 1907), pp. 2–5.

8. See Korten, *When Corporations Rule the World.*

9. Discussion of Theodore Roosevelt's administration is drawn from Kane, *Facts about the Presidents;* and Levy and Fisher, *Encyclopedia of the American Presidency,* vol. 3.

10. See Vaclav Smil, *Cycles of Life: Civilization and the Biosphere* (New York: W. H. Freeman, 1997).

11. See World Bank, *World Development Report, 1993: Investing in Health* (Oxford: Oxford University Press, 1993).

2. Synopsis of SEED-SCALE

1. Grace L. Boggs, "A Question of Place," *Monthly Review* 52 (June 2000): 18–20.

2. A variety of websites are helpful here:

   www.future.org: Future Generations, a nongovernmental organization promoting the concepts and projects described in this book, with continual updating of relevant information

   www.sustainablemeasures.com: Sustainable Measures, a consulting firm that develops indicators for measuring progress toward a sustainable society, economy, and environment

   www.rprogress.org/progrsum/cip/cip_main.html: Redefining Progress, a public policy organization balancing economy, environment, and social equity and including a U.S.-based group of communities seeking indicators for monitoring change

   http://iisd1.iisd.ca/ca/measure.compindex.asp: International Institute for Sustainable Development, maintaining an international compendium of initiatives and indicators on sustainable development www.loka.org: Loka Institue, a base of information on how to use science and technology for community-based action

3.   See Harry C. Boyte and Nancy N. Kari, *Building America: The Democratic Promise of Public Work* (Philadelphia: Temple University Press, 1996).

4.   See Carl E. Taylor, "Surveillance for Equity in Primary Health Care: Policy Implications from International Experience," *International Journal of Epidemiology* 21 (1992): 1043–9.

5.   See Tom Athanasiou, *Divided Planet: The Ecology of Rich and Poor* (Athens: University of Georgia Press, 1998).

3. Making a Large and Lasting Impact

1.   For other discussions of approaches for going to scale, see David C. Korten, "Community Organization and Rural Development: A Learning Process Approach," *Public Administration Review,* September/October 1990, pp. 480–511; Robert Myers, *The Twelve Who Survive: Strengthening Programmes of Early Childhood Development in the Third World* (London: Routledge and UNESCO, 1992); Samuel Paul, *Managing Development Programs: The Lessons of Success* (Boulder: Westview, 1982); and David Pyle, *Life after Project: A Multi-Dimensional Analysis of Implementing Social Development Program at the Community Level* (Boston: John Snow, 1984).

2.   Donald E. Ingber, "The Architecture of Life," *Scientific American* 278 (January 1998).

4. Our Maturing Understanding of Community Change

1.   Donald T. Phillips, *Lincoln on Leadership* (New York: Warner, 1992).

2.   See Paolo Freire, *Pedagogy of the Oppressed* (New York: Seabury Press, 1970) and *Education for Critical Consciousness* (London: Sheed and Ward, 1974).

3.   Robert Chambers, *Whose Reality Counts? Putting the First Last* (London: Intermediate Technology, 1997), p. 106.

4.   Walt W. Rostow, *Stages of Economic Growth: A Non-Communist Manifesto* (New York: Cambridge University Press, 1960).

5.   Lester C. Thurow, *The Future of Capitalism: How Today's Economic Forces Shape the World* (New York: Morrow, 1996), pp. 6–8.

6.   United Nations, *Report of the United Nations Conference on the Human Environment,* document A/Conf.48/14/Revision 1 (New York, 1972), preamble, clause 1.

7.   WHO/UNICEF, *Primary Health Care: A Joint Report by the Director Gen-*

eral of the World Health Organization and the Executive Director of the United Nations Children's Fund; International Conference on Primary Health (Alma Ata, U.S.S.R., 1978).

8. Santosh Mehrota and Richard Jolly, *Development with a Human Face: Experiences in Social Achievement and Economic Growth* (Oxford: Clarendon Press, 1997); John Rohde, Monica Chatterjee, and David Morley, *Reaching Health for All* (New Delhi: Oxford University Press, 1993); Robert Myers, *The Twelve Who Survive: Strengthening Programmes of Early Childhood Development in the Third World* (London: Routledge and UNESCO, 1992).

9. David C. Korten, *When Corporations Rule the World* (West Hartford: Kumarian Press; San Francisco: Berrett-Koehler, 1995).

10. Thurow, *The Future of Capitalism,* pp. 43–64.

5. Assuring Accountability through Better Paperwork

1. Mary Jordan, "School Reform: Promise or Threat?" *Washington Post,* February 14, 1993.

2. Sean Reardon and Katherine Merseth, *Augusta County—Beech Mountain Institute,* MacDougall Case Studies (Cambridge, Mass.: Harvard Graduate School of Education, 1993).

6. A Crisis Can Become an Opportunity

1. Intergovernmental Panel on Climate Change, *Report to the General Assembly* (New York: United Nations, 1995).

2. *Pendleton Times,* November 14, 1985.

3. See K. M. A. Aziz and W. Henry Mosley, "The History, Methodologies, and Findings of the Matlab Project in Bangladesh," in *Prospective Community Studies in Developing Countries,* ed. M. Das Gupta, P. Aaby, M. Garenne, and G. Pision (Oxford: Clarendon Press, 1997), pp. 28–53; James F. Phillips, W. S. Stinson, Susham Bhatia, M. Rahman, and J. Chakraborty, "The Demographic Impact of the Family Planning–Health Services Project in Matlab," *Studies in Family Planning* 12, no. 5 (1982): 131–40; James F. Phillips, H. Chakraborty, and A. Chowdhury, "Integrating Health Services into an MCH-FP Program: Lessons from Matlab," *Studies in Family Planning* 15, no. 4 (1984):153–61.

4. J. Cleland, J. Philips, S. Amin, and G. M. Kamal, *The Determinants of Reproductive Change in Bangladesh: Success in a Challenging Environment* (Washington, D.C.: World Bank, 1994).

5. Henry B. Perry, *Health for All in Bangladesh: Lessons in Primary Health Care*

for the Twenty-first Century (Dhaka, Bangladesh: University Press, 2000), pp. 7–25.

6.   Ibid., pp. 88–90.

7.   F. H. Abed and M. R. Chowdhury, "The Bangladesh Rural Advancement Committee: How BRAC Learned to Meet Rural People's Needs through Local Action," in *Reasons for Hope: Instructive Experiences in Rural Development*, ed. A. Krishna, N. Uphoff, and M. J. Esman (West Hartford: Kumarian Press, 1996).

8.   Carl E. Taylor, "How Care for Childhood Psychological Trauma in Wartime May Contribute to Peace," *International Review of Psychiatry* 10 (1998): 175–8.

9.   K. Nader and R. S. Pynoos, "The Children of Kuwait after the Gulf Crisis," in *The Psychological Effects of War and Violence on Children*, ed. L. A. Leavitt and N. A. Fox (Hillsdale, N.J.: Lawrence Erlbaum, 1993), pp. 181–95.

10. See James P. Grant, "Children, Wars, and the Responsibility of the International Community," in *War and Public Health*, ed. B. S. Levy and V. W. Sidel (New York: Oxford University Press, 1997), pp. 12–24; UNICEF, *The State of the World's Children* (New York, 1996).

11. Atle Dyregrov and Magne Raundalen, "Children and War in the Contemporary World," *International Child Health* 7 (1996): 43–52.

12. R. J. Apfel and B. Simon, *Minefields in the Hearts: The Mental Health of Children in War and Communal Violence* (New Haven: Yale University Press, 1996), p. 244.

13. See Peter R. Berke and Timothy Beatley, *After the Hurricane: Linking Recovery to Sustainable Development in the Caribbean* (Baltimore: Johns Hopkins University Press, 1997).

7. Ding Xian

Epigraph: Yangchu C. James Yen, *Y. C. James Yen's Thoughts on Mass Education and Rural Reconstruction—China and Beyond*, ed. Martha M. Keehn (New York: International Institute of Rural Reconstruction, 1993), p. i.

1.   Pearl S. Buck, *Tell the People: Talks with James Yen about the Mass Education Movement* (New York: Harper & Row and the International Institute of Rural Reconstruction, 1959).

2.   Gerald F. Winfield, *China—The Land and the People* (New York: W. Sloane Associates, 1948), p. 437.

3.   Marjorie B. Bullock, *An American Transplant: The Rockefeller Foundation and Peking Union Medical College* (Berkeley: University of California Press, 1986), pp. 134–89.

4.   Conrad Seipp, ed., *Health Care for the Community: Selected Papers of Dr. John B. Grant* (Baltimore: Johns Hopkins Press, 1963), pp. 148–66.

5.   C. C. Chen, *Medicine in Rural China* (Berkeley: University of California Press, 1989); idem, "A Personal Remembrance," in Yen, *Yen's Thoughts on Mass Education.*

6.   James B. Mayfield, "Sustainable Development: Integration of Dr. Yen's Thought and the Concept of Sustainability," ibid., pp. 77–90.

7.   Jimmy Yen, personal communication to Carl Taylor, spring 1964.

8.   Hsing-Huang M. Hsiao, "The Farmers' Movement in Taiwan: Retrospects and Prospects," in Yen, *Yen's Thoughts on Mass Education,* p. 171.

9.   Juan M. Flavier, "Implementing Dr. Yen's Reconstruction Credo," ibid., p. 121.

8. Kerala

1.   T. N. Krishnan, "Health Statistics in Kerala State, India," in *Good Health at Low Cost,* ed. Scott B. Halstead, Julia A. Walsh, and Kenneth S. Warren (New York: Rockefeller Foundation, 1985), p. 39.

2.   P. G. R. Panikar, "Health Care System in Kerala and Its Impact on Infant Mortality," ibid., p. 47.

3.   Richard W. Franke and Barbara H. Chasin, *Kerala: Development through Radical Reform* (New Dehli: Promilla Press; and San Francisco: Institute for Food and Development Policy, 1994).

4.   Charlotte Wiser and William Wiser, *Behind Mud Walls in India* (London: George Allen and Unwin, 1934), p. 180.

5.   Verrier Elwin, *A Philosophy for NEFA,* 2d ed. (Itanagar, Arunachal Pradesh: Directorate of Research, 1957), p. 2.

6.   T. N. Krishnan, "The Route to Social Development in Kerala: Social Intermediation and Public Action," in *Development with a Human Face: Experiences in Social Achievement and Economic Growth,* ed. Santosh Mehrotra and Richard Jolly (Oxford: Clarendon Press, 1997), p. 204; Panikar, "Health Care System in Kerala," p. 49.

7.   Moni Nag, "The Impact of Social and Economic Development on Mortality: Comparative Study of Kerala and West Bengal," in Halstead, Walsh, and Warren, *Good Health at Low Cost.*

8.   Franke and Chasin, *Kerala.*

9.   Nag, "Impact of Social and Economic Development."

10. Panikar, "Health Care System in Kerala," p. 48.

11. Krishnan, "Health Statistics in Kerala State."

12. Bill McKibben, *Hope, Human and Wild* (Boston: Little, Brown, 1995).

9. The Adirondacks

1. Barbara McMartin, "The Adirondacks: It's Not a Model; It's a Mess," *Adirondacks Journal of Environmental Studies*, Spring/Summer 1999.
2. Bill McKibben, *Hope, Human and Wild* (Boston: Little, Brown, 1995).
3. Rockefeller Institute of Government, *Employment and Payrolls in the Adirondack Park* (Albany: New York State Department of Labor and Statistics, State University of New York, 1994).
4. Alston Chase, *Playing God in Yellowstone* (San Diego: Harcourt Brace Jovanovich, 1986).
5. New York State, Department of Labor Statistics, "Longer-Term Developments, 1985–1992," in *Employment in New York State* (Albany, 1996, 1998).
6. Commission on the Adirondacks in the Twenty-first Century, *The Adirondack Park in the Twenty-first Century* (Albany: State of New York, 1990), pp. 17–25.
7. See Chase, *Playing God in Yellowstone*.
8. See Philip G. Terrie, *Contested Terrain: A New History of Nature and People in the Adirondacks* (Syracuse: Adirondack Museum/Syracuse University Press, 1997).
9. Commission on the Adirondacks, *Adirondack Park in Twenty-first Century*.

10. Narangwal

1. See Arnfried A. Kielmann et al., *Child and Maternal Health Services in Rural India—The Narangwal Experiment*, vol. 1: *Integrated Nutrition and Health Care*, World Bank Research Publications (Baltimore: Johns Hopkins University Press, 1984), p. 256.
2. Colin McCord and Arnfried A. Kielmann, "A Successful Program for Medical Auxiliaries Treating Childhood Diarrhea and Pneumonia," *Tropical Doctor* 8 (1978): 220–25.
3. F. Shann, K. Hart, and D. Thomas, "Lower Respiratory Tract Infection in Children: Possible Criteria for Selection of Patients for Antibiotic Therapy and Hospital Admission," *Bulletin of the World Health Organization* 62 (1984): 577–85.
4. Abhay B. Bang et al., "Reduction in Pneumonia Mortality and Total Childhood Mortality by Means of Community Based Intervention Trials in Gadchiroli, India," *Lancet* 336 (1990): 204–6; Mrigendra R. Pandey et al., "Reduction in Total under Five Mortality in Western Nepal through Community Based Antimicrobial Treatment of Pneumonia," *Lancet* 338 (1990): 993–97.

5. "Water with Sugar and Salt," editorial, *Lancet* 2 (1978): 300–1.

6. Nevin S. Scrimshaw, N.S., Carl E. Taylor, and John E. Gordon, *Interaction of Nutrition and Infection,* WHO Monograph Series no. 57 (Geneva: World Health Organization, 1968).

7. Carl E. Taylor and Cecile DeSweemer, "Lessons from Narangwal about Primary Health Care, Family Planning and Nutrition," in *Prospective Community Studies in Developing Countries,* ed. Monica Das Gupta, Peter Paaby, Michel Garenne, and Gilles Pison (Oxford: Clarendon Press, 1997), pp. 101–29.

8. See World Bank, *World Development Report, 1993: Investing in Health* (New York: Oxford University Press, 1993).

9. Charles C. J. Carpenter, "Treatment of Cholera—Tradition and Authority versus Science, Reason and Humanity," *Johns Hopkins Medical Journal* 132 (1973): 197; Dalip Mahalanobis et al., "Oral Fluid Therapy of Cholera among Bangladesh Refugees," ibid., pp. 197–205.

10. Colin McCord and Arnfried A. Kielmann, "Home Treatment of Childhood Diarrhea and Pneumonia in Punjab Villages," *Journal of Tropical Pediatrics and Environmental Child Health* 23 (1977): 197–201.

11. Nathaniel F. Pierce et al., "Replacement of Water and Electrolyte Losses in Cholera by an Oral Glucose-Electrolyte Solution," *Annals of Internal Medicine* 70 (1969): 1173; Richard A. Cash et al., "A Clinical Trial of Oral Therapy in a Rural Cholera Treatment Center," *American Journal of Tropical Medicine and Hygiene* 19 (1970): 653.

12. John B. Wyon and John E. Gordon, *The Khanna Study: Population Problems in the Rural Punjab* (Cambridge, Mass: Harvard University Press, 1971), p. 437.

13. Scrimshaw, Taylor, and Gordon, *Interaction of Nutrition and Infection*; Nevin S. Scrimshaw et al., "Synergism of Malnutrition and Infections: Evidence from Field Studies in Guatemala," *Journal of the American Medical Association* 212 (1970): 685–92.

14. Kielmann et al., *Child and Maternal Health Services,* 1: 123.

15. Wyon and Gordon, *The Khanna Study,* p. 184; Helen Gideon, "A Baby Is Born in the Punjab," *American Anthropologist* 64 (1962): 1220–34.

16. Arnfried A. Kielmann and Sanyukta R.Vohra, S.R., "Control of Tetanus Neonatorum in Rural Communities—Immunization Effects of High-Dose Calcium Phosphate-Adsorbed Tetanus Toxoid," *Indian Journal of Medical Research* 66 (1977): 906–16.

17. Carl E. Taylor et al., *Child and Maternal Health Services in Rural India—The Narangwal Experiment,* vol. 2: *Integrated Family Planning and Health Care,*

World Bank Research Publications (Baltimore: Johns Hopkins University Press, 1984), p. 252.

18. Carl E. Taylor, "Surveillance for Equity in Primary Health Care: Policy Implications from International Experience," *International Journal of Epidemiology* 21 (1992): 1045–49.

19. Carl E. Taylor, "Primary Health Care in India: Relationships with the Indigenous Health Systems," in *Science and Technology in South Asia* (Philadelphia: South Asia Regional Studies, University of Pennsylvania, 1985), pp. 77–89.

20. Commission on Health Research for Development, *Health Research: Essential Link to Equity in Development* (New York: Oxford University Press, 1990), p. 1.

11. Curitiba, Brazil

1. United Nations, *Long-Range World Population Projections: Two Centuries of Population Growth, 1950–2150* (New York, 1992); idem, *World Urbanization Prospects: The 1992 Revision* (New York, 1993), p. 3.

2. Daniel Taylor-Ide and Carl E. Taylor, "The Interrelationships of Population Growth with Health and Human Habitat," in *International Perspectives on Environment, Development, and Health,* ed. Gurinder S. Shahi et al. (New York: Springer, 1997), pp. 63–78.

3. S. Buckley, "Despite Economic Gains, Disparities in Care Remain," *Washington Post,* September 17, 1999.

4. Bill McKibben, *Hope, Human and Wild* (Boston: Little, Brown, 1995).

5. Website: www.dismantle.org/curitiba.htm, September 11, 1999.

6. Eugene Linden, "The Exploding Cities of the Developing World," *Foreign Affairs,* January/February 1996.

7. McKibben, *Hope, Human and Wild.*

8. Ibid.

9. Donella Meadows, "The City of First Priorities," *Whole Earth Review,* Spring 1995.

10. McKibben, *Hope, Human and Wild.*

11. Ibid.

12. Jamkhed, India

1. Mabelle Arole and Raj Arole, *Jamkhed* (London: Macmillan, 1992), distributed by Teaching Aids at Low Cost, 226 Hatfield Rd., St. Albans, Herts.

AL1 4LW, England; and CHRP, Jamkhed, Admednagar, Maharashtra 413201, India.

2. Connie Gates, "Evaluation of the Jamkhed Training Center," 1998, Jamkhed Center, Jamkhed, Ahmednagar, Maharashtra 413201, India

14. Kakamega, Kenya

1. See Miriam K. Were, *Organization and Management of Community-Based Health Care* (Nairobi: UNICEF, 1982).

15. The White Mountain Apache, United States

1. Keith Basso, *Wisdom Sits in Places: Landscape and Language among the Western Apache* (Albuquerque: University of New Mexico Press, 1996).
2. White Mountain Apache Tribe v. U.S. Government, 614 (11th Circ., 1987).
3. State of Arizona, Watershed Management Division of the State Land Department, "Proceedings of the First Meeting of Federal, State, and Private Agencies Contributing to Arizona Watershed Research and Management," Phoenix, 1957; R. E. Robinson, "The Cibecue Project: A Review," in *Watershed Review: Proceedings of the 1965 Watershed Symposium* (1966), pp. 24–25, quoted in Jonathan W. Long, "Cibecue Watershed Projects: Then, Now, and in the Future," *USDA Forest Service Proceedings*, RMRS-P-13 (Washington, D.C., 2000).
4. Delbin Enfield, White Mountain Apache Planning Department, personal communication, October 2000.
5. U. S. Bureau of the Census, *Summary Report of the Census, 1990* (Washington, D.C.: U.S. Government Printing Office, 1992).
6. Arizona Center for Health Statistics, *Health Status Profile of American Indians in Arizona: 1996 Data Book* (Phoenix: Arizona Department of Health Services, 1998), p. 89.

16. Urban Agriculture

1. This chapter synthesizes Jac Smit's lifetime of work around the world. Useful references on urban agriculture include A. G. Egziabher et al., *Cities Feeding People: An Examination of Urban Agriculture in East Africa* (Ottawa: International Development Research Centre, 1994); P. Henderson and J. Orange, *Gardening for Profit* (American Botanist, 1991); M. Koc, R. McRea, L. Mougeot, and J. Walsh, eds., *For Hunger-Proof Cities: Sustainable Urban Food Systems* (Ottawa: International Development Research

Centre, 1999); M. Olson, *Metrofarm* (TS Books, 1996); I. Sachs and D. Silk, *Food and Energy: Strategies for Sustainable Development* (United Nations University, 1990) (www.cityfarmer.org/UNPress.html#UNPress); and J. Smit, A. Ratta, and J. Nast, 1996; *Urban Agriculture: Food, Jobs, and Sustainable Cities* (New York: United Nations Development Program, 1996). For more information on specific topics, contact Jac Smit, President, Urban Agriculture Network, Washington, D.C.; e-mail: urbanag@compu serve.com.

17. Peru

1. R. Cortez, *Reformas de descentralizacion en el sector salud la equidad y calidad de la prestacion de servicios de los centros locales de salud bajo Administracion Compartida en el Peru*, Programa de Investigacion Sobre Reformas Sociales en Educacion y Salud en America Latina y el Caribe, Instituto Latinoamericano de Doctrina y Estudios Sociales, Centro Internacional de Investigaciones para el Desarollo, Banco Interamericano de Desarollo (Washington, D.C.: Mayo, 1998); R. Cortez and P. Phumpiu, *Policy Brief: The Delivery of Health Services in Shared Community-State Adminstrative Centers: The Case of Peru* (Ottawa: International Development Research Centre, 1999) (www.seminario-reformas.cl/policyeng/cortez.htm.).
2. Cortez and Phumpiu, *Policy Brief;* L. C. Altobelli, *Report on Health Reform, Community Participation and Social Inclusion: The Shared Administration Program* (Lima: UNICEF, 1998).
3. Carol Graham, 1998, "New Stakeholders in the Management of Health Services," in *Private Markets for Public Goods: Raising the Stakes in Economic Reform* (Washington, D.C: Brookings Institution Press, 1998), pp. 109–13.
4. Daniel Taylor-Ide and Carl E. Taylor, *Community Based Sustainable Human Development: Going to Scale with Self-Reliant Social Devlopment*, UNICEF Working Paper on Environment no. 1 (New York, 1995).
5. Carol Graham, "Social Services, Social Security, and Privatization in Peru," in *Private Markets for Public Goods*, pp. 83–138.
6. Ministerio de la Presidencia, "The Peruvian Strategy: From the Struggle against Poverty to the Creation of Opportunities," Government of Peru, Avenida Paseo de la Republica 4297, Surquilla Lima, Peru, February 2000.

18. Tibet, China

1. D. Winkler, "Deforestation in Eastern Tibet: Human Impact—Past and Present," in *Development, Society, and Environment in Tibet*, ed. G. E.

Clarke, Proceedings of the Seventh Seminar of the International Association of Tibetan Studies, Graz 1995 (Vienna, 1998), pp. 79–96.

2. Carl E. Taylor et al., "Health Survey of Tibetan Villages North of Mount
Everest," *National Geographic Research and Exploration* 8 (1992): 372–77.

3. PuChong, "Pendeba Action in the Qomolangma (Mt. Everest) National
Nature Preserve," in *Sustainable Development International* (London: ICG,
1999).

4. Robert L. Fleming Jr., "A Summary of Biodiversity: The Great River Ecosystems of Asia Region," Future Generations Technical Report, Franklin,
W.Va.; also online at www.future.org/reports.

5. National Oceanic and Atmospheric Administration, "Flooding in China
Summer 1998," November 20, 1998; online at www.ncdc.noaa.gov/ol/
reports/chinaflooding.html.

19. China's Model Counties

1. Conrad Seipp, ed., *Health Care for the Community: Selected Papers of Dr.
John B. Grant* (Baltimore: Johns Hopkins Press, 1963); Victor W. Sidel and
Ruth Sidel, *Serve the People: Observations on Medicine in the People's Re-
public of China* (Boston: Beacon Press, 1974).

2. Kadriye Yurdadok and Tuna Yavuz, "Swaddling and Acute Respiratory
Infections," *American Journal of Public Health* 80 (1990): 873–75.

3. Carl E. Taylor and Xu Zhao Yu, "Oral Rehydration in China," *American
Journal of Public Health* 76 (1986): 186–88.

4. Carl E. Taylor, Robert Parker, and Zeng DongLu, "Public Health Policies
and Strategies in China," in *Oxford Textbook of Public Health*, ed. W. W.
Holland et al. (Oxford: Oxford University Press, 1991), pp. 261–70.

20. SEED-SCALE Principles and Criteria

1. Robert Chambers, *Whose Reality Counts? Putting the First Last* (London:
Intermediate Technology, 1997), pp. 31–32.

2. Daniel C. Taylor-Ide and Carl E. Taylor, "Population, Environment, and
Development: A New Method for Research, a Starting Point for Action," in
International Perspectives on Environment, Development, and Health, ed.
Gurinder S. Shahi et al. (New York: Springer, 1997); D. A. Schon, *Educating
the Reflective Practitioner* (San Francisco: Jossey-Bass, 1987).

3. Nevin S. Scrimshaw and G. R. Gleason, *RAP Rapid Assessment Procedures:
Qualitative Methodologies for Planning and Evaluation of Health-Related*

Programmes (Boston: International Nutrition Foundation for Developing Countries, 1992).

4. Carl E. Taylor, "Surveillance for Equity in Primary Health Care: Policy Implications from International Experience," *International Journal of Epidemiology* 21: (1992) 1045–49.

5. United Nations, *Agenda 21: Programme of Action for Sustainable Development*, Publication E.93.1.11 (New York); World Commission on Environment and Development, *Our Common Future* (Oxford: Oxford University Press, 1987).

6. World Bank Operations Evaluation Department, *Rural Development: World Bank Experience, 1968–86* (Washington, D.C., 1988), pp. 286–307.

7. David C. Korten, *When Corporations Rule the World* (West Hartford: Kumarian and Barrett-Koehler, 1995).

21. Community-Based Action through SEED

1. Robert Chambers, *Rural Development: Putting the Last First* (Essex: Addison-Wesley Longman, 1983); Robert Chambers, *Whose Reality Counts? Putting the First Last* (London: Intermediate Technology Publications, 1997).

2. Nevin S. Scrimshaw and Gary R. Gleason, *RAP Rapid Assessment Procedures: Qualitative Methodologies for Planning and Evaluation of Health-Related Programmes* (Boston: International Nutrition Foundation for Developing Countries, 1992).

3. William Reinke, *The Functional Analysis of Health Needs and Services* (London: Asia Publishing House, 1976).

4. Daniel C. Taylor-Ide and Carl E. Taylor, "Population, Environment, and Development: A New Method for Research, a Starting Point for Action," in *International Perspectives on Environment, Development, and Health*, ed. Gurinder S. Shahi et al. (New York: Springer, 1997), pp. 676–97; Donald A. Schon, *Educating the Reflective Practitioner* (San Francisco: Jossey-Bass, 1987).

22. How to Go to SCALE

1. Daniel Taylor-Ide and Carl E. Taylor, "Population, Environment, and Development: A New Method for Research, a Starting Point for Action," in *International Perspectives on Environment, Development and Health*, ed. G. S. Shahi et al. (New York: Springer, 1997); idem, *Community Based*

Sustainable Development: A Proposal for Going to Scale with Self-Reliant Social Development, UNCEF Children, Environment, and Sustainable Development Series, no. 1 (New York: UNICEF, 1995).

Conclusion

1. M. Giampetro, "Sustainability and Technological Development in Agriculture," *BioScience* 44 (1994): 677–89.
2. P. Link, "China in Transformation," *Daedalus* 122 (Spring 1993).
3. Government of Punjab, Economic and Statistical Organization, *Statistical Abstract of Punjab* (Chandigarh, 1999), p.162.
4. David Seckler, quoted in "Is the Joy Ride Over?" *Down to Earth* 9 (August 15, 2000): 32.
5. Government of Punjab, *Statistical Abstract of Punjab*, p. 215.
6. "Is the Joy Ride Over?"
7. M. S. Swaminathan, keynote address at the Indian Science Congress, Varanasi, January 1968.
8. Amartya Sen, *Development as Freedom* (New York: Alfred A. Knopf, 1999).

ACKNOWLEDGMENTS

A multiple-perspective conversation has shaped this book, one that surely must have started soon after our species started speaking, as our forebears sat around fires wondering how to cope with the wilderness and improve their circumstances. Development is not a new concern, nor is it an impersonal, technical discourse; it is at the core of our transgenerational growth as people. We are heirs to the decisions of others, and we inevitably bequeath the landscape shaped by our thinking and actions to generations that follow.

For us, this conversation took shape in John and Elizabeth Taylor's going to India nearly a century ago. For fifty-four years they wove together at the village level a concern with values, health, and habitat. Through these years Jesse and Elizabeth Daniels were teachers in poor communities in central Pennsylvania, and from them we learned the impact of hands-on education. Their ideas grew within an expanding family circle—Mary, Betsy, Henry, Jennifer, Carter, Helen, Nancy, and Herb—all of whom are professionals in fields that this book investigates. The fact that all are also family enabled us to continue this conversation across decades and to braid together some complex issues.

We are particularly grateful to those who joined this discussion, sharing time and patience as chapter authors. The pioneering work of Mabelle and Raj Arole, Abhay and Rani Bang, Patricia Paredes, Robert Parker, Jac Smit, Betsy and Henry Taylor, Miriam Were, and Zeng DongLu speaks for itself and undergirds the concepts of this book. Kevin Starr's considerable help also qualifies him as a member of this writing group.

Drafting these concepts began in 1994, when the Independent Task Force on Community Action for Social Development met at the Rockefeller Foundation offices in New York City and wrapped up at UNICEF's International

Child Development Center in Florence, Italy. Those discussions led to the two monographs upon which this book is built: *Partnerships for Social Development: A Casebook* (Franklin, W.Va.: Future Generations, 1995) and *Community Based Sustainable Human Development* (New York: UNICEF, 1995). Both were presented at the World Summit on Social Development in Copenhagen in 1995, and the feedback that came in from around the world must also be acknowledged. We are grateful to each task force member: Mabelle Arole, Deepak Bajracharya, Elzbieta Dec, Aditi Desai, Lucia Dube, Kul Gautam, Muriel Glasgow, Dan Kaseje, Kausar Khan, Karl-Eric and Pauline Knutsson, Bob Lawrence, Sauni ole-Ngulay, Philomena O'Dea, Margarita Pacheco, Gurinder Shahi, and Draisid Tontsirin.

The design for the SEED process that lies at the heart of this book grew from the Evergreen House Seminars of Future Generations. Participating in this seminar with us were Chun-Wuei Su Chien, Huang Wenhuan, Li Bosheng, Bina Pradhan, Mohan Man Sainju, and Reds Wolman.

Since we began working on the manuscript, a number of colleagues have been particularly helpful: Omak and Audrey Apang, Seth Berkeley, Jared Blumenfeld, Jack Bryant, Chris Cluett, Wade Davis, R.W. Francke, Jim Grant, Nawang Gurung, Peter Ide, Dan Jantzen, Richard Jolly, Ramesh Khadka, Y. P. Kohli, Flora MacDonald, Halfdan Mahler, Bill McKibben, Henry Mosley, Hemmo Mutingh, Gordon Perkin, Ping Chin, Puchong, Jed Purdy, Mike Rechlin, Herbert Reid, Peykom Ringu, K. D. Singh, Sohan Singh, Mike Stranahan, Sal Werner, and Yan Yinliang.

Early discussions with several people informed this book: Ernie Campbell, Bob Fleming *pere et fils,* Clarence Gamble, Helen Gideon, John B. Grant, Sushila Nayar, Nevin Scrimshaw, and John Wyon. Key colleagues debated these topics with us through the 1960s, 1970s, and 1980s: Tim Baker, Bob Black, Chen MingZhan, Cecile DeSweemer, John Gordon, Jim Grant, John Hume, Arnfried Kielmann, Colin McCord, V. Ramalingaswami, Koye Ransom-Kuti, Bill Reinke, Mathu Santhosham, Ernest Stebbins, and all the members of our Narangwal team. Also challenging our thinking were Spencer Beebe, David Burleson, Bill Coperthwaite, John and Derek Craighead, Adam Curle, David Kinsey, King Seegar, Peter Seligmann, Narayan Shrestha, Dan and Seija Terry, and Bekh and Rita Thapa. Many students have recently become particularly involved with using our ideas; of these, Barry Bialek,

Sekhar Bono, Pippa Brashear, Jaime Castillo, Delbin Enfield, Christy Fong, Jonathan Long, Anbarasi Edward Raj, Mary Skarie, and Mark Stibich sent in particularly helpful critiques.

Many loose ends pop up in a process such as this. For help in tying these down and snipping them off, we gratefully remember the labors of Manjit Bali, Mandakini Banerjee, Steve Green, Rita Gurung, Maggie and Art Hooton, Carol Mick, Arun Seth, Bishu and Bijaya Shah, Lito Tejada-Flores, and, in a host of special ways, Jennifer, Jesse, Tara, and Luke Taylor-Ide. Fifteen-year-old Anthony Steele did the illustrations of the seven steps.

Publishing a book has many beginnings. Early on, we were blessed with two special and talented partners. Howard Boyer urged us to create the book and gave us invaluable encouragement. Through the several drafts of the book, our editor, Ann Hawthorne, has been a dedicated friend, never allowing us to give less than our best, from first word, and first thought, to last. Jim Jordan, director of Johns Hopkins University Press, and George Thompson and Randy Jones, president and editor of the Center for American Places, made sure that the book became a reality and showed themselves to be paragons of flexibility and precision, as great publishers should be.

Thank you all.

AUTHORS AND CONTRIBUTORS

Authors

Daniel Taylor-Ide spent the past fifteen years helping design and set up large nature preserves in China, Nepal, and India; for the fifteen years before that, he designed and led a variety of nonformal educational projects. Currently he is president of Future Generations, a "school for communities" that teaches the processes outlined in this book, and a senior associate at the Johns Hopkins University, School of Public Health. His doctoral degree from Harvard is in education and development planning, and his awards include being knighted by the King of Nepal and receiving an honorary professorship from the Chinese Academy of Sciences. Avocations include wilderness photography, raising the KyiApso, a rare Tibetan dog, building and flying high performance airplanes, and designing energy-efficient houses. He is married and has three children.

Carl E. Taylor is professor emeritus at the Johns Hopkins University, School of Public Health, and was chairman of the school's Department of International Health from 1961–84. From 1984–87 Carl was a UNICEF representative in China. Earlier, he held faculty positions at the Harvard School of Public Health and Christian Medical College in Ludhiana, India. Carl has worked in seventy countries over a period of six decades, promoting community-based primary health care. He holds numerous honorary professorships, doctorates, and professional accolades, including a Presidential Citation from the United States. He has seven grandchildren in whom he takes particular pleasure, especially when he can go trekking in the Himalaya with them.

Contributors

Raj and Mabelle Arole founded the Comprehensive Health and Development Project in Jamkhed, India. Trained as physicians and then in public health at Johns Hopkins, parts of their life stories can be glimpsed in their chapter. What is not told is the international acclaim they have received, including India's premier civil award, Padma Bhushan, as well as Asia's prestigious Ramon Magsasay Award. Sadly for us all, Mabelle died in 1999.

Abhay and Rani Bang founded and lead the Society for Education, Action, and Research in Community Health (SEARCH) based in Gadchiroli, India. Both husband and wife are scholars as well as physicians with public health training. Their community-based work has made a number of conceptual breakthroughs, including gynecological disease burdens and, most recently how to reduce neonatal mortality in poor, village-based situations. Their awards include the Gold Medal from the Indian Council of Medical Research and the prestigious Mahatma Gandhi Award.

Zeng DongLu is a physician with public health training from Johns Hopkins. She was with the Maternal and Child Health Bureau of China's Ministry of Health for many years, and then became a health officer with UNICEF in Beijing. During her career she was deeply involved in the growth of the model counties project described in Chapter 19.

Patricia Paredes is a Peruvian physician with graduate training in public health from the London School of Hygiene and from Johns Hopkins. She has been doing field-based research focusing on evaluating essential drugs for applications in developing countries. She was a member of Peru's Ministry of Health during the evolution of the community-based work described in Chapter 17 and is now on the staff of Management Sciences for Health based in Washington, D.C.

Robert Parker has combined a career of academic medicine on the faculty of the Johns Hopkins University, School of Public Health, with extended periods of fieldwork in health projects in India, China, Nepal, Puerto Rico, and the rural United States. His particular interest in China began during childhood, when he spent the first years of his life there; then he returned for seven years to be head of the health office for UNICEF/China.

Jac Smit is president and founder of the Urban Agriculture Network. He grew up working in poultry, dairy, fruit, and ornamental horticulture and went on for academic training in agriculture and urban design. He began his professional career as a city planner and, while working in thirty countries on five continents, became increasingly involved with urban agriculture. He is the author of the seminal *Urban Agriculture: Food, Jobs, and Sustainable Cities.*

Betsy Taylor is an anthropologist and research director of the Appalachian Center at the University of Kentucky. Her work there has focused on developing community-based information systems and starting programs that foster community/academic/government partnerships in the Appalachian region of the United States. She has also worked in India, Nigeria, the Philippines, and Nepal.

Henry Taylor is commissioner of public health for the state of West Virginia. Before entering public health, he was a physician for thirteen years in rural America with a wide-ranging practice that called upon him to care for individuals in need and respond to communities in crisis. Now leading a state public health system, his focus is on how to shape the larger environment so that it may systematically enable better health and be prepared to respond to crises.

Miriam K. Were recently retired after being in charge of population activities for the United Nations in east, central, and Anglophone west Africa. Prior to this, she served as the World Health Organization's representative for Ethiopia. Earlier, she was head of the Department of Community Health at the University of Nairobi, where she helped set up the Master of Public Health degree program. For her work, described in Chapter 14, she received UNICEF's Maurice Pate Award.

INDEX